# Community and the Economy

# Community and the Economy

## The theory of public co-operation

Jonathan Boswell

with a foreword by Bernard Crick

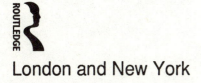

London and New York

First published 1990
by Routledge
11 New Fetter Lane, London EC4P 4EE
29 West 35th Street, New York, NY 10001

© 1990 Jonathan Boswell

Typeset by LaserScript Limited, Mitcham, Surrey
Printed in Great Britain by Billing & Sons Ltd, Worcester

*British Library Cataloguing in Publication Data*
Boswell, Jonathan
Community and the economy: the theory of public co-operation.
1. Politics.
I. Title
330
ISBN 0-415-05556-3

*Library of Congress Cataloging in Publication Data*

Boswell, Jonathan.
Community and the economy: the theory of public co-operation / Jonathan
Boswell; with a foreword by Bernard Crick.
    p.  cm.
Includes bibliographical references.
1.Consensus (Social sciences)  2.Political participation.  3.Social
participation.  4.Community.  5.Co-operation.  I.Title.
JC328.2.B67 1990
306.2—dc20
ISBN 0-415-05556-3
90-31658
CIP

# Contents

# Foreword

The author wrote to me out of the blue. I did not know him. He said that he had produced a manuscript that cut across disciplinary lines and, to make matters worse, was written for a general intelligent public not for disciplinary specialists. So he was genuinely worried about it, and friends of his in Oxford, he said, had suggested that my opinion should be sought as to whether it was any good. Having few friends at Oxford, I took this to be a donnish put-off to Mr Boswell: that Crick was Jack of all trades and master of none and *wrote in the newspapers* and had edited *Political Quarterly*, which is neither one thing nor the other. For that reason, on a false hypothesis, I agreed to read it if only to spite them.

What I found was extraordinary. What he has done is to attempt a general theory of a mixed economy. Everyone has talked about it – on what principle should the mix be mixed? – but no one has made a plausible attempt since Tony Crosland's (dare one now say?) slightly over-rated *The Future of Socialism*, except perhaps David Marquand's recent *The Unprincipled Society* (1988). 'Political economy' in the nineteenth century was once a whole subject, I mean an integral, holistic subject. But for most of this century 'political economy' has been either a Marxist reduction of the political to the economic in theory (vice versa in practice) or an Hayekian total subordination by theory of the political to the economic (which liberal project in practice has needed a great deal of political power, force even, by an ever-more-centralized state).

In a sense Boswell tries to cut through the perceptions of rival extreme models and to make (if I may recycle a phrase from the first lines of my own *In Defence of Politics*) 'a platitude pregnant': that advanced economies can only be mixed economies. So here is a general political and economic theory of the factors needed for a good mixture.

Such a general theory must embrace economic and political considerations, as well as, it quickly emerges, ethical and sociological ones too; it must also draw on academic knowledge but without technicality. Mr Boswell regards the rival models of central state direction and of a completely free market as not merely extreme, but as absurd and fundamentally misleading about actual advanced economies and the actual behaviour of people in economic activity. On the first point he has no difficulty in showing that the two models so interlock in practice that privatization, for example, leads to more and not less regulation; and on the second point he uses a wide range of studies of actual management and business situations to show that they all involve some community institutions and some sense of community. Some sense of 'community' by managers already limits some possibilities of profit maximization, as well as social factors other than legal or political control. Some are external, the repute of the firm, for instance, among its customers, clients or shareholders and even among its competitors; and some are internal, congeniality, tradition, work-place environment, etc. He distinguishes very clearly between profit maximization and being in profit.

He says 'two cheers' for the price mechanism and points to already existing areas of 'fraternity' or 'community', even in apparently tough and unlikely circumstances (at any rate 'economically irrational' factors that can be explained in no other way). These factors can be built on if people choose. The margin for intervention in the public good in a free society and a market economy is wider than Thatcherites will allow or can imagine, but narrower than socialists have traditionally believed. He also makes a massively simple but important sociological point: that any kind of economic enterprise depends on high levels of public co-operation. What is also impressive is that while his argument has an important moral element (owing something to a distinctively continental European Christian democracy that is rarely understood or taken seriously in this country – Federal Germany has a more efficient capitalism *and* a better welfare society than ours), it is not anti-business.

'Economic community depends partly on the right kinds of structures and institutions'. These he tries to specify, not in terms of ideal or ideological criteria but of developmental principles that can be observed in the best contemporary practice. In general terms he takes these to be: (1) what he calls 'threshold continuities among key frontiers between economic sectors' (that is a reasonable stability in the institutions for public influence); (2) 'village-type numbers' in the principal organizations at national levels; (3) 'all-round organizational transparency' or 'openness' ensured both by laws and social monitoring and (4) 'extensive institutions for interdependence and contact across social divisions and economic gulfs'.

At a time when a Prime Minister has declared that 'there is no such thing as society' and actually tries to create disrespect for public, non-privatized spheres (except the police and the army), it is salutory as well as bold to have it argued from an economic perspective that 'fraternity' is the most neglected moral value (and to him a more acceptable social value than equality). He shows how fraternity could be enhanced from existing best-practices in economic life. An economy with more fraternity would, in the long run, he argues, be more productive and balanced. The society/individual dichotomy is a false dichotomy both ethically and economically. Boswell is not, very much not, a negative growth or 'small is beautiful' man; rather the not-too-big is both efficient and comfortable.

Overall he has produced, I think, the most convincing theory of a mixed economy that I've read in my lifetime. And he presents it well. It could be read (I am not entirely sure if the author would wish us to) as a theory of social democracy. Sweden is often in his mind, though he is no robotic Swedophile, as one sometimes finds; his theory is more general and its applications would be more diverse. In some ways it is very close to Labour's new thinking, but far more coherent. He would welcome their new economic 'revisionism' and stress on decentralization, etc., but may well fear that it could remain mere words on paper unless there is a coherent economic theory as well as a political one. I think Labour should steal his clothes although he would seem to prefer a voluntary share-out across Left and Centre. However, there is a lot to be found in his pockets. His grasp, indeed use of, relevant political and sociological theory is excellent. Coming with a fresh mind he has gone to the heart of the matter of Durkheim on the need for 'community', and extracted what is relevant for public policy, not engaged in internalized professional debate. All this he relates to economic practice.

I have already mentioned another strand in his thinking. His social democracy is influenced by continental Christian democratic thinking, at least in its earlier idealistic forms (not always the recent practice of Christian Democratic parties). He tunes in, as it were, to a tradition of social consciousness which has produced a rich literature on social and economic responsibility. On the continent it has even influenced some conservatives, though here it has more obvious relevance to a recent evolution towards common ground (however much the political leaders deny it) in the thinking of large elements of both Left and Centre. In some ways his attempted synthesis of economics and an ethics of responsibility (with the knowledge of society that this entails) is reminiscent of Bertrand de Jouvenel. His critique of single factor explanations (*the* market, *the* community, etc), is reminiscent of Karl Popper.

He refers several times, with qualified admiration, to Crosland's *The Future of Socialism*. But he makes an unusual but important criticism of it: that fundamentally it is a model of moral imperatives working on the individual consciences of leaders who are also economically realistic. But Boswell argues that morality must be conceived as social inter-actions, not the good will of gentlemen socialists. However, I refer to this in passing so that I can end by saying that I think (with astonishment) that he has produced the Crosland of the 1990s – and in many ways a work more profound, wide-ranging and politically more flexible and less inhibited. Few readers will agree with everything this book says – I don't believe, for instance, that a fraternal society is possible without a greater diminishment of inequalities by public power than Mr Boswell apparently either thinks necessary or possible to envisage. But no one could read this book without emerging wiser, or if very resistant both to reason or fellow-feeling, without being greatly stimulated.

Bernard Crick
University of Edinburgh

# Acknowledgements

This book springs from investigation over many years of the relationships between economic institutions, politics and social ethics. I started work on it when I was at the City University, London, researching business and society themes. I owe a lot to the stable base provided by that institution and its friendly atmosphere. Later, as a senior associate member of St. Antony's College, Oxford, I was able to work more concentratedly on issues related to public co-operation in democratic mixed economies. I am very grateful to the College: its hospitality and intellectual stimulus, along with Oxford's facilities generally, were invaluable as I completed the book.

I would like to thank the following organizations for assistance over sources or logistics at various times: the (US) Association for Social Economics; Harvard University Business School; the International Jacques Maritain Institute, Rome; the (UK) Christendom Trust.

Many people helped along the way with comments and suggestions: scholars, sometimes from afar, colleagues and friends. Kenneth E. Boulding generously commented on some initial, primitive efforts, as did Peter Danner and the late Robert Faulhaber. The following were good enough to give their views on a complete early draft: Sir Charles Carter, John Grieve Smith, Jack Hayward, Maurice Kirby, Philip Nind, Sig Prais, Ray Thomas. Helpful comments on various parts came from Kenneth Andrews, Volker Berghahn, Antony Black, Sir Ralf Dahrendorf, Carlos Davila, Ronald Dore, Michael Freeden, Frances Kelly, Sir Arthur Knight, Michael Knight, Ronnie Lessem, Keith Macmillan, Peter Pulzer. Towards the end, helpful points on presentation were made by the Rt. Hon. Aubrey Jones, Adrian Leftwich, the late Patrick McLaughlin, and Ian Mordaunt.

My sincere thanks go to all these people. I emphasize that none of them can be held accountable in any way for the book's viewpoints, let alone its imperfections or any errors I have made.

I am grateful to Alan Jarvis of Routledge for being so efficient and supportive over the final lap. Finally, I owe a great debt to the many students who unknowingly helped me to test out much of the material in lectures and seminars both at home and overseas.

Jonathan Boswell

# Chapter 1

# The recovery of community

This book is about the magnetic yet elusive subject of community. It investigates community as an ideal, a phenomenon which struggles to express itself in the most unlikely places, and an object of action in modern times. In this book I relate community mainly to economic life. This is because community meets many of its most daunting tests in a modern economy. Community values and institutions are vital for their own sake, in the economic system as elsewhere. They are also important for balanced and sustained economic success.

In advanced western societies our consciousness of community has become threadbare. There is an impoverishment in our sense of what it is to be social beings and members one of another, and builders of community.

This poverty in community thinking affects our intellects, our imaginations and our consciences. It confines and restricts our everyday assumptions about the sort of people we are, how we relate to each other, and the directions we ought to go in. Our interpretations of social processes are deeply affected by it; so are the approaches we rely on to redress social problems. In economic life the sense of solidarity and social responsibility has retreated most of all. In the advanced economic systems of the west, our stock of communal perceptions, sentiments and prescriptions has sunk particularly low.

## THE CONVENTIONAL VIEW OF SOCIETY

This is how a detached contemporary observer might describe the dominant ideas about society held in the advanced western democracies in our times.

At root, social reality consists of separate units, both individuals and, often, groups or classes. It is these separatisms which form the most basic and fundamental factor. Social constraints have to be accepted in order to prevent some people's freedom being trampled on by others, and for purposes of collective defence, economic prosperity and common services; also, many would add, to prevent a minority from gaining too much power and wealth, and to promote greater equality. But people's desires for freedom, equality and prosperity characteristically conflict, and the groupings set up for these purposes also tend to be class bound, fractious and competitive.

Our detached observer would go on to explain western society's mainstream idea of how social order is ensured, in practice, against these tremendous odds.

First, people's and groups' separatist inclinations can be socially canalized and made creative; this is true even of their selfishness. Second, democratically elected governments impose laws and constraints. Thus, either the base metal of separatism and rivalry is transformed into copper, or even gold, or it is curbed by legitimate regulation and fear.

In modern economic systems, these tendencies reach a climax. As individuals and sectional interests jostle for livelihoods, possessions or profits, there are grave risks of waste, anarchy and exploitation. So it is in the economic system that the primary methodologies just mentioned move into top gear. Competition and acquisitiveness are rendered socially useful through the working of appropriately guided market forces. Central direction operates through laws and through government's directive power over taxes and public spending, and over credit and money. These 'hard' mechanical-type processes are what keep a large, sophisticated economic system on the road and moving forward.

Finally our observer might summarize western society's dominant social ideals.

In this society, certain classic controversies dominate the ethical agenda. The deeply cherished value of freedom is interpreted in differing ways. Attitudes towards equality and social justice vary intensely, with deep divisions between egalitarians and others, and between 'haves' and 'have-nots'. People dispute the relationships between freedom, equality and economic prosperity, and the nature of prosperity itself, particularly as between private goods and collective welfare. They argue incessantly about the scope of private enterprise, the extent of centralization and decentralization, and the role of the state.

Now whatever its apparent disagreements, this set of ideas about society is more coherent and consistent than is often thought. There are strong, though often unexplained, connections between its principal parts, particularly between 'freedom', 'equality', 'prosperity', 'competition' and 'state direction'. These ideas spring from common roots in a certain fundamental conception of human nature. Even when in conflict, they complement one another. Their frequent conten-. tiousness does not destroy an underlying unity.

But my main point relates to a gigantic omission. This concerns the place of community. If readers look again at the brief portrayal above, they will find no reference to community as an important value in itself. They will discover no hint of its part in human nature, its ethical role, its key contribution to social cohesion. What they will find are repeated implications that community is secondary, constrained, merely instrumental, even inferior.

The conventional set of ideas goes along with such typical interpretations as these. 'Community is an addition or follow-on, something which comes *after* some original state of separateness, even as a come-down or a second best.' 'Community is a necessity for survival, as when we huddle together in a storm, or as a preventive against the evils of anarchy or dictatorship.' 'True community is restricted to family and personal friendship – it is impossible in a wider sense, in larger units, or under "capitalism".' 'In such wider contexts, community may be a constraint, even a danger to privacy, diversity, liberty, democracy.' 'Community is useful as a subordinate instrument; it is valuable only in so far as it assists towards individual freedom, or equality between individuals or classes, or increased prosperity.'

In contrast to all this, however, another view of community exists, one which puts community at the *centre* of its social thinking; and it is this view which is going to be explored in this book.

In this book, I am going to identify 'community' with values directly related to its etymology and roots. Here a number of vaguely overlapping terms jostle uncertainly; for example, 'solidarity', 'social responsibility', 'fellowship', 'communion'. I propose to highlight three such closely related terms: (1) 'fraternity', (2) 'associativeness', and (3) (civic or democratic) 'participation'. I will use these three concepts in order to flesh out 'community', retaining the latter only as an umbrella term for this more specific family of ideas. I will apply the label 'democratic communitarianism' to the social philosophy which actively seeks to promote the values of fraternity, associativeness and participation.[1]

It is this interpretation of community which suffers above all in the conventional picture, this family of ideas of fraternity, associativeness and civic participation which is persistently mistreated.

## THE BELITTLEMENT OF COMMUNITY

To start with, there is flagrant misappropriation when certain would-be community-defining values turn out to be xenophobic, racist or totalitarian. 'Destroy foreigners', 'exclude blacks' or 'glorify the state' are obvious perversions of community. Clearly, too, community is truncated when it is restricted to the 'true believers' of some religious, revolutionary or idealistic sect. But usually the belittlement is more subtle and plausible. It takes place under the aegis of the dominant ideals outlined above. In effect, community is commandeered by one or more of these ideals, typically by 'liberty' or 'equality'.

The most common case is when 'community' is defined as a society where freedom exists, or where people agree that freedom is vital. Our fondness for many facets of 'freedom' makes this idea specially attractive to us. But two major difficulties arise. However valuable and essential 'freedom' may be, it diverts attention from thinking about 'community' as such. Moreover, 'freedom' may be, and often is, interpreted in a- or even *anti*-communal ways.

Suppose, for instance, that 'freedom' is interpreted in terms of people going all out for private enrichment, or behaving atomistically, or 'keeping themselves to themselves'. However strong a popular consensus behind this view, we would hardly accept it as a good or even a minimal basis for a community. Were such an acquisitive or atomistic society to exist, we would probably see it as flagrantly contradicting community. We might have similar reservations about a 'freedom' obsessed with people's 'rights' or privacy or separate development, to the neglect of ideas of interdependence, mutual obligation and social responsibility. We might wonder whether a liberal-minded 'tolerance of diversity' is really enough, either. Whether this value, for all its importance, is an adequate foundation for community in the sense of fraternity, associativeness or participation is open to doubt.

Another form of subtle appropriation often occurs when we seek to define community in terms of equality or equality seeking. We then see a community as essentially built on a consensus as to what is 'just' or 'fair', or on the attainment of 'justice' or 'fairness' in practice. But again, these terms may be, and often are, interpreted anti-communally. In fact, the conventional view, as sketched above, tends towards a highly individualistic concept of 'equality', even a rather possessive one. Typically, it concentrates on 'equality' in the distribution of income, wealth and opportunity as between individuals. Again, we may well see such redistribution as desirable. Yet its pursuit, even its actualization, is consistent with highly acquisitive behaviour on the part of the individuals and social classes in question.[2]

Community is not only commandeered by values drawn from the conventional repertoire, it is also overshadowed by them.

In the conventional picture of society summarized above, giant status is given to concepts of liberty, equality and prosperity. Competition and state control come closely behind. Every one of these ideas has long been the intense object of (1) definition and measurement, (2) philosophical interpretation, and (3) ideological debate. Controversies about the meaning of liberty, equality and prosperity, competition and coercion, not to mention their relationships and their conflicts, leave little room for anything else. By comparison, concepts of fraternity, associativeness and civic participation have been relegated to a pygmy role.

My contention is that this imbalance badly needs to be redressed. Community should not be treated as a residual, an ancillary or a derivative. At the very least, community as fraternity, associativeness and civic participation calls for investigation in its own right.

Yet paradoxically, such exploration is further hindered not by the complete absence of community ideas but by their pervasiveness. In fact, they are all around us but in immature, secondary or emasculated forms. This produces a widespread illusion that they are alive and well, and do not need intellectual effort.

Hard thinking about community concepts is not helped by the mystique often attached to them. At one level, they are sanctified by morality and religion. Scriptures and Commandments enshrine and elevate them. Christians see them as forming the essence of spiritual events and sacraments. The doctrine of the Trinity applies the idea of a community of persons to the very nature of God. At another level, community concepts are identified with such sentiment, loyalty and ceremony as a modern nation state still evokes. For some people community still has local meanings, as in a village fête, a parish council or a street party. Often, it is equated with sheer sociability, as experienced in pubs, cafés or sporting events. Many invest community concepts with a nostalgic regret for some imaginary long-vanished golden age. Nearly everywhere, they have mythic and folkloric overtones.

Thus, community concepts often possess not only an elusive dignity but also emotive power. They come not as invitations to explore or argue, but rather as assumptions or datum lines. In their higher forms, they often become honorific or ritualistic; elsewhere, they slide easily towards the sentimental and the pretty. Community ideas appear as primordial or rudimentary, occupying either the attics or the basements of our minds, but seldom, if ever, the hurly-burly middle floors. If subjects are distinguished as 'hard' or 'soft', community typically emerges as 'soft'. Neither a clear definition nor an extended pattern of ideas seems able to be attached to it.

The conventional ideas about society mentioned above first of all discard the idea that community has a potential for disciplined analysis and interpretation as a social value. Then, freedom, equality, prosperity, competition and coercion are regarded as readily observable and empirically measurable; but community is not. Above all, these obsessively rehearsed social phenomena are regarded as relatively explainable. At least, they are seen as amenable to hypothesis setting, theorizing and model building. But approximations to community definitely are *not*. Correspondingly, the idea that community can be an object of deliberate policy also tends to fall to the ground. For if community cannot be defined or measured, and above all if it is unexplainable, there is little point in discussing the specifics of its pursuit.

As against all this, I intend to show that it makes sense to think of community in a systematic way, first as a social ideal (indeed as the *supreme* social ideal), second as a measurable phenomenon which can also be reasonably explained, at least in the area covered in this book, and third as an object of action.

## WHY INVESTIGATE COMMUNITY IN THE ECONOMY?

I should now explain why this book concentrates on community within economic life, and in that context, on relationships between sectional interests (business, labour, pressure groups, etc.), public opinion and the state.

At first sight, modern economic life appears a highly unpromising field for exploring community. The advanced economic systems of the west are hardly models of social solidarity or civic participation. These values seem to have little to do with many of the powerful forces at work; for example, with fluctuations in employment, production or prices, with advancing technology, or with the chronic imbalances between rich and poor regions, nations and continents.

In the economy, both individuals and groups tend to be divided from each other by the vast scale of activity, the minute specialization of tasks, and an incessant mobility. Consultation, participation and a sense of involvement are hard to induce. The large majority of people are passive or even apathetic: any power to affect either market forces or public economic policies largely rests with a few.

There is much to be said for the view that modern economic systems are not just inhospitable to fraternity, but breeding grounds for social irresponsibility. Trade unionists, managers, professional people and pressure groups all scramble for scarce resources. Each group seems merely to jostle for itself, with scant regard for its neighbours, let alone for society's outcasts, future generations or those public purposes which enjoin restraint. Cumulatively, such sectionalist behaviour defeats many vital collective interests. Unintentionally, it exacerbates a wide array of social evils, ranging from sweated labour through pollution and congestion to 'stagflation'. At worst, there is deliberate wrongdoing; for example, shady marketing practices, rackets in scarce goods, dumping of poisonous wastes, industrial espionage, attempts to bribe public officials.

It is easy to conclude that these hard-bitten, fractious and sometimes even immoral systems can only be properly controlled, let alone improved, by the 'hardest' of instruments. Surely there is no alternative to larger and ever more refined doses of competition and/or state direction? Does not an enquiry into self-discipline, social responsibility and public spirit in (of all places) the economy defy realities and run clean against the grain?

Yet the reasons for such an investigation are compelling. As I have said, relationships of community are not wholly lacking in modern economic systems. Through the twentieth century, in various countries and contexts, public ties and interests have exerted some distinctive pulls on economic organizations. However, not only is the evidence on these phenomena highly scattered and often hidden. Conventional doctrines have disguised their very existence. Academic compartmentalizations badly fragment our recognition of them. Community phenomena in the economy classically fall between the stools of economics, politics, sociology, social ethics, management, and policy studies.

The first reason for a study of community in modern economic systems, then, is to fill a major gap in knowledge. Community in economic systems has been much less investigated that its counterparts in, say, villages, urban life or social welfare. Even in the economy, attention has mainly concentrated on communal relationships *within* the main organizations or sectors; associativeness *between* them has hardly featured. The communal ties between sectional economic interests, public opinion and government have been seriously neglected. Of course, my aim is not to fill the whole of this gap; but I hope to uncover a sample of the data and to open up the field.

The second reason for investigation is pragmatic, and more urgent. In the political economies of the west, the problems which require sectional interest restraint or public collaboration crowd in on every side. They range from aspects of stagflation through industrial reorganization to training and retraining for skills. They include pressing issues of human health and safety, environmental pollution, racial discrimination, and business ethics. Readers can readily think of examples of such problems. In some cases, co-operative approaches are suitable only in the longer term; in others they are useful immediate adjuncts to competition or state direction. Sometimes, these other methods badly need complementing by voluntary collaboration; sometimes, the latter's role is unique and irreplaceable so that without it no solution whatever is likely.

Careful investigation of collaborative and non-collaborative phenomena over long periods should be able to shed light on these problems. It may well show that certain types of institutions, cultures or political situations have been favourable to economic community. This should have significance for long-term policy thinking. At present the field is confused by vague and partly overlapping ideas. These include 'sectional interest restraint' or 'participation', 'self-regulation', 'business social responsibility', 'business ethics', and 'the private pursuit of public interests'. Further examples are 'informal social control'; 'public suasion'; *freiwillige Disziplin*; *Sozialpartnerschaft*; social co-ordination *via* 'integration' as compared with competition or coercion.[3] These ideas, and the phenomena relating to them, badly need to be considered as a whole.

The third reason for this study's emphasis connects with a particular standpoint on social values and public policy, one which significantly differs from both the 'New Right' and the 'Old Left', and also from the merely pragmatic 'centre'.

Many people seek a third way between the excesses of competition and centralization. They are suspicious of both market-privatist panaceas and an over-mighty state, and horrified when these two combine, as in some manifestations of the 'New Right'. They are shocked by the meanness and crudity of a fast buck, 'I'm all right, Jack' society, but also wary of addictive dependences on laws and government controls. These people's desire, though, is not simply for 'moderation' between ideological extremes or a splitting down 'the middle'. They are dissatisfied with mere pragmatism. What they want is a principled pursuit of greater public spirit, collaboration and democratic participation in both politics and social life.

Such a standpoint, however, has marked implications for economic institutions and behaviour as well. It suggests that if politics cannot be left, safely or ethically, to the naked play of class division, acquisitiveness or a leviathan state, neither can the economy. It implies that our economic systems, too, should be made more publicly responsible and fraternal, and participative.

This desire for a communitarian 'third way' is still largely amorphous. Whether it translates itself into something politically coherent and forceful remains to be seen. As to its validity, I expect readers to make up their own minds in due course. For the moment, my point is simply that no search for greater fraternity, associativeness and democratic participation can ignore the economic system. A communitarian effort in society and politics would critically depend on a vigorous new co-operative fabric in the economy. Yet the likely shape of such a fabric is largely mysterious. It requires detailed exploration in the light of both theory and historical experience.

A final consideration takes us back to the undernourished, underprivileged state of community thinking as a whole. To redress the huge imbalance I have referred to will take a long time, diverse approaches, and many contributors. But the very abrasiveness of modern economic life offers particular promise in pursuing it. For this is ground which tests and stretches communitarian concepts, observations and hypotheses to the very limit. An analogy is with pilot testing a new car or training a commando military force. The car has to be tested through the toughest climates, the roughest surfaces, the sharpest gradients, bends and curves. The commando recruits have to surmount 'worst scenario' obstacles, appalling physical conditions, and severe emotional stresses.

The very fact that economic life exhibits so much competitiveness, coerciveness and sheer impersonality makes it an ideal cutting edge for clarifying community ideals. The relative tangibility of both competition and state direction sets such limited community as exists in the economy in sharper relief. It becomes easier to single out and measure, by way of contrast, community related phenomena which fit into neither of these camps.

As for the search for explanations of economic community, this involves high risks, but also the potential for high rewards. If certain institutional, structural or ideological forces are found to favour community-related behaviour in the economy, however imperfectly, it is almost inconceivable that such findings will be irrelevant elsewhere. Any factors which can be shown to have helped community to survive against such tremendous odds, as with the super-tested cars and commando soldiers, cannot fail to illuminate our wider understanding of community and its pursuit.

## SHAPE OF THE ARGUMENT

In an initial outline, I suggest that the value of community is capable of occupying, coherently and consistently, the summit of our thinking about social ideals. I invoke a venerable tradition here which has deep roots in western culture even though it has fallen into disrepair and neglect. I show how, once we begin to unpack 'community', we find the rich and interrelated principles of fraternity, complementary association and democratic participation. These have wide implications for the economy as well as for social life and politics. I also suggest that if these principles are taken seriously, certain other ideals have to be downgraded and refurbished, particularly the conventional interpretations of liberty and equality.

Next, I am going to argue that, contrary to conventional doctrines, approximations to community *do* exist in modern economies, and that these can be both defined and observed more easily than is usually thought. This defies the common assumption that business, trade union and sectional interest behaviour has already been fully classified. It contests the exclusive hold of concepts of 'competition', 'maximizing', 'class' and 'coercion'. By contrast, I will define a phenomenon of partial and imperfect economic community: 'public co-operation'. I will suggest that 'public co-operation' is an important additional classifier not only of organizational behaviour at the grass roots but also of whole economic systems. It is badly needed, I believe, in order to supplement our present polarized (and arguably misleading) obsessions with competition and state direction.

Then comes the riskiest part of the enterprise, the attempt to 'explain' public co-operation in the economy, which takes up the main bulk of the book. Here my argument will revolve around three sets of factors: facilitative structures, emergencies, and communitarian beliefs.

I am going to argue, first, that economic community partly depends on the right kinds of structures and institutions. It helps if organizations and people in key sectors do not come and go too rapidly. It is useful to have most activity organized by units which are of the right size, publicly speaking: not 'too big', 'too small' or 'too numerous'. Further, it is a help if economic units are appropriately visible both to each other and to an active public opinion. Yet a further facilitator is institutions which promote a lot of background contact between members of different social classes and economic groups. I take the view that these four structural factors go a fair way towards explaining such community behaviour as exists in advanced economic systems. Although not the main explanation, they are quite important. And they have been badly neglected.

This 'structural' analysis concentrates on the organizational, logistical or communication obstacles: obstacles to be reduced, I suggest, if economic community is to have a chance, although their reduction alone does not guarantee its success. In a positive sense, the principal 'structural' features of a publicly co-operative economy emerge as fourfold: (1) threshold continuity along certain key frontiers between sectors, (2) village-type numbers of the principal organizations at national levels, (3) all-round organizational transparency ensured both by laws and by active social monitoring, and (4) extensive institutions for interdependence and contact across social divisions and economic gulfs.

Two further factors tend to be more significant. It is crucial for public co-operation to be sustained by appropriate beliefs. I emphasize the motivational inadequacy of economic pragmatism, or the idea that community and collaboration are good mainly because they help to solve specific economic problems, to increase profits, earnings, national production, etc. To regard public co-operation in the economy as an instrument or mechanism produces, I maintain, little support for it and even some confusion. Rather, the most effective cultural and attitudinal nurture for public co-operation comes from a deeper source. It springs from a conviction that public co-operation forms part of a wider search for community which has value in itself, indeed supreme value; from an assignation of top priority, in its own right, to the quality of inter-personal and intergroup relationships.

Without this sort of conviction, the structures just referred to become all the more resistant; the will to improve them is lacking. Without such overriding communitarian beliefs, too, it becomes harder to handle the third main influence on community in economic systems which I am going to highlight: the national emergency factor, the sort of crisis which can help to push a country's economic co-operation upwards on a sustained basis, but which can also bring about disaster.

Some ideologies have clearly been antipathetic: Marxism and extreme collectivism, classical individualism, cults of competition and 'spontaneous order'. Other currents of thinking have been inadequate: the purely economic rationale for public co-operation; utilitarianism; conventional materialism and managerialism. I am also going to suggest that, for complex conceptual and historical reasons, mainstream democratic socialism has been distinctly ambivalent.

The experience of those countries which have exhibited high levels of public co-operation is illuminating. We have to look carefully at the fairly positive records of Sweden, Belgium and The Netherlands over long periods, and of Austria and West Germany after 1945. In these countries, the favourable ideologies were those approximating, albeit highly imperfectly, to communitarian values: national pride specifically associated with democracy and participation; the co-operativist thrust of Scandinavian social democracy from the 1930s; personalist Christian democracy in its best initial phase in some of the other countries.

These beliefs helped certain crucial phases of public co-operation building in the respective economies. They acted in conjunction with favourable structural factors (often partly linked to a small size of country), and with national emergencies. However, the mixture of these elements varied a good deal. In some cases a critical movement upwards was relatively peaceful. It was helped mainly by favourable starting structures, and more especially by a communitarian ideology, even though emergency played a part. In other cases, a more stormy transition was mainly emergency propelled. But where all these factors were lacking, a sustained phase of intensive public co-operation did not emerge. This was the case, we will find, in both the USA and the UK.

At all these stages, this book is exploratory, not exhaustive. For example, it does not provide a detailed country-by-country history or comparison of public co-operation; rather, a framework for further work on these fronts is assembled. The book does not cover the multinational or supranational dimension (although some helpful inferences arise there). Nor does it develop the detailed implications for policy. However, my belief is that the essential way to make progress at this stage is to engage quite robustly and unashamedly in breadth. My aim is to open up the field, to stake out a lot of ground, and to offer a 'helicopter view' of the whole.

## STRUCTURE OF THE BOOK

As already indicated, this book starts out from values; it then moves through historical and contemporary phenomena to a heavy emphasis on explanations, ending up with long-term implications for thinking about community.

First, I outline the background principles of community. Chapter 2 identifies the main historical roots of these principles over the past century: Durkheim's libertarian solidarism, personalist Christian democracy, and various strands of civic humanism. The position I call democratic communitarian has a proud, albeit dispersed, heritage; its distinguished but half-buried roots are worthy of reclamation and recovery. In chapter 3, I briefly develop the key principles, namely, fraternity, complementary association and democratic participation. I also introduce their economic counterpart: the ideal of an associateship or basic solidarity between diverse economic interests, public opinion and the state. This would be an economic system's archway and crown, surmounting the still necessary but subordinate pillars of competition and state direction.

We then move across to the realities of an advanced mixed economy. Chapter 4 identifies the imperfect real-life form of economic community which already exists as 'public co-operation': that is, processes whereby business, trade union and other sectional organizations freely collaborate with each other and with external groups or government in the cause of public interests. I discuss examples of public co-operation in practice, at the levels of an individual organization or locality, a sector, or a national economic system. I also examine the ways in which public co-operation can be measured.

The main bulk of the book then follows: an exploration of those forces which appear to have aided or impeded public co-operation in the twentieth-century advanced economies of the west. Chapter 5 introduces my explanatory framework, centring round institutional structures, national emergencies, and communitarian beliefs. Chapter 6 examines the relevance of two sorts of structure: threshold continuity among organizations and their decision makers, and conformable size, or a co-operatively favourable size distribution of economic organizations, relative to public authority and size of country. Organizational trans- parency and social monitoring, as further aids to public co-operation, are discussed in chapter 7. Relevant institutions for background social mixing and contact are explored in chapter 8. Particular attention is given to 'forums': representative bodies where decision makers or envoys from different economic sectors, sometimes also from government, engage in colloquy about public interests.

This still leaves the crucial explanatory role of ideology and culture to be dealt with, also of emergency. The historical nature of public co-operation's ideological opponents and allies, as already mentioned, is considered in chapter 9. Finally, chapter 10 adds the emergency factor and briefly tests the complete model against the twentieth-century experience of seven countries: The Netherlands, Belgium, Sweden, Austria, West Germany, the USA and the UK. These countries' patterns of long-run success or failure in public co-operation are found to be consistent with the explanatory model. Further, I believe the model emerges as a promising one for further applications and research.

Chapter 11 considers the implications of the argument for policy thinking, assuming that more public co-operation is desired on both ethical and economic grounds. Priorities for long-term structural change and for new or improved institutions for interdependence (but not, I should emphasize, detailed policy recipes) are brought together. The turn-of-the-century prospects for democratic communitarianism, with or without catalytic emergencies, are briefly assessed.

# Chapter 2

# The roots of democratic communitarianism

No interpretation of political economy can escape from making strong assumptions about the meaning of human nature and the aims of society. These assumptions, in turn, involve value judgements and ethics. To fail to own up to one's value preconceptions verges on unfairness to the readers. To fail to make them reasonably clear at the outset is to risk confusion and inconsistency later on.

This task of clarifying value foundations could be got out of the way quickly if it were possible to draw on a single, well-established and well-known set of teachings. It would be convenient to be able to point to a large, homogeneous bundle of writings such as those which have inspired, say, Marxism or the 'New Right'. But then, perhaps, many of the problems addressed in this book would not have arisen in the first place, whereas a large part of the difficulty we are faced with is precisely that no unified and widely pervasive movement of thought in favour of this book's affiliation has existed in modern times.

The cause we are concerned with has for long been ideologically underprivileged. It has boasted no coherent modern *summa*, no world-famous prophet. Worse, the concepts surrounding free associativeness and solidarity have often been exploited ideologically. For this a combination of seductive attractiveness with elasticity is much to blame. The concept of 'community' has come to be employed so loosely and variably as to be virtually useless on its own. The no less vague and protean idea of 'fraternity' has been inviting to the extent of attracting swarms of unlikely allies. 'Fraternity' and its correlate concepts have even been dragged into the service of essentially antipathetic ideals.

Thus, traditional conservatives may invoke notions of 'colla-boration', 'social harmony' or 'partnership'. Yet it soon becomes clear that, far from being paramount, these notions are dragged into the service of other ideas which are more important for conservatives. A sense of 'community' is to be promoted within a largely accepted status quo. No major reform of existing social arrangements or cultures is envisaged, although this might well be needed if 'fraternity' were genuinely to be put first. Instead, a greater degree of good feeling is to be sought within a context of hierarchy and inequality. 'Community' is to be pursued in the midst of, or despite, or even for the sake of, an existing social system.[1]

Ideas of 'fraternity', 'solidarity' or 'brotherhood' are still more widespread on the extreme left. That these ideas are being commandeered or highjacked emerges no less clearly than with the conservatives. Even intellectually they are marginalized. 'Community' in the sense we are going to discuss it turns out to be a far distant ideal for the extreme left; it is viewed as a mechanical outcome of other changes which grab far greater attention. A communitarian rhetoric may be widespread and sincere. But even in theory the foreground is taken up with notions of class war, proletariat or revolution.

Indeed, it is difficult to find a single system of beliefs which gives the central place, unambiguously and consistently, to free associativeness. It is hard to find a single structure of ideas which puts this value at the heart of its interpretation of human nature and the social world, and of moral rightness and ethics, and which then goes on to draw out implications for reform consistently and coherently.

We have to do the best we can with dispersed approximations. Yet although there is no single clear parenthood for the ideas developed in this book, sources of inspiration are available which, if put together, begin to form a reasonable substitute. Within the past 100 years several broad families of ideas have been highly relevant. Once these scattered contributions have been recovered and reconsidered, and, what is more, juxtaposed, a coherent set of underlying principles begins to emerge. I propose to apply to these principles the deliberately broad, umbrella-type label, 'democratic communitarianism'.[2]

## LIBERTARIAN SOLIDARISM (DURKHEIM AND OTHERS)

A first set of pointers comes from the immensely creative social thinker Emile Durkheim (1858–1917). Neither the defects of some of Durkheim's theories, nor the subsequent and often esoteric controversies about his writings, should be allowed to obscure his giant standing in the field of ideas about free associativeness.[3]

In some form or other the principle of associativeness consistently claimed the attention of this brilliant French sociologist. Durkheim occupied himself continuously and creatively with the idea of 'solidarity'; that is, relationships of affection, trust, reciprocity and moral obligation between human beings.[4] No other idea rivalled this one for its sheer hold on his mind. Durkheim advocated libertarian values and greater equality, too. But for him, significantly, liberty and equality could not stand on their own; nor could they claim primacy, separately or even together: instead, both liberty and equality were essentially correlates, even instruments, of the central vision of 'solidarity'.

For the purposes of this book Durkheim's significance lies equally in the fact that he went on to grapple with the implications of a 'solidarity' with libertarian and egalitarian overtones specifically for economic life and for an evolving industrial society. It was the way in which Durkheim tried to relate the central concept of free associativeness to actual trends in modern economic institutions which makes him particularly seminal from our point of view.

Durkheim was convinced that the primary need was for economic life to become more ethical, civilized and humane. It was vital for economic institutions to express and encourage certain 'durable and profound needs' of human beings for 'communing'. A more moral society meant, above all, one which would develop solidarity in freedom between both individuals and sectors. After all, it was this sort of nexus of freely accepted mutual linkages which had been 'forever the fundamental basis of social life'. 'What gives unity to organised societies . . . is the spontaneous consensus of parts.'[5]

According to Durkheim, classical liberal theories of individualism, contract and competition, for all their huge influence, were grossly inadequate. Even in bare historical and explanatory terms, they were caricatures of reality. 'Individuals' were not, and never had been, understandable other than in terms of personal and social relationships. The classic liberal concept to the effect that initially separate, isolated and 'free' individuals had somehow created a historic, original 'contract' as a basis for an organized society was a myth; and not even a useful myth.

The value of the individual personality was crucial for Durkheim; but this could be understood only in terms of its relationships with others, interpreted far more subtly than by crude theories of exchange or contract, let alone competition. The values of 'contract' could not form a sustainable basis for society. 'A contract is only a truce, and very precarious; it suspends hostility only for a time.' There could be 'no stable equilibrium' founded on so thin a basis. 'The conquered do not go away.' Only deeper and more lasting cultural and institutional bonds could effectively moderate conflict and create the basis for people to have mutual confidence and trust, to work together, and to find personal dignity and meaning in their lives.[6]

Durkheim went on to relate these (to some extent timeless) assertions to a specific view of the way things were going in advanced industrial societies. A strong vision of contemporary historical trends was central to his thought. Durkheim believed that the endemic issue of free solidarity *versus* conflict and coercion was being played out on a new stage. A new twist was being added to this perennial moral drama in the modern context of mass production and giant organization, vast populations, and increasing economic specialization.

A central feature was the increasing importance of economic institutions in people's lives. 'Economic functions', it seemed, were becoming 'steadily more important'. As a corollary, Durkheim thought, people would continue to devote less and less time to military, religious and territorial concerns. A still more fundamental tendency was that of *increasing interdependence*. Economic, technological and social influences were ceaselessly multiplying the interactions between both individuals and social groups. The impacts which different sections could have on each other, both for good and ill, were endlessly proliferating. 'Happenings', Durkheim claimed, 'are much more contagious'; and, moreover, that 'contagiousness' would go on spreading.[7]

Durkheim ventured into highly contestable territory when he attempted to pin down rather precisely the exact nature of this interdependence. He identified it overwhelmingly with just one factor, the division and specialization of labour. The tendency for people's jobs, and for economic activities generally, to subdivide in ever more intricate ways was, he suggested, the chief cause of the hugely increasing potential for mutual benefit or damage. A contemporary critique of Durkheim would contest this. It would probably assign greater importance to other forms of 'contagiousness': on the virtuous side, for example, to the social benefits of people getting training and education; on the negative side, to the bad 'spillovers' caused by pollution or, more subtly, the ways in which competing sectional groups' aggressive claims on resources have exacerbated both inflation and unemployment.

Durkheim went on to make arguably a bigger mistake in connection with the long-term implications of interdependence. Like many other thinkers of his time, he was an optimist and a believer in moral progress. Durkheim went so far as to believe that, in the long run, the increasing division of labour would improve the prospects for social morality. He thought it would produce greater mutual recognition and sensitivity between the different groupings; indeed, his idea was that it would create greater solidarity in an 'organic' way which would be superior to, or at least more advanced than, previous 'mechanical' solidarities based on mere consanguinity, race or physical contiguity.

Even at the turn of the century such sweeping optimism might have been intuitively suspect. Certainly, Durkheim's 'organic' *versus* 'mechanical' terminology has (rightly) been much criticized subsequently. Yet the fact that Durkheim drew such fragile and romantic implications for the future, and his use of certain highly contestable analogies, should not detract from his fruitful emphasis on the deep-seated interdependence trends in advanced industrial societies. To mis-specify aspects of these trends, let alone to credit them with such potent capacity for good, were, no doubt, serious faults; but they were arguably far outweighed by Durkheim's broad-ranging vision.

Durkheim emphasized that increasing interdependence posed a huge moral challenge. There was a stark, sombre gap between the needs for solidarity which interdependence increasingly threw up, and the brute realities of conflict and division in advanced economic systems. Economic forces had largely destroyed traditional solidarities without putting anything intelligible or reliable in their place. Industrialization, mass urbanization and the capitalist ethos had wrought grave damage to the social fabric. Injustice and exploitation abounded. The existing 'moral conscience of trades' was pathetically inadequate. Conflict and social stress were endemic, particularly as between labour and employers. There was widespread *anomie*: an absence of recognized and accepted norms to regulate affairs.

What, then, was the solution? Durkheim was convinced that the state would need to play a central role. Government action was required in order to promote greater social justice and a major redistribution of wealth (which Durkheim saw as one prerequisite of greater solidarity in freedom). The state should provide certain of the conditions for greater personal freedom to be exercised in positive ways, for individuals to develop their capacities, particularly for 'communing'. But Durkheim was convinced that too much state action would be 'tyrannical' and 'oppressive', and also inefficient.

The state's ability to promote social unity in freedom was limited. It was 'too remote from individuals' and often heavy-handed. Moreover, economic life was far too specialized, intricate and fluid to be amenable to detailed central control. So it would be a great mistake merely to rush from competitive conflict to an all-enveloping state. Only one route offered a viable alternative to both disunity and central tyranny; and that was the building-up of a civilized, sustainable network of institutions *between* individuals and the state.

What was needed here, Durkheim thought, was the formation of 'professional ethics', the exercise of responsible self-discipline by occupational groups, above all the emergence of new 'corporations' with public responsibilities and duties. In Durkheim's view, in the Roman Empire and again in the Middle Ages, a 'corporative' organization of economic affairs had been largely socially beneficial. It had fulfilled perennial needs for people to work together and to feel that their roles were meaningful. At their best, corporations had been moral regulators, and had integrated economic life into the wider social and political community. Subsequently, of course, the corporations or guilds had fallen into decay and (largely justified) disrepute. But now, Durkheim insisted, they needed to be restored to life in modern forms.

Durkheim's manifesto for corporations as 'public institutions', as it emerged by 1902, had six main components. (1) New or reformed corporations should provide a wide range of participation and solidarity-enhancing services for the people inside them, through welfare, education and recreation as well as work patterns and economic decision making. (2) The corporations should be national or even international in scope, and mobile and enterprising, unlike the previous more rigid guilds. (3) The corporations would need to be in direct contact with the state, but emphatically not so as to be absorbed by it. (4) They should be able to educate their members towards a wider social life and public involvements, thereby playing an indispensable 'moralizing' and 'socializing' role. (5) They should (and probably anyway would) develop into 'one of the essential bases of our political organization', perhaps even 'the elementary division of the state'.[8] A further implication was (6) an overcoming of the employer/trade union conflict, and the emergence of new or restored forms of self-regulation or associative management of enterprises.

This was a manifesto for what came to be called 'corporatism'. Yet the usage of that term soon wandered far from Durkheim's intention. Ideologists of a very different colour were to tear the 'corporate' element of Durkheim's programme from the moral context of libertarian solidarity in which he had placed it. 'Strong corporations' were to become the centrepieces of authoritarianism (as with Salazar and Pétain) or even Fascism (as with Mussolini's and Franco's regimes).[9]

Yet Durkheim's libertarian solidarism found some genuine echoes and counterparts. Much of his programme was paralleled by guild socialism in Britain, which challenged centralized ideas of socialism. Similar themes resounded in Richard Tawney's seminal book, *Acquisitive Society*; in co-operativist mutations of social democracy in Scandinavia from the 1930s onwards; in Harold Macmillan's social Toryism in the 1930s.[10] The linkages were still stronger with Christian democratic thinking in its heyday (see p.26). By the early 1930s a leading American liberal and social economist was saying many similar things in a series of eloquent and accessible books – John Maurice Clark. Clark's ideas on the economics of 'interdependence', and individual and group 'responsibility', were close in spirit to much of Durkheim. By the 1960s, the British economist Andrew Shonfield was elaborating on similar themes of economy-wide co-operation among mutually responsive corporate groups, although Shonfield put less emphasis on ethical relationships, and more on wealth creation, than Durkheim had done (and a greater stress on the role of the state).[11]

The brand of libertarian solidarism propounded by Durkheim forms an important part of the intellectual heritage of this book. Yet from the viewpoint of a fully fledged democratic communitarianism, it had several major faults. Durkheim pinned too many hopes just on 'corporations'. He did not fully explain how 'solidarity' would work between the various sectional units. He gave little attention to the overall resource management or 'co-ordination problem' in a modern political economy. Also, Durkheim's ideas on government and political reform were less well developed. He tended to discount unduly the continued role and socio-ethical importance of both the family and the local community.

There were confusions between prediction and prescription in Durkheim's thought. It was sometimes unclear whether he was saying that something *was* happening or *would* happen in the future (perhaps even in some inexorable, deterministic way), or that it *should* happen. Durkheim's ethical preconceptions were not fully clarified, a grave deficiency. For all its brilliance and fervour, his passion for the core value of free associativeness lost something through not being traced back to coherent philosophical roots. Neither Durkheim's understanding of human nature, nor his interpretations of human value and purpose, were perhaps quite ample enough to carry the weight of theory and prescription he built upon them, giant thinker though he was. It fell to other movements of thought to make up for at least some of these deficiencies.

## PERSONALIST CHRISTIAN DEMOCRACY

Although this book's assumptions owe much to this next tradition, there are several reasons why the contribution of personalist Christian democracy has become shrouded and neglected.

One barrier to understanding is created by the fact that this tendency originally drew heavily on Christian interpretations of human nature, and more particularly on Catholic inspirations and institutions, a suspect linkage for many. Equally if not more important, since the 1950s the Christian democratic parties in Western Europe have tended to become less idealistic and reformist. Their earlier links with communitarian (and Christian social) ideas have receded.[12]

Christian democratic ideas originally flowed out from four main sources. First came some nineteenth-century pioneers of politically liberal social catholicism: Lamennais, Lacordaire, Ozanam, Von Ketteler. Then, starting with Leo XIII's historic social encyclical, *Rerum Novarum* (1891), the papacy's major pronouncements became more favourable. They sonorously condemned capitalism, state socialism, and materialism. They expressed a yearning for a reformist, associationalist third way (although it should be added that the papacy was far from consistent in following up this line politically).[13] Less well known but highly seminal were the writings of philosophers and social reformers: in Italy Giuseppe Toniolo and more especially Luigi Sturzo; Heinrich Pesch in Germany; and in France Albert de Mun and Marc Sangnier, and, by the 1930s, the radical personalist, Emanuel Mounier, and more particularly the philosopher, Jacques Maritain. Finally, in the period immediately after 1945, there emerged a series of political platforms in a brief phase of high promise and noble intentions.[14]

Personalist Christian democratic thinking started out from a concept of the infinite worth of each and every human person. The belief was that because human beings were capable of moral choice, and because they were spiritual beings destined for eternal life, they were of infinite value. Through their life spans, human persons had the right and responsibility to develop themselves to the fullest extent as a preparation for eternity. The necessity for democracy and personal liberty followed critically from this. For considerations of choice, self-development and human dignity made it essential that everyone should have certain basic freedoms and an active share in their own government. All of these values, however, had to be understood in terms of relationships. Personal development and the enhancement of human dignity were unthinkable except along (diversely interpreted) communal routes.

Neither freedom nor democracy could be achieved, let alone morally justified, on a basis of 'individualism'.

According to this thinking, the person and the community were intimately interlinked, economically, politically, morally, spiritually. 'The person is a whole, but ... it is an open whole which tends by its very nature to social life, and to communion.' 'The goal of society is the perfection of the person ... the perfection of the human person is possible only in and by society.' Thus, community experiences were thought to be crucial not simply because of needs for survival, mutual support or socio-economic complementarity. Above all, relationships with others, involving 'intelligence', 'generosity' and 'love', were essential for each human person's moral and spiritual growth.[15]

Personalist Christian democracy was even more explicit about the moral primacy of communal relationships than a thinker like Durkheim. It was first and foremost by virtue of 'love of neighbour as of oneself' that persons would fulfil their truest selves and best prepare themselves for the life beyond. Thus, religion was held to provide a super-mandate for (inevitably imperfect) efforts at 'love' or 'fraternity' through secular society. By the same test, certain other concerns emerged still more sharply as subordinate, for example economic growth, power over nature, technical progress. Not that such activities were to be despised in an 'other worldly', earth-denying or escapist fashion. For they, too, were capable of contributing to people's development, by presenting still further challenges to moral choice and free communality as well as human ingenuity. But the cause of economic development in a broad sense was clearly far from primary in the hierarchy of values on which these thinkers insisted.

Democracy itself was to be justified mainly because of its moral potential for 'each person's civic conscience and responsibility'. It was recognized as still primitive, so Christian democracy's early programmes called for extensive reforms: votes for women, regional decentralization, proportional representation. But the viewpoint equally implied that democracy would always be an aspiration, never an accomplished fact. It involved a spiritual dimension, a persistent challenge to consciences, a constant personal renewal, so that people really would take responsibility and participate communally.[16]

This group of ideas was eloquently expressed by the Christian philosopher Jacques Maritain (1883–1971). Maritain was a thinker of great breadth, a lucid modern interpreter of Aristotle and St Thomas Aquinas. His 'Christian humanism' offered much ground to those with different presuppositions. He developed it not only from religious assumptions but also with reference to an updated concept of 'natural law': basic, perennial axioms which, he suggested, any thinking person could derive through reason and reflection. On this basis, Maritain expounded the themes of person and society, freedom, social justice and 'fraternity', but with 'fraternity' in various forms at the peak. He advocated a new 'post-capitalist' social order which would incorporate, among other things, extensive 'social' as well as 'political' rights; a diversity of participation and conscience-raising institutions; a form of associative ownership through much of the economy.[17]

Maritain was not a utopian, let alone a detailed policy maker. He emphasized that this 'new order' might be defeated or at least long delayed (a sombre contrast with Durkheim). Even then (reflecting a Christian reading of human nature and history), it would still be *en route*, provisional, exigent of 'tension and movement', a new form of 'pilgrimage'.[18] Maritain did not develop 'the details of concrete realization'. Rather, he sought to provide a broad sense of mission, an ethos for change, as well as an architecture of the relevant value concepts (although his handling of political ideas had some flaws and blurred edges, partly the price of his breadth).

From a communitarian viewpoint, Maritain's significance was two-fold. He sought to portray (convincingly to many) an intimate relationship between the beliefs of orthodox Catholic Christianity and the idea of a more socially just, participative and fraternal society in modern conditions.[19] And he argued, consistently and cogently, that it would be difficult properly to project such a society without 'an explicit philosophy and an explicitly formulated ideal'. In his hands, this emerged as a core interpretation of human nature and purpose, a philosophical anthropology, a base-point view of the human person and its value and destiny. This view was teleological, not emotivist or utilitarian. It Maritain's terms, it was also a universally and perennially valid view (contrary to relativism), and a synthesizing, would-be 'integral' one, thus defying modern tendencies towards 'dispersion', 'polymorphism' or 'decomposition' in our understanding of human nature.[20]

Maritain's ideas in one field, the notion of 'the common good', were developed by his associate, Yves Simon. As Simon explained, two individuals, a handicraftsman and a moneylender, may speak of their 'common interest' in going after 'prosperous returns'; say, 10 per cent and 20 per cent respectively. But

30 per cent as the sum total of the coveted return is a sum of private

goods which looks like a common good but is not . . . In order that a good be common, it is not enough that it should concern, in some way or other, several persons; it is necessary that it be of such nature as to cause . . . a common life of desire and action.

Indeed, 'the common good' could be understood only in relation to 'community'. And 'community', according to Simon, meant (1) some members being able to act for the whole, (2) all members desiring the same overall objects, (3) their knowing that the others, too, desired those objects, and their being involved with each other in actually pursuing them, and (4) exchanges between them of 'communications' or signs aimed at producing 'communions'.[21]

For Simon, Maritain and the rest, this made for a stark conflict not only with totalitarian ideas of community but also with the classic liberal individualist's concept of the 'common good' as a mere aggregate of atomistic units or private possessions. Their view also went well beyond mere 'consensus' or the idea that for a 'common good' to exist, or indeed 'community', all that is needed is a general agreement on some object (even though that object might be a-communal or even anti-communal in itself), or just a shared intellectual perception (as though communion in action and experience were not also important).

Next came an implication which marked off personalist Christian democracy perhaps more controversially. This was its pluralistic communalism, its belief that people's moral development through associativeness required certain 'natural groupings'. 'From his birth to his death, each man is involved in a multiplicity of natural social structures outside of which he could neither live nor achieve his full development.'[22] There was not one society but a series of societies: initially and chiefly the family; then the local community, the voluntary welfare association, the religious organization, the trade union, the corporate enterprise. All of these, since they could help to promote the moral development of human beings in communion with one another, had essential rights as well as responsibilities.

This viewpoint was traditionalist in some ways, particularly in relation to family, locality and region; but it was not conservative in a Burke-ean sense. There was much that was wrong, it was felt, about the existing situation so that additions, subtractions and recastings were needed. The intermediate organizations had obligations to respect their members' personal rights, to share power internally, to avoid exploiting other groups. Their social conduct would always need improving. Their structures sometimes required revision. In some respects, too, the balance of power between them would need changing; in particular, downwards to smaller political communities, and away from capital and towards labour (also towards transnational entities – the early Christian democrats were already interested in European integration). As for the state, it would have a lot to do by way of adapting, arbitrating between and co-ordinating the various groupings (but emphatically not replacing them). It would also have an important reserve power to limit any sectional organizations that threatened its own role or oppressed other groups and, corrrespondingly, it had a duty to give special assistance to the weaker groups.

This brings us to the final plank of personalist Christian democracy: its concern for humanism in economic life. The movement's historical roots, after all, went back to protests against the evils of industrial capitalism, family insecurity, class warfare, and the denial of human dignity at work. As a leading Christian democratic party, the French MRP, put it in 1945, an 'economic democracy' was needed: 'the effective participation of everyone in the management of economic affairs . . . a more equal distribution of income . . . the primacy of labour over capital'.[23]

The desire to combine economic decentralization with social responsibility came to a head over the issue of property. Here Christian democracy drew on a long tradition which owed much to Judaism, Aristotle and, more particularly, medieval Christian thought. Resources were to be distributed as widely as possible, both to persons and groups (the principle of 'subsidiarity'), yet also deployed in communal ways from day to day (the principle of 'common use' or 'the universal destination of goods'). Every person had a right to some property in the interests of security, creativity and justice; a wide diffusion of initiative to corporate units was also vital. But equally, property of every sort implied social duties. It was supposed to go along with restraint in both acquisition and consumption; with a subordination to communal needs, particularly those of the poorest; with a constant solicitude for relationships.

How could this subtle equipoise be promoted in modern conditions? One obvious priority, it seemed, was a much wider spread of personal or familial property, partly in housing or through small enterprises. In agriculture, systems of peasant family proprietorship, buttressed by co-operation and collective services, were to be restored. In the most problematic field, large-scale industry, 'capitalism' was to be replaced largely by associative forms of ownership or a 'vocational group order', variously described as ending the supremacy of finance and

shareholders, linking capital and labour, advancing worker participation, transcending class conflicts.

There were major gaps in this prospectus. The ethos was far stronger
than the analysis. There was much vagueness about the institutional,
structural and cultural changes required for *une économie personnaliste
et communautaire* (Maritain's phrase). It was far from clear what sort of
economic problems would be faced on the way, how far existing control
methods would still be needed, or to what extent economic community
would complement, or replace, competition and direction.

A decentralizing, property-diffusing emphasis was not too difficult,
at least in theory; the overall co-ordination issue was another matter. If
the broad direction of reform for the individual enterprise was clear, the
nature of a new participative, associative nexus across a whole
decentralized system emphatically was *not*. What social fabric or con-
nective tissue of pressures, encouragements and obligations would be
needed in order to facilitate the primacy of 'common use', a socially
'functional' and 'responsible' property, an integration of the poor, a
'co-operation for the common good'?

These hiatuses left wide scope for dispute once political
responsibilities and economic pressures had to be faced. They weakened
the radical, reforming impetus. They contributed to the political
fragmentation and declining idealism which were to follow.[24]

None the less, democratic communitarianism stands heavily in this
movement's debt. Personalist Christian democracy reaffirmed, in a
modern form, age-old communitarian ideas of Hebrew, Greek and more
particularly Christian provenance, which are still important through
western culture. To those who sought a religious and philosophical basis
for their communitarian values, it provided one, along with an 'integral
humanism', a unified doctrine of the human person.[25] Unless
communitarian values were regarded as self-evident or self-sufficient,
such a wider (although not necessarily Christian) framework was bound
to be sought and might even be construed as a necessity if communitarian values were not to become merely marginal and if they were to
avoid subtle take-over by the conventional ideologies.

Personalist Christian democracy was less utopian than the other
tendencies discussed in this chapter, more alert to human tragedy and
fallibility. It showed concern for more varied dimensions of
communality, as well as pointing to their complementarity (see chapter
3). In the economic field, its ordering of value priorities was well worth
having, from the viewpoint of this book, although the gravest defect was
undoubtedly the inability to think this through.

## VARIETIES OF CIVIC HUMANISM

One thing was rather neglected by both Durkheimian solidarism and personalist Christian democracy: this was a fully developed theory of citizenship and the state. They sketched one out, but no more. To address this task would have meant working yet again over familiar questions which had always occupied political theorists, such as the role of the individual citizen, the rights and obligations of government, and the rationale of political activity.

Yet answers to such questions are available which accord well with communitarian values. They can be found in the writings of various political philosophers over the past 100 years, who have insisted that politics is first and foremost about the pursuit of personal virtue in community. Drawing on much the same axioms about human nature as personalist Christian democracy (although usually less fully), these thinkers have emphasized that it is the conditions for virtue among citizens that ought to be the primary priority of the state. Equally, they have asserted that it is civic activity, in varying forms, which has the potential to draw out people's best qualities. In the view of these philosophers, then, civic participation is at once the linchpin of democracy and a cornerstone of the good life.

Historically, civic humanists were among those who argued that 'enabling' state action was vital to secure many of the conditions for people to develop their full capacities, particularly for relating well together. Such conditions included safeguards against chronic poverty, unemployment and ill health, and the encouragement of many smaller associations. But government was to promote personal virtue only in these sorts of barrier-removing ways. The scope for personal moral choice was to be enhanced. It would still be up to individuals to decide how to use their extended freedoms.

The civic humanists argued that, in the absence of much public-spirited participation by citizens, selfish factionalism would prevail. From there it was but a small step to elitism or overcentralization, by way of reaction, or even tyranny. Effective democracy and lots of citizens being actively involved were held to be virtually synonymous. Again, such citizen participation could not be commandeered; but state action could and should remove certain specific obstacles to it. Among the necessary measures would be widespread and much improved education, including civic education; a public ethos which commended and celebrated participation whilst reprobating both self-seeking and supine obedience; and reforms in both political structures and electoral systems.

These themes have been expressed under a confusing variety of banners.[26] More than with Durkheimian solidarism and personalist Christian democracy, the main emphasis has been philosophical in a rather abstract sense. The role of the state has sometimes been overplayed. The practical workings of civic participation have received little attention. Its links with economic life have seldom been confronted. The political economy dimension has been almost wholly lacking. Yet the civic humanists have much to offer towards a democratic communitarian synthesis. They have combated rival, currently more dominant, theories of democracy in terms familiar to those who study political ideas. Their twin themes, personal virtue's facilitation as the primary object of government, and civic action as a key to personal virtue, nicely round out the ideological prelude to the argument of this book.

In England, civic humanism was expounded philosophically in the late nineteenth century by the Oxford idealists. As a recent study puts it: 'These men saw the State as the focus of a sense of community and citizenship, an institution in which a good common to all classes and recognizable by all interest groups could be articulated.' As to the nature of that 'common good', T.H. Green, the leading Oxford idealist, wrote:

Human society presupposes persons in capacity – subjects capable each of conceiving himself and the bettering of his life as an end to himself; but it is only in the intercourse of men, each recognised by each as an end, not merely a means, and each as having reciprocal claims, that the capacity is actualised and we really live as persons.

Again

The social order, the community, are the spheres within which our characters develop. Such character-developing social environments are possible only under conditions in which individuals are prepared to accept one another as persons and to treat one another as ends in themselves; a mutual recognition which actually forms and defines 'a common good'.[27]

If 'democratic citizenship for all men' was the highest social ideal, both rights and responsibilities were involved. 'As well as the State providing the preconditions for citizenship, citizenship carried certain duties to the welfare of the community.' 'Citizenship was active and orientated to community life.' Even the value of freedom was to be interpreted in this light. 'Real freedom was not the absence of compulsion but the maximum of power for all members of society to make the best of themselves' ('the best' being interpreted, significantly, in communal terms). 'A man must be given a sphere of responsible action in order to exercise his moral faculties.'[28]

This way of thinking has found new expression over recent years in the USA under the label of 'civic or biblical republicanism'. To cite one theorist, what is at stake is 'an emphasis on the value of politics as moral cultivation of responsible selves'; 'the recovery of a sense of civic life as a form of personal development'; a concept of 'civic virtue' as 'a life that enables individuals to know themselves in regard to the social interdependence in which they live and to respond actively to and share in shaping that wider community'. 'A public life develops only when a society realizes that reciprocity and mutual aid are worth of cultivation both as good in themselves and as providing the basis of the individual self.'[29]

It has been suggested that this viewpoint is a recovery or 'reappropriation' of a long-lived tradition of thinking in the United States. Market liberalism and separatist individualism are held to have dominated over this tradition but never completely effaced it. John Winthrop's active godly commonwealth in seventeenth-century Massachusetts; George Washington's eloquent personification of public virtue as 'the modern Cincinnatus, forming the new nation, ruling without excess, and returning to ordinary life'; the Founders' belief that 'without civic virtue . . . the Republic would decline into factional chaos and probably end in authoritarian rule'; Jefferson's ideal of a self-governing society of relative equals, of an educated people actively participating in government as the only true guarantee of liberty; de Tocqueville's argument 'that the heart of democracy was active civic association'; all these have been invoked as part of an extended historical as well as philosophical argument.[30]

A closely linked idea is 'participatory democracy'. Here again, democracy's chief merit is seen as its potential for stretching human faculties. If democracy is to survive, let alone prosper, a widespread involvement of ordinary citizens in national affairs is vital. Just possessing representative national institutions is inadequate. Moreover, participation at national levels is unlikely to develop without 'social training' for democracy in the shape of participation in other and smaller spheres, including industry. Indeed, smaller groupings are regarded as schools or training grounds for the leading pursuit. Empirical evidence is adduced to the effect that participation in grass roots, specialized communities can indeed help to prepare for participation in the wider national sphere.[31]

The participatory democracy model has been sharply contrasted with the view which sees democracy primarily as an output mechanism, a begetter of wealth or economic growth. It has been said that this latter concept essentially views human beings as 'infinite consumers and accumulators' (surely an impoverishment or distortion); whereas under the participatory model we are to regard ourselves primarily as 'exerters and enjoyers of our capacities'. And from this, once again, a communitarian moral is drawn.

> One can acquire and consume by oneself, for one's own satisfaction or to show one's superiority to others . . . whereas the enjoyment and development of one's capacities is to be done for the most part in conjunction with others, in some relation of community. And it will not be doubted that the operation of a participatory democracy would require a stronger sense of community than now prevails.[32]

## THE SEARCH FOR ASSOCIATIVENESS IN LIBERTY

A guiding thread runs through all these streams of thinking, and that is the concept of a search for associativeness among distinct parts (whether these be persons or social groups).

That ideal is common to Durkheimian solidarism, personalist Christian democracy and civic humanism, despite their differences of emphasis and detail. They are united in the three following beliefs: (1) that there are distinct and unique components (above all individual persons, but also person-enhancing groupings) whose diversity and freedom are crucial; (2) that these units are to be brought together in mutually fulfilling (not just convenient or necessary) relationships of community; and (3) that since such a balance is never perfectly attained, it always needs to be striven for. Thus, separate decision units are to be helped to make a constant effort to converge and collaborate communally while still preserving, indeed enhancing, their distinctness. Through persistent endeavour, a whole is to be composed of still free parts. The keynote is to be a pursuit of associativeness in liberty. All else is secondary or subordinate.

This model of the social world differs radically from those which have dominated throughout several centuries in the west. The social principles which have come to be most widely taken for granted are not at all of this kind.

One conventional model concentrates on a concept of separate and isolated individuals, their material desires, liberties or expressive pursuits. Often these individuals' 'interests', still conceived as essentially private, are seen as reconciled and promoted by a process of 'spontaneous order', an 'order' which is typically credited to the 'invisible hand' of the market and competition. But separatist individualism also takes a gentler form through concepts of private personal growth. By contrast, another set of models concentrates on aggregates, notably class, race, nation or, more abstractly, mankind, 'evolution', the march of history. Here the individual persons of particular times and places are viewed merely as members or subunits, links in a chain, or stepping stones in a collective ascent.

Yet a further influential focus returns to separate individuals as the fundamental units of account and policy objects. But this time the central questions are, 'what is, and what *should* be, the division of resources among individuals?' The concern is with the interpersonal distribution of incomes and wealth, status or power. The ethical yardstick becomes greater equality, still individualistically conceived. Finally, a further and ubiquitous idea tends to be (usually implicitly) subscribed to by believers in all of the above, despite their many conflicts. This is the notion of an indefinite enlargement, acquisition or conquest of resources, whether in terms of inventing new things, exploring space, or acquiring more individual or collective wealth.

Separatist individualism, freedom, spontaneous order, collectivism, equality, material advancement: these ideas are so culturally pervasive that it would be surprising if readers of this book did not confess to much fondness for one or more of them. Their prestige has for long been enormous. That these models can or should be subordinated to a principle of a higher order is hard to conceive. That some of them might even have to be cast aside in the interests of such a higher value may seem daringly radical. Yet it should be clear that the principle of a search for associativeness in liberty, if it is taken seriously, is more or less irreconcilable with every one of them.

This antipathy becomes more evident when we consider the underlying notion of associativeness in liberty rather more closely. If one asserts that the unity in diversity of human beings is fundamental, this is but another way of putting at the centre a concept of good human relationships. One is claiming that the starting point of enquiry, the overarching model and the ultimate evaluative yardstick in social affairs is the standard of relationships between persons. That human beings should relate well together, thereby developing their distinctness, is thought to matter most of all.

In varied or overlapping ways, libertarian solidarism, personalist Christian democracy and civic humanism all insisted on this axiom. For Durkheim, such prescriptions as publicly orientated corporations or reduced inequalities of wealth were no more than stepping stones towards more and better 'communing'. For personalist Christian democrats, such causes as family social security, local and regional decentralization, and co-determination in industry were likewise no more than facilitators. For them the overarching goal was the development of the unique and infinitely valuable human being (on the way to its eternal destiny) through diverse communities. For civic humanism, again, the chief virtue and rationale of political life, and especially of democracy, was to be exercise grounds for communal participation, extending human beings in a particularly vital way.

Such a common vision is fundamentally opposed to certain long-dominant cults of individualism, 'spontaneous order' and collectivism. With these the chasm is unbridgeable, the incompatibility complete. There is a fundamental philosophical and even logical contradiction. You cannot accord primacy to the interaction of distinct, infinitely valuable persons and yet at the same time embrace enthusiastically the ideas of omnipotent, all-enveloping, diversity-destroying processes or wholes. You cannot found your social philosophy on associativeness in liberty and yet think continuously of 'the individual' as fundamentally separate, atomistic and self-contained. You cannot see as crucial a conscious, deliberate moral effort to improve the quality of recognition, communication and mutual regard between persons, and between their vital groupings, and yet at the same time sweepingly rely on the idea of a social order which is to be achieved automatically, mechanically or 'spontaneously', primarily through, even by a process of deliberately exacerbating, selfish pursuits.

If the quality of human and group relationships really is the basic building block in one's view of the social world, then it is simply not possible to adhere to overarching cults either of super-collectivities, or of individuals as islands, or of an 'invisible hand' in social life.

With regard to liberty, equality and material progress the opposition is less complete. The situation here is more subtle, and much obviously depends on the definition of terms. Indeed, we will find that unity in diversity among persons and groups demands elements of both liberty and equality as prerequisites. Here a synthesis may well be needed within which, on certain definitions, liberty and equality find an honoured place, and material progress, too. But such a synthesis is to be constructed first and foremost in terms of personal and intergroup relationships. It is this emphasis which is to frame the context, this model which is to set the pace.

Of course, the search for an associativeness-in-liberty model lacks some of the beguiling properties of its ideological rivals. It cannot emulate the elegant simplicity of the market optimality theory, the equality of measurable resources criterion, or the idea of material progress. It does not offer the shapely satisfactions of mathematical equalities, semi-geometric expression, simple functions or lines. It can hardly be expressed in terms of, say, chemistry, deterministic physics, mechanics or cybernetics (although some of its predecessors drew extensively, if misleadingly, on biological or organic analogies, strong traces of which exist in Durkheim). But perhaps this imperviousness to mathematical expression, and to (narrowly conceived) natural-science-linked interpretations, is a positive boon.

The search for the associativeness-in-liberty model has aesthetic attractions of a different kind. It has strong links with millennial cultural traditions. Its absorption with human and social relationships echoes, after all, the principal focus of interest of novelists, playwrights and poets. There is an enormous amount of imaginativeness, romanticism, sentiment and also religious symbolism on its side.

Whether a particular work of art illuminates the search for associativeness in liberty is another matter. A visual linkage could well imply too much symmetry or stability, and is unlikely to do justice to the dynamics of the search. Persistent, perhaps even restless, movement would have to be portrayed, also elements of fragility, tension, frustration. Among paintings, Raphael's *Disputà* invokes (at least indirectly) an important facet of the model. The *Disputà* depicts a key arena (in this case a theological one); namely the forum, where committed individuals persistently and sometimes fiersly argue about a tradition which they all espouse and about an interminable search that none the less unites them, if only in embryo.

A better aesthetic analogy comes from music. It is the process of attempting an ideal orchestral performance of a major musical work. The work itself expresses some ideal of unity in diversity. Each interpretation by a particular orchestra or conductor is always an approximation, never a 'perfect' expression of the composer's idea, even assuming that that is definable by the very composer himself. And the search for 'perfection' involves an active, creative interdependence among diverse personalities, the orchestra's members, and its varied instruments.[33]

The orchestral analogy suggests a lot about the conditions of the community experience and its effects on those involved. For the orchestra's members and the conductor, the conditions for practising and performing the work include elements of background structure, ritual, belief and accident. Perhaps most important, there is the potential for self-fulfilment through self-transcendence, in so far as these persons are 'lifted out of themselves'. Both the work and its performance are experienced as 'bigger than all of us'. Those involved are united not only with each other, but also with the audience and the composer. Going still wider, there is a sense in which they are united, too, with other performers and enjoyers of the work, both living and dead, indeed as yet unborn. But none of this involves any diminution of their stature or uniqueness. On the contrary, and perhaps most significantly of all, the communal process extends each performer's distinctness as both a person and a musician.

# Chapter 3

# Fraternity, associativeness and participation

Behind all the streams of thinking considered in the previous chapter lies the idea that human beings possess a real capacity to understand and appreciate each other. Equally, the belief is that the ability to commune is crucial not just for human survival but also for our growth as persons, indeed our whole personal identity. This potential for communion is viewed as part of the very definition of being human, and perhaps the most essential part.

The deepest form of communion is love, and here an element of mystery is inescapable. The German philosopher of community, Max Scheler, suggests that we should at least be clear what love is *not*. Scheler argues that the following notions are excluded: total absorption in or by the other; complete fusion; the disappearance of personal identity and distinctiveness; sympathy with others merely by analogy or empathy; fellow feeling as a mere emotional sentiment, or as infection or imitation; the idea that love for others must mean a desire for their material well-being; a 'love of mankind' in abstraction from, or as a substitute for, particular loving relationships.

Scheler claims that the experience of love finds a value simply in sharing ('a joy shared is a joy doubled, a sorrow shared is a sorrow halved'). More radically, he suggests that love or 'sympathy' can extend even to a sense of shame and complicity in the behaviour of far distant or long-dead criminals. According to Scheler, every human person possesses a nature which is 'just as originally a matter of being, living and acting "together" as a matter of existing "for himself": a communal nature which is spiritually as well as biologically determined from the start'.[1]

The reality of interpersonal communion is a matter of basic human experience, confirmed by deep reflection. The phenomenon is no less real than antipathy or dominance; no more elusive than any other idea about a social world that anyway has to be interpreted; no less solid than, say, 'competition', 'power', 'influence' or 'authority'.

The concept of communion as fundamental and constitutive immediately excludes the atomistic individualism of Hobbes, Locke, Hume, Bentham and their modern disciples. It rejects the language of 'individual interests' as the central, let alone exclusive, way of thinking about society and social ethics. It regards as grossly inadequate the economic theory that 'preferences' for goods and services, as held by so-called independent, autonomous individuals, are the basis of 'social welfare'.

Once we accept communion as crucially formative, we are able to perceive, and to welcome, many lesser forms of free associativeness. We become capable of recognizing the faint approximations to communion which appear in wider, sometimes unlikely places. We begin to see more clearly how communion filters through in a variety of paler, less complete or more fleeting forms; for example, in neighbourhoods, at workbenches or on playing fields, in political colloquy or religious acts, also in a bus queue, a thunderstorm, a national celebration. This brings us to the wider principle of fraternity which plays such a large part in this book.

## THE BASIC PRINCIPLE OF FRATERNITY

Fraternity has three components: (1) conviviality, (2) mutual aid and (3) shared commitment. In this sense, fraternity corresponds to Aristotle's definition of 'friendship'. According to Aristotle, friends must enjoy each other's company, be useful to each other, and share a commitment to the good (the latter including a duty to help one another to become better persons in an ethical sense). A key implication is that people's different talents should be greeted as a source of fruitful complementarity, indeed that we should celebrate each other's uniqueness. As the political theorist Bernard Crick suggests, fraternity means not only accepting others as they are but 'an exultant recognition of diversity of character'.[2]

The word 'fraternity' may be criticized as referring only to men, even as 'sexist'. Of course, the term itself is not sacrosanct, as distinct from the idea it expresses, and its best defence is severely practical. It so happens that 'fraternity' is well established and culturally widespread. The available alternatives tend to be cumbrous, culture bound or historically tainted. The 'sexist' objection is neatly dealt with by Crick. He comments that 'sisterhood' would be as good as 'fraternity', indeed perhaps better; 'but it would be still better to desex, even to feminise, old "fraternity", rather than to rewrite most languages or impede them with more neologisms'.[3]

Fraternity's ethical centrality follows from what has already been said. Because it approximates to communion, fraternity is fundamental to personal development and moral value. As William Morris put it, 'Fellowship is life, and lack of fellowship is death.' There follows a crucial need to ensure opportunities for fraternity through our social structures, to provide a 'more companionable environment', 'to invest our technological know-how into the growth of convivial institutions'.[4]

Many existing social structures tend to make fraternity unnecessarily difficult. One classic example is the atomistic new housing estate. There a young wife could say, 'It's like being in a box to die out here'. Another classic case is the standard production line in a large factory. There a young worker could say, 'When I came here first I couldn't talk at all. Now I manage a few words with the man opposite me'.[5]

Fraternity is obstructed by large distances between people's living spaces; by shortage of time (as when much of the day has to be spent on exhausting commuter travel); by the absence of cafés, pubs or public meeting places; by restless geographical mobility and 'the pressure to keep moving upward' which 'often forces the middle class individual, however reluctantly, to break the bonds of commitment forged with a community'. Other impediments to fraternity are the divisions between 'staff' and 'labour', the isolation of elderly and disabled people in specialist institutions, and the existence of ghetto communities not only of the underprivileged, but also in leafy, single-class, single-generation suburbs and in the 'life-style enclave' where what is celebrated is not human complementariness (as just mentioned) but 'the narcissism of similarity'.[6]

These examples show that, although fraternity is a fundamental impulse, all too many forces indirectly obstruct it. The first test of a democratic communitarian society is that it constantly attacks the needless obstacles to fraternity. Such a society would try, for example, to enable people to live reasonably close to their workplaces. It would provide for social spaces between dwellings, and public places so that people could mix more freely. Jobs and work processes would be restructured; socially balanced neighbourhoods would be encouraged; opportunities would be built in for different classes and social groups to mingle across barriers, at least at certain critical points in everyone's life.

None of these things would ensure fraternity for it cannot be socially engineered; but the effort to destroy impediments to it is fundamental.

As Richard Tawney suggested, the first priority is to reform institutions at least so that human beings can be brought 'within reach of each other'. 'The mutual relationships of all citizens should be the yardstick for all social and economic decisions.'[7]

In the framework we are discussing fraternity plays a special part. Whereas the fundamental axioms about personal relationships and communion are starting points, no more and no less, the fraternity principle constitutes a first crucial guideline for both social analysis and public policy. In its light various needless social defects can be pinpointed, and ways of tackling them. The insistence on removing obstacles to conviviality, mutual aid and community service is crucial, and on this foundation further key principles are built.

## COMPLEMENTARY ASSOCIATION

The streams of thinking outlined in the previous chapter tended to assume that fraternity requires varied social groupings: the family, the local community, the cultural or religious group, the economic enterprise, the trade union or profession, the nation state.

Of course, they differed in emphasis. Durkheim and his counterparts, including the guild socialists, concentrated heavily on economic groupings; the civic humanists emphasized national politics and, in some cases, the state; the personalist Christian democrats sought a balance. They all agreed, however, in preferring a pluralistic way. A single, all-purpose, all-enveloping grouping was excluded, whether large or small, a guild or a commune, a tiny village, or the nation state. Instead, different forms of communities were to promote different aspects of fraternity. Indeed, there was more than a hint that the diverse groupings should be *complementary*. These implications, though, were not always made clear, and they need to be spelt out.

Many communitarians are attached to the related notions that fraternity works best when social groupings are (1) multi-purpose or even all-inclusive, and (2) small. Some have even suggested that only thus can 'community' exist at all. The small 'face-to-face' grouping, where relationships are close and multi-faceted, is viewed as best for fraternity or indispensable to it. The optimal community would be seen as the Welsh village Glynceniog Hall: virtually every contact between the villagers was an overlapping one, where the organizer of the village play turned out to be also 'a cousin, a fellow church or chapel member, a friend or just a fellow villager'.[8]

According to this view, the ideal is still the Greek *polis* or city state, encapsulating 'the whole communal life of the people, political, cultural and moral', where so many activities that were 'necessary, interesting and exciting' were enjoyed 'in the open air, within sight of the same acropolis'.[9]

This is an understandable reaction in face of the giantism and impersonality of advanced industrial societies. Yet it is, at least in part, an emotional reaction, and not a necessary deduction from the principle of fraternity.

If it is true that fraternity unfolds through a diversity of social groupings, then each grouping merits some degree of independence within a larger society. Not only should the social groupings have separate identities and powers in order to avoid excessive centralization (an argument on which De Tocqueville and others insisted); each grouping has a better chance of developing people fully if it is not completely engulfed and has room to breathe.

Personal choice is important. No doubt it is salutary that for each of us some groupings are inherited, given, pre-decided. Even within such groupings many moral choices arise, as do wide opportunities for personal growth. Only a restless, roots-denying radicalism always prefers freshly chosen communities. None the less, personal development through fraternity also requires extended choices, and elements of novelty and exploration: choosing between groups, balancing priorities of personal time and effort among them and, for some people, joining with others to create new groups.

Small, close, all-purpose groupings are not necessarily best for a person's moral growth. A tiny mountain village, like medieval Montaillou, bred festering, unrelieved hatreds as well as intense loves. The single grouping which purports to provide for all forms of communality easily ends up by starving some forms, overemphasizing others, or even undermining the requisite that community must not be coerced. The 'godly commonwealths' or 'peaceable kingdoms' of seventeenth- and eighteenth-century New England did not tolerate dissent; seriously divergent thinkers had to leave. The American small town in the nineteenth century could be conformist, oppressive, stultifying.[10] Indeed, one might readily predict from first principles that a small, all-purpose grouping would be too restricted for many diversities of character to cross-fertilize or even to emerge at all.

The groupings may well require some free-standing apartness in order fully to express their particular forms of fraternity. A different quality of encounter is then discovered in each. In a sense, each must be experienced separately for its distinctiveness to be appreciated.

Suppose I go to work or attend a professional gathering, a political meeting or church, and meet James, who is also an immediate neighbour whose family has known my family for several generations. Then my relationship with James as a fellow worker, colleague or co-believer is likely to be clouded by, or even subordinate to, my relationship with him as neighbour or family friend. Compare my contact with another person, John, whom I encounter only at work, professionally, politically or in church, synagogue or mosque. It is likely that this will help me to appreciate a further aspect of fraternity the more clearly because this aspect stands alone.

There are fraternity-based arguments in favour of larger as well as smaller forms of associativeness. In wider social contexts, fraternity tends to become more diffused; but it is no less real, and not necessarily less positive. Its value for human development persists and sometimes expands.

These arguments crystallize around the vexed issued of the nation state. Neither Emile Durkheim nor the personalist Christian democrats nor the civic humanists opposed the nation state. Their ideas are far removed from simplistic 'anti-statism', anarchism, or an overarching cult of 'small is beautiful'. To begin with, a larger framework is indispensable for the diverse social groupings themselves. Without a large container entity like the nation state, how could these groupings perform their complementary work for fraternity in the distinctive, free-standing ways just suggested? But the nation state itself has some more directly communitarian potentials: to act as a focus for a further form of fraternity related to citizenship and politics (see p. 52); to extend the search for free association beyond merely parochial forms. For all its dangers, the nation state can still be viewed as 'a focus of primary allegiance', 'an area in which the common good achieves greater density', 'a point of reference for morals'.[11]

There is yet a further argument for a loose-knit, confederal pattern of social groupings, large as well as small, and extending upwards to the nation state, indeed beyond. This argument has to do with social inclusiveness and openness to change.

Omnibus communality, particularly on a tiny scale, may easily breed a narrow conservatism which simply leaves a lot of people out. Barriers to entry may proliferate, as also exiles and even expulsions. There 'small' is *not* 'beautiful'; it is insular and selfish. A diversity of social groupings and a larger nation-state grouping do not guarantee that things will be better. But they increase the chances of keeping the frontiers open, of accommodating immigrants, of integrating the most deprived.

They are rather more likely to be flexible, and to innovate new forms of search for community in liberty.

Thus, once it is thought through, the principle of fraternity has little sympathy for notions of community which are monopolizing, focused exclusively on the grass roots, or opposed in principle to large-scale organization and to the nation state. Such ideas cannot be reconciled with the diversity of social groupings which is needed if fraternity is to unfold fully, in complementary ways, for each and every person. Only a pluralistic pattern within a substantially sized society can allow the diverse groupings room to develop. Only such a pattern, too, is consistent with considerations of diffused power, personal choice, social inclusiveness and openness to change – considerations on which democratic communitarianism equally insists.

## PARTICIPATION AS A RIGHT AND A DUTY

This third key principle, which is very much a logical outcome of both fraternity and complementary association, provides further cutting edges. It is also more liable to be misunderstood.

Participation means to share freely in activities which shape or express democratic community. It has to be voluntary. Coerced or conscripted involvements do not qualify; nor do services which are paid for. Although elements of giving and receiving, sacrifice and reward, are present, such terms may be inappropriate for experiences which tend to 'take people out of themselves'. As a more inclusive and elastic term, 'sharing' is preferable. Participation has both 'shaping' and 'expressing' dimensions. It involves the *shaping* of democratic community through active contributions to decision making or administration at all levels. But it also involves the expression of communality through public events, shared symbols, celebrations, processions or festivities.

The idea of participation may seem pious or prim. It may suggest lives dominated by the local sports club, trade union branch or welfare association, by ballots, petitions and demos. One is reminded of Oscar Wilde's reported objection to socialism: that 'it would take too many evenings'. There are dangers of hyperactivism or 'do-goodism', of mutations of the puritan or Protestant 'work ethic'; also of trivial forms of sociability or participative 'outgoing' devoid of inward depth.

The notion of 'duty' (which I shall argue is closely linked to participation) has enjoyed even greater disfavour. To many social theories such a notion is foreign. Morals tend to be seen as purely 'private'. Life in wider society is viewed as implying deference to force, the mere observance of laws, or 'pursuing pleasure' and 'avoiding pain'. Less crudely, collective activities are explained in terms of bargains, quasi-contracts or rational compromises, often for the sake of increased (individual or collective) wealth. In the civic–political sphere at least, the notion of 'duty' has even acquired a certain stigma. The dominant concept has been 'rights' cut adrift from obligations; and 'duties' may be conceded only in terms of standing up for some other person's 'rights'.

The concentration on 'rights' may well be allied with separatist individualism or sectionalism, and with cults of 'going it alone'. Indeed, it has been suggested that 'rights' tend to have 'a certain divisive effect, since their function is to mark the bounds of autonomous spheres within society'.[12] At the very least, a huge emphasis on 'rights' distracts attention from the supreme importance, for the communitarian, of *relationships*.

Both participation and 'duty' are invoked by the communitarian traditions discussed in the previous chapter. Both clearly follow from the principles of fraternity and complementary association, as just outlined. If fraternity is fundamental to the development of one's personality, and if it is best drawn out through diverse forms of associativeness, the clear implication is that we all have both the right and the duty to participate in the various groupings. Moreover, once participation and 'duty' are correctly interpreted, the stereotypes described above emerge as travesties.

For example, participation involves not only *acting* together but also *being* together, not just common struggles or sufferings but also common enjoyments. It has spiritual, intellectual and recreational dimensions, and involves play and dialogue as well as 'work'.

A penetrating study of contemporary culture in the United States offers some grass roots examples of people who 'got involved' and explained why. Angelo Donatello first re-established his identity within his own ethnic community and then engaged in local politics in his Boston suburb, 'seeing it as his duty to represent not only Italian Americans but also the welfare of the town as a whole'. Cecilia Dougherty was an elected city official and social activist in Santa Monica, expressing her 'sense of self' in terms of 'a narrative illustrative of long-term commitments rather than desires or feelings', and of virtues in a 'tradition of solidarity with working people and "have-nots"'.

Again, Ed Schwartz in Philadelphia had pioneered co-operative self-help projects in poor neighbourhoods and at work, believing that 'people's political development – their capacity to organize their common life – is both an end and a means'. For Mary Taylor, in California, who had taken a strong stand on environmental issues,

> the pursuit of short-term interest is what is killing us . . . . The public good is based on the responsibility of one generation to the next . . . . It is important for all people to live as happy persons . . . . The way to do that is to realize that you have a debt to society.[13]

These are examples of the more intense, 'shaping' modes of participation. Its 'expressive' forms are typically more casual, informal or relaxed. They include the factory outing, the village fête, the annual street party, the religious procession. A British national symbol, the Coronation, has been described as 'the ceremonial occasion for the affirmation of the moral values by which the society lives', even as 'an act of national communion'. This recalls Durkheim's attribution of 'moral remaking' to quasi-religious 'reunions, assemblies and meetings', and his strictures on modern societies for missing out so badly on these things. However, the more sinister potentials of 'the crowd', with its risks of aggressiveness as well as anonymity, must not be forgotten.[14]

Even purely ad hoc social activities may include forms of expressive participation. A bus queue conversation, an evening in the local pub or leisure time in a café may involve discussion of political events. 'Watching the news' on television does not qualify; but conversing about it with a workmate or a neighbour does. The public domain is shared; a common civic concern is expressed; communal viewpoints may be formed.[15]

## PARTICIPATION AS AN INTRINSIC GOOD

The commonly accepted view is that participation is needed for its 'outputs'; for example, winning a game, building a dam, increasing productivity. From a communitarian standpoint, this view is seriously inadequate. Of course, we participate in activities which have their own rationale, such as wealth creation, sport and art. But success in these fields is not the whole point or even, perhaps, the main one. Although participation is needed to secure good results in them, the reverse proposition is applicable, too: that is to say, those things are particularly good which involve the maximum of associative participation, whether of the 'being together' or 'doing together' kind, as well as serving other useful ends.

This is a claim which turns conventional wisdom upside down. The modern custom, drenched as it is in economic–utilitarian ideas, is to say 'We participate in joint activities in order to get X, Y or Z done.' To which democratic communitarianism replies, 'Yes; but it is also true, and arguably more important, that X, Y or Z are worth doing precisely because we participate associatively in them and so develop ourselves as human beings'.

In similar vein, John Stuart Mill suggested that participation was a good in itself, not a mere means to a (utilitarian) end. He believed that it would 'guard against passivity, inertia, timidity, and intellectual stagnation'. More recently, it has been said that 'increased self-awareness ought to be counted as a "benefit" from participation, independently of its instrumental efficiency'. Environmental crises, which stimulate people to protest, then to contribute to public policy formation, have been cited as an example.

> In these crises citizens view participation no longer merely as an effort, costly in time and money, that is required for the production of a desired policy, but rather regard action in the public interest as part of their consumption, as directly pleasurable.[16]

Conventional economic thinking about 'costs' and 'benefits' is not helpful here. At least for some people some of the time, the so-called 'costs' or 'sacrifices' of public involvement are nothing of the kind. On the contrary, as Albert Hirschman suggests, they constitute 'benefits' to such an extent that 'one can raise one's benefit by raising one's input'. This, Hirschman says, is something which so-called 'free riders' miss out on. '"Free riders" don't just cheat the community . . . they cheat themselves first of all.'

Hirschman goes on to talk of 'the fusion of – or confusion between – striving and attaining'. He cites Pascal on activities which 'carry their own rewards', and invokes the venerable tradition of the religious pilgrimage.

> Obviously, it would make no sense to categorize the travel as the cost of the pilgrimage, and the sojourn and prayers at the holy site as benefit. The discomforts suffered and perils confronted during the trip were part and parcel of the total 'liminal experience' sought by the pilgrim, and distance from the site often acted as a stimulant to the decision to go forth rather than as a brake.[17]

The communitarian view of participation challenges some influential notions about the aims of politics, for example the 'output', consumerist notion that even democracy itself is primarily an instrument for delivering such things as national safety, increased wealth or public facilities to the electors. Communitarianism does not deny these desiderata. But it does insist, by contrast, that democracy's highest value comes from its communally participative attributes. Participation, then, is not just part of the mechanism or paraphernalia of a democracy which is otherwise useful. Rather, participation largely defines what democracy is *about*, even what democracy is *for*.

Participation is a right in the sense that every person is entitled to the various groupings wherewith to develop his or her personality to the full. Society must ensure full access to such groupings. This requires the vote, free speech, a multi-party system, and other components of political citizenship. It also implies the protection of family life; a situation where everybody can belong to a defined locality, region and state; a rich plurality of voluntary, cultural and recreational groups; and not least, access to employment.

But it should be equally obvious that participation is also a *duty*. If social groupings and civic life are fundamental for self-development, involvement in them becomes a moral imperative. Democratic communitarianism nearly always prefers more participation, not less. It takes issue with the many modern trends which encourage passivity. These trends reinforce most people's tendency to underutilize, indeed to undervalue, their potentials for participation. It is not just laziness or alternative diversions which hold us back, but also our lack of self-belief.

In most social groupings there are critical thresholds between minimal and much fuller degrees of participation. There is a major jump, for example, between spectator and active sport, between watching television and entertaining ourselves. A large gulf has to be negotiated between voting in elections and, say, turning out to a political meeting on a cold November night. Deciding that Jones the shop steward or Robinson the manager are 'OK people' to trust is very different from actually contributing to workplace decisions. There is a major leap, too, from giving money to charity to spending time with an old person or a sick neighbour.

Democratic communitarianism is concerned that people should make such jumps. But we are bound to differ in our degrees of participation, and the particular mixtures we choose. Certain modes carry risks of 'overcommitment', destruction of private life, 'burn-out', eventual 'disappointment', even a 'rebound effect' back to purely private pursuits. Moreover, in most groupings, intense involvement is only possible for minorities. The concern is to ensure that these are substantial minorities. In civic life, there should always be an honoured place for partial participators if only because, as Michael Walzer has suggested, there is 'a need for second guessers whole role is precisely that they didn't attend meetings in the first place'. There should always be a place, too, for a political audience which, as Walzer says, 'can be critical as well as admiring, enlightened as well as mystified'.[18] Not only sprinters or long-distance runners are required for civic participation, but also joggers, ramblers, casual strollers, as also informed, appraising spectators. To summarize, then, a democratic communitarian society would spare no effort to encourage participation. The implications are enormous for family and employment policy and support to voluntary groups, for education in general and civic education in particular, for the media, and for voting systems.

A more subtle requirement is that the social ethos should celebrate participation. This means recovering the concept of duty: not an enforced duty; not duty towards a social abstraction or some collective Moloch; not duty that is necessarily uncomfortable or one-sidedly 'altruistic'; but duty which recognizes the indivisibility of the personal and social ... duty related to one's own development through free associativeness, pursued through participation in diverse social groupings and in civic life ... duty which is as often relaxed, convivial or even festive as it is sober and determined.

## LIBERTY AND EQUALITY AS MEANS, NOT ENDS

Much of what we call liberty constitutes an essential prerequisite for fraternity, complementary association and participation. The main forebears of a democratic communitarian perspective, Durkheimian solidarism, personalist Christian democracy and civic humanism, never faltered in their adherence to concepts of personal and group freedom. They were devoted to political democracy, limited central government, and extensive civil rights. Indeed, a democratic communitarian prospectus would be concerned to enhance these things. Otherwise, how could persons and groups exercise the choice out of which, at best, true community is wrought?

None the less, once fraternity, complementary association and participation are placed at the centre, 'liberty' cannot be accepted as the ultimate rallying cry, even in its more congenial forms.

One sort of enthusiastic libertarian goes out of his way to contradict communitarian values. His system of ideas makes no provision for them. His fundamental axioms as to 'the individual', 'welfare', 'progress' and 'competition' discount or exclude them from the start. His belief that social good can be conjured out of 'spontaneous order' or the market's 'invisible hand' pushes them aside, or even threatens to castrate them.[19]

If the public benefit really is identified with a myriad of self-seeking practices, then the struggle to strengthen free associativeness in all its forms, through social life, politics and the economy, can only be viewed as superfluous, perhaps even damaging. The ascription of social virtue to insular, atomistic behaviour cuts at the very heart of community concepts. By this elegant and still influential theory, not only is liberty exalted above fraternity; the former is defined in terms which directly undermine and corrode the latter. Acquisitive or possessive individualism is celebrated. 'Competition', 'markets' and 'privatism' become panaceas rather than useful instruments. It even becomes possible to justify a combination of private acquisitiveness with a magnified central power. The losers from this are likely to be intermediary institutions, future generations and the poor, not to mention the mutual affections and intergroup solidarities on whose patient enhancement community depends.

Other brands of libertarianism discount fraternity, associativeness and participation in more partial ways. These values are nudged aside in the interests of something gentler: not possessive but expressive individualism; not the strident accents of the 'New Right' but the gentle seductions of anti-politics or contracting-out; not materialism but social escapism. The call may be to Emerson's 'trust thyself' or to 'doing one's own thing', to a quasi-oriental abdication from worldly concerns, to a 'therapy' purely of the self, to a 'moving away from institutional claims and other people's agendas . . . in search of an inner validation'.[20]

Sometimes talk about 'community' is retained but in a contracted or fragmented form. It is reserved for neighbourhood units, small communes or 'life-style enclaves', for worker co-operatives or self-managed enterprises, or the cause of industrial democracy. This, too, impoverishes the fraternity factor. The problems of wider political economy are shrugged off; broader concepts of building up free associativeness are abandoned; the dangers of economic parochialism and of small, tight, omnibus groupings (see pp. 40 and 41) are ignored.

However, where community values are merely narrowed down, rather than philosophically negated, at least a fragmented search for free associativeness persists. For the communitarian, the challenge is to reunite the fragments and to show how they lead on to more expansive aims. Patient dialogue is preferable to rejection; to discover a new synthesis would be best of all.

Some reinterpretations of 'liberty' edge close to this. They abandon an exclusive emphasis on 'negative freedom' or mere freedom from constraints (which often implies atomistic individualism, a disregard for social responsibilities, an unconcern about poverty and inequality). Instead, their emphasis is on 'positive freedom' or the idea of enabling people to develop their full potential. Then, edging still closer to the communitarian position, they sometimes interpret that potential mainly in terms of community, thus recalling the ideas of the leading civic humanist, T.H. Green (see chapter 2).

But having travelled this far, the communally minded new libertarians gib at taking the final step. They are not ready to substitute 'fraternity' for 'freedom' as the highest goal. Having opened the envelope of 'freedom', and found that its best contents are communitarian, they persist in proclaiming the envelope as their leading principle, not the contents. Yet once 'freedom' is redefined so as to point chiefly towards personal fulfilment through relationships, surely nothing less than this latter objective deserves the central place?

Thus, liberty needs to be rescued from its inherent inadequacies as a supreme cult. It requires to be demoted, in a sense, before its best strengths can come into play. Although indispensable, it cannot be the prime guiding principle. Once liberty is juxtaposed with a fully understood community, their inescapable linkage becomes clearer; but so also does a major qualitative difference between them. This is something like the difference between a minimum and an optimum or between a trial and a performance. Indeed, what appears to be at stake is nothing less than the contrast between a prerequisite for social morality and social morality itself.

According to the communitarian perspective, liberty acutely needs the context of fraternity, complementary association and democratic participation; then it is seen as an essential precondition, a guarantor of personal and organizational moral choice, but never as the final end.

As with liberty, so with *equality*, democratic communitarianism finds much to embrace but also much to reject.

Fraternal, associative and participative values imply, first, that people are entitled to access to social organizations and to a share in decision making in economic, social and political affairs. Second, communitarian values equally support those public services which reduce, or at least cut across, social divisions; notably communal schools, hospitals, health services and networks for the elderly and disabled. Third, fraternity, associativeness and democratic participation possess a redistributive cutting edge. They require a redistribution of resources in order to combat poverty and to help to integrate communally the most deprived and the excluded. All of these priorities can be abundantly justified on democratic communitarian grounds alone. Other validations are superfluous, even confusing.

Thus, greater equality of access to social organizations and to policy formation is welcomed because it gives more chances for people to develop their distinctive talents, primarily in association with others. It is mainly because of their potential for 'mixing', for the sharing of experience and the bridging of social chasms, that communal education, health and other basic facilities are favoured. Again, it is mainly because the existence of deprived and excluded minorities is a blot on community, that 'anti-poverty' would be given such high priority.

For people to be left out or marginalized, whether they are the long-term unemployed, disadvantaged ethnic groups, immigrants, single-parent families or, more generally, the chronic poor, is offensive to community. Their integration demands both redistributive taxation and voluntary, decentralized forms of action. In terms of fraternity, associativeness and participation, the effort to 'include them in' would be seen as a never-ending challenge, but one spurred on, above all, by the search for associativeness in liberty.[21]

Readers are asked to note what categories of egalitarianism these priorities do *not* include. They do not justify the idea that complete or greater equality is somehow good in itself. They provide no mandate for redistributive taxation purporting to favour a majority of the population in the advanced economies, as in the rhetoric of 'raising up the working class'; nor for general battles to squeeze indefinitely either 'the capitalists' or a bonanza state. A communally driven redistribution furnishes no sanction for what Bernard Crick describes as 'jealous levelling' or a thrust to maximize 'simple arithmetical equality', which is consistent with 'a totalitarian society', and which 'could conceivably create even fiercer competitiveness'.[22]

The contrast goes further. There is no support for the notion that fraternity will eventually emerge as a by-product of egalitarian preoccupations over a long period. Nor is there even acceptance of the more subtle idea that axioms for 'justice' or 'fairness' in the allocation of resources between individuals, if only these could be agreed by a rational consensus, would themselves constitute a sufficient basis for 'community'.[23]

Most of these ideas typically rest on the very assumptions which characterize narrow individualism. Here, too, pre-social or a-social individuals with isolable interests are taken as the basic entities or guiding norms. It is between such individuals that increased or complete equality is sought. Here, too, appropriable private goods are accorded moral centrality. The one-sided emphasis on individual rights and entitlements, to the neglect of responsibilities, persists.

Once democratic communitarian principles are adopted, the anti-poverty cause has no need for these particular egalitarian, individualist or materialist rationalizations. It may even be harmed by them. Anti-poverty finds abundant justification, instead, on the ethically firmer ground of fraternity, associativeness and participation. These provide the acid test, not an abstract concept of justice, or a utilitarian pseudo-calculus. In their light, selected aspects of equality are seen to be crucial: those categories of redistribution which incorporate and promote free communality in concrete ways.

## COMMUNITARIAN POLITICS

I now conclude by drawing some of the implications of these communitarian principles, very briefly, first for politics, then for a modern economic system.

Democratic communitarianism suggests that it is a vital priority to nurture public traditions. A sense of identification with both the dead and the unborn should be fostered. This reflects De Tocqueville's dictum that a culture which 'makes men forget their ancestors . . . clouds their view of their descendants and isolates them from their contemporaries'.[24]

An important part of communitarian politics is to debate public traditions and what these mean. This is a dynamic process. As Alastair Macintyre puts it, 'a living tradition is an historically extended, socially embodied argument, and an argument precisely in part about the goods which constitute that tradition'. Macintyre adds that even political community itself can be regarded as sort of 'enquiry', a continuing process of discovery in which differing viewpoints are necessary. Another modern philosopher calls political discussion of this sort 'rational community', as distinct from the 'affective community' of a shared culture and the 'productive community' of co-operation at places of work.[25]

But democratic communitarianism goes further than other view-points in insisting that associativeness in politics is, to a major degree, an end in itself. Here again, as in the earlier discussion of social groupings and participation, the conventional view is reversed. According to that view, political civility and consensus are essentially lubricants: instruments for the final delivery of 'outputs' such as defence, national power, private consumption, public welfare spending. Democratic communitarian principles suggest, however, that associativeness in politics is 'a good thing' in itself.

What this means is that politics, too, is a theatre for the pursuit of free community. It is yet another testing place for the personal virtues, and for the communal growth of the people involved, in this case particularly the politicians. Partnership in politics is also a scene setter for fraternity, associativeness and participation in the other arenas, not least the economic arena – as we shall see.

To quote a modern social philosopher:

> To be sure, good consequences for each and for all may flow from the dialogue – and there may be men sufficiently impoverished in their political imagination to suppose that such an instrumental value is the only merit of rational community. But men may take an interest in the existence of the dialogue itself, and if they do, they will strive to create a political order whose essence just *is* that dialogue.[26]

A major obstacle arises when party ideologies are not only polarized but such as to exclude or upstage communitarian beliefs. This happens, for example, when there are just two hegemonic parties, one professing competition, privatism and economic freedom as a cult, the other venerating state direction, collective ownership and economic equality. The intricacy and excitement of these ideas, and their conflict, tend to crowd out fraternity in the public mind. Moreover, for all their antipathy, both sets of beliefs tend to share the assumptions of separatist individualism. Paradoxically, it is the parties' very agreement on these assumptions which embitters their strife. A political consensus steeped in concepts of personal separateness and 'rights', of possession and 'choice', has, in the last resort, a particularly divisive effect.[27]

## ECONOMIC COMMUNITY AS AN IDEAL

As we saw in the previous chapter, all elements of the democratic communitarian heritage insisted that an advanced economic system could not be exempted from the search for free solidarity. It would not be possible to separate 'society' and 'the economy' so that democratic community would be increased in society, while the economy remained untouched. But most of the forebears went a lot further. They believed that the economic system stands in particular need of change, and that its reform on democratic communitarian lines constituted the biggest and probably the most challenging task.

But how would this be done? By replacing markets and state direction? If not, how should they be complemented or corrected? What alternative methods of co-ordination would be available? And how far could democratic community and economic efficiency be reconciled?

The precursors mainly concentrated on reforms within the enterprise. Their emphasis was chiefly on achieving more fraternity and participation in the workplace, changing the balance of power within economic institutions, and creating co-operative units which would be more or less separate and self-contained. On the bigger issues of political economy the pioneers offered, in the main, only a broad rhetoric related to 'solidary ties' between corporations and the state (Durkheim), or 'social co-operation' (the personalist Christian democrats) or 'participation in national policy making' (some of the civic humanists).

Clearly, this was inadequate and is, if anything, still more inadequate today. Greater fraternity and participation within economic organizations are important aims, but far from enough. The most ambitious programme of employee partnership, of intra-enterprise co-determination or industrial democracy, would still fall far short of democratic communitarian imperatives. Much more is needed than changes within each organization considered separately. Parochialism and sectionalism would persist and might even worsen. The quality of relationships among the different economic interests, other social groupings, public opinion and government, would be left untouched. Nothing would have been done to address a persistent array of problems which call for co-operative solutions *across* these gulfs.

According to democratic communitarian principles, there is no question of sweeping away either markets or state direction. On the contrary, both have to be maintained in important roles. Communitarian principles even provide a limited ethical case for markets and state direction, one which goes well beyond a mere grudging acceptance. None the less, if fraternity, complementary association and democratic participation are accorded primacy, and their implications followed through, it becomes evident that a lot more than markets and state direction is called for across a whole economy.

The ideal of economic community implies that neither markets nor state direction can be more than subordinate instruments at best. If markets and state direction constitute the two indispensable pillars of an advanced economic system, some form of associativeness in liberty has to be, as it were, the surmounting arch. The arch is to bridge and unite the pillars. It is needed in order to give coherence to the whole and to provide a sense of upward thrust in ethical terms, to say nothing of pleasing the eye.

Fraternity, associativeness and participation are to extend, in modified forms, to the relationships between economic organizations, social organs and the state. The economic system is to be seen, in major part, as a complex of connecting cells whose mutual sensitivities represent a vital force. Island concepts of management and ideas of purely corporate utopias are to be abandoned. The principle of enterprise both *for* and *in* community is to take over the central ground. The economic organizations themselves are to be associates or social partners.

Economic community implies a looser relationships than small-circle fraternity. Neither intimacy nor a constant huddling together is envisaged, let alone unanimity. The social partners are to be strung together by elastic bands, not cords or chains. On the other hand, analogies from conventional political understandings, international relations or the sports field are too slack. Economic community involves a lot more than, say, common membership of a nation state, non-belligerent co-existence or joint involvement in a competitive game, even a game with the most elaborate rules. Analogies with market relationships are particularly inept. Even a generalized language of bargaining, contract or mutual convenience is too shallow.

Value is attached not only to each separate organization, but also to the quality of their relationships. Their legitimacy is to be traced not just to each one's power to facilitate free associativeness inside itself, but also to reciprocal duties which should exist among them. The whole network is to be interwoven by mutual responsibilities. No 'invisible hand' is expected to harmonize the different parts. Mere balance or competition among the separate interests contributes little to, may often detract from, the common good. Nor is obedience to the state and the law to be loaded with the inordinate burden of producing that common good, let alone identified with it. Rather, public responsibilities as well as powers are to be widely diffused among economic agents.

Clearly, the relational duties of organizations differ from those of individual persons. Organizations do not 'grow in virtue' nor 'become more truly themselves' through communal relationships. None the less, a constant effort is to be poured into bridge building and associative linkages within the triangle of economic organizations, society and government. This is particularly vital where the organizations form up into competing economic interests or social classes, or rival claimants on public resources. Like individual citizens, economic organizations should be involved in consultation about public policies. For them, too, civic participation is not only a right but also a duty. They are to be active contributors to national policy making, although in this field their associateship or partnership is to be a junior one.

Thus, the ideal of economic community implies a new or renovated fabric of recognitions, connections and affiliations across the system. A nexus of mutual obligations and loyalties would stretch across the political economy or at least its leading parts. Public responsibilities would be enshrined in organizations' objects and codes, ratified by the democratic community, sustained through the economic culture.

Democratic communitarianism objects to the moral attenuation of persons inside economic organizations. It takes issue with the cultural and institutional forces which often put these persons in thrall, unwittingly, to a pseudo-pragmatism, a quasi-technical detachment, a real or apparent cut-offness from ethical choice. The widespread immunity of managers, workers and economic 'operators' from civic and socio-ethical appraisal is deplored. Equally deplored is the frequent stunting of moral *opportunities* for them in terms of interpersonal fraternity, inter-group associativeness, and participation in public policy.

Economic community would be full of potentials for extended fraternity. Both inside and around organizations, and along their interfaces with society, through relationships with peers, neighbours and public arbiters, there would be many opportunities for people to make the sort of choices which can lead to personal moral growth. Between economic organizations themselves, there would be many openings for complementary association, for partnership-type modifications of the same themes of companionship, mutual help and shared civic–ethical commitment. As for relationships 'upwards' towards the social and public arbiters, the keynote would be democratic participation. Many channels would exist for both persons and organizations to contribute to democratic community, expressively and actively.

Even then, as free agents, both the persons and the organizations involved might frequently duck the opportunities. But from a democratic communitarian viewpoint, that would be no excuse for failing to provide them.

# Chapter 4

# Public co-operation in the economy

It seems a far cry from the high ideals of fraternity, complementary association and democratic participation to the earthy realities of a modern economic system. The attainability of these ideals in a modern economy, with all its conflict, coercion and impersonality, seems implausible. That versions of community ideals may already have appeared there, if only palely and falteringly, is difficult to accept.

Scepticism here takes us back to the many background influences on our thinking which insist on making a radical, irredeemable split between 'community' and 'the economy' (see chapter 1). If there is one thing that vast numbers of people find it easy to agree on, it is that there is a huge, even yawning, chasm between modern economic systems and the sort of community values discussed in the previous chapter. Such a chasm is constantly assumed on both 'right' and 'left', by economists and students of society, and by both pragmatists and idealists.

None the less, I intend to show in this chapter that there is a partial connection between democratic communitarian values and certain limited phenomena which have existed in modern economic systems. I intend to demonstrate that these phenomena at least offer clues, stepping stones or bridgeheads to the ideal of economic community.

The relevant phenomena will be identified in aggregate terms as 'public co-operation'; that is, processes whereby economic decision units freely collaborate with each other, and with external groups or government, in the cause of public interests. It is this phenomenon, with its various ramifications, which provides the next stage in my argument: the claim that the associative ideal is already present in advanced economic systems, if highly fragmentedly and imperfectly, and that an enormous amount can be learnt from the rough-and-ready approximations to economic community which already lie around us.

Before this can be done, though, a lot of preparatory investigation and analysis is needed. We first have to examine the co-operative phenomena in some detail, both at national levels and on the ground, drawing on a lot of historical evidence. Next, we have to see whether these phenomena are measurable and whether they form a pattern. Only then can we begin to compare realities with ideals. Readers should be warned that all this makes for a big jump from the discussion of social principles pursued so far in this book. It involves a major change from the conceptual to the empirical; from the discussion of values to a detailed grappling with many aspects of economic organization and functioning as they have actually existed.

## 'CORPORATIST' PARTICIPATION, INDUSTRIAL PEACE, PAY RESTRAINT

In 1965 Andrew Shonfield, a leading economist, published a path-breaking book, *Modern Capitalism*.[1] In it he said a lot about the phenomena of collaboration in democratic mixed economies. Shonfield saw public aims for the economy as achieved not only by vigorous competition, not only through laws, nor just through fiscal or monetary controls. According to his analysis, a major part had also been played by processes of consultation, negotiation and persuasion, drawing both business and labour into voluntary convergences with public policies.

Shonfield explained how, through the post-war years, governments had repeatedly tried to get their way through methods falling well short of coercion: by convoking and conciliating between economic interests, by making deals and compacts with them, by persuading, 'jogging' or 'nudging'. In response, big business and big labour, exercising variable power towards each other and society, had sometimes collaborated as junior partners with government. Varying roles in bringing all three together had been played by planning agencies, organs of public opinion, financial institutions, and (more or less well-organized) intermediary organizations of business and labour.

According to Shonfield, these collaborative networks were ubiquitous, but they varied a lot in style and effectiveness between countries. They could be more or less directly state led, centralized or decentralized, formal or informal. Rhetorically, they might have star ratings or low profiles; sometimes, they were ideologically disguised. The collaboration might partly rely on direct financial inducements (for example, conditional public subsidies). An important feature had been the economy-wide moral compact, its classic form being a government commitment to work for growth and full employment 'in return' for pay–price restraint by trade unions and business. Co-operation often depended on the disciplines of publicity and information flows to the other partners, government and, sometimes, the public ('the principle of the goldfish bowl'). A crucial factor had been the 'active search for consensus'; 'organised colloquy'; 'informality and close personal contact'; 'a system of wide-ranging consultation and organised argument'.[2]

It is not generally realized how far, since Shonfield's book appeared in 1965, scholars have pushed ahead with the study of co-operative processes in modern mixed economies. True, their work has been highly fragmented and a unifying conceptual framework has been lacking. Yet three important indicators of economy-wide 'co-operativeness' have emerged.

The first indicator is often discussed under the heading of ('liberal') 'corporatism'. It is the extent to which sectional economic interests participate in public policy processes within a broadly democratic system, through representative institutions endowed with public rights and duties.

Do most workers, farmers, companies and other economic agents belong to representative national organizations? Does each part of such a network have a publicly recognized special status or monopoly in its part of the field? Do the intermediary bodies (trade unions and labour federations, employers' associations, professional groups, etc.) have the right to be consulted by government and parliament, and to be included in the discussion of public policies? While remaining fairly autonomous and separate from government, do these bodies have wide public responsibilities to carry out specific economic tasks, to work with each other, and to help implement public policies?

Scholars have reached a broad measure of agreement that, according to these tests, the principle western economies have tended to exhibit three levels of 'corporatism': 'high', 'intermediate' and 'low'.[3]

A second indicator of economy-wide co-operativeness is industrial peace, measured by a low incidence of strikes and days lost through industrial disputes. Of course, a good no-strike record is not an infallible guide to the dominance of conciliatory, consensual or pacific ways of resolving industrial conflicts. It may be that strikes are discouraged by legal controls and penalties, or by a situation of large-scale unemployment where people are deterred from striking through fear of losing their jobs. However, barring legal repression and large-scale unemployment (and subject to the statistics being comparable and covering suitably long periods), it is reasonable to take major contrasts in the incidence of strikes and days lost through disputes as a broad indicator of the 'co-operativeness' of a country's industrial relations. Again, this is a test on which some countries have had consistently better records than others.[4]

A third criterion is effective voluntary incomes policies, measured by moderate rates of increase in pay. Such policies became a major objective in many mixed economies after 1945. Incomes restraint was regarded as a crucial test of labour's and business's collaborativeness with public interests in securing steady economic growth without excessive inflation.

Once again, we have to be circumspect about the likely causes and effects. Moderate pay increases could signal an incomes policy enforced by law, severe penalties and a highly coercive state. They could reflect severe recession and unemployment, equally undermining the 'voluntariness'. Thus, it is only reasonable to attribute 'success' to voluntary incomes policies where these were non-coerced and where they co-existed with reasonable growth and high employment (as was usually the aim). Yet again, there is no doubt that some success stories of this kind occurred between the late 1940s and the 1970s.[5]

Now suppose that a particular country is found to have performed well on all of the above tests over a long period. To excel in economic interest participation, industrial peace and voluntary pay restraint – all within a context of non-coercion and steady non-inflationary growth – would be a major achievement. Such a combination would say a lot about the political economy's quality. It would surely merit special recognition. No longer could we measure such a system's social co-ordination along purely competitive or *dirigiste* lines. Indeed, if a number of such cases emerged, our present, crudely two-dimensional method of classifying economic systems would become seriously inadequate. A third force would have to be allowed for, a third type of characterization added.

In fact, several national systems did achieve precisely this combination during much of the period after 1945. An example worth quoting is that of Austria.[6]

In Austria, highly inclusive organizations of labour and business enjoyed semi-constitutional status. They had considerable powers and representational rights. But as a correlate, both business and labour were meshed into an intricate pattern of social obligations: internally, mutually, and towards public authorities and the state. There was wide acceptance of the principle that, within a broad consensus about public interests, sectional units should take account of neighbouring groups, the other 'social partners', government's wishes, the whole economy. There were extensive and entrenched processes of direct contact, negotiation and consultation.

A high level of industrial peace was a notable achievement in Austria, a moderate rate of pay and price inflation was another; both in conditions of reasonable economic growth and without draconian controls. A perceptive study of the system emphasized that all these features – the networks for representation, 'participation' and 'consultation', the 'remarkable record of industrial peace', the successful wage–price policy, 'the absence of detailed rules and prohibitions', 'the great reliance on voluntariness and co-operation' – interlocked.[7]

Taking our cue from the Austrian case and similar ones, is it reasonable to rank whole economic systems as 'more or less co-operative'? The first indications would appear to be, 'yes'. Of course, fine, cardinal measures are not feasible, only broad-gauge comparisons. All the indicators I have mentioned have flaws, and they are not fully comparable. A purist may object that participative networks or activities describe a 'process' or 'input' into the system, whereas industrial peace and pay restraint for stable growth represent some of its hoped-for achievements or 'outputs'. The three measures are far from comprehensive. They exclude sectional interest co-operation with many other public aims, for example in relation to environmental protection, anti-poverty, or non-discrimination in employment, or in connection with 'soft laws' or (non-coerced) tax obligations.

However, none of these objections is fundamental. Problems of broad-gauge measurement, incommensurability and partial coverage are inescapable in virtually every social field. They constantly afflict the analysis of both state direction and competition. Anyone who thinks it is easy to measure off economic systems as more or less 'state controlled' or 'competition driven' had better look at the evidence! Even the long-established, apparently 'hard' business of measuring competition between industries suffers from these defects. By contrast, the assessment of economic co-operativeness is still in its infancy. It is not difficult to envisage improvements in the measures I have singled out or the addition of further ones, perhaps related to civic contributions or environmental policy.[8]

No suggestion is being made as to the overall frequency of the co-operative processes. Their intense forms may well have been rare. Moreover, it is clear that they did not replace either competition or state direction, although they appear to have reduced these counterparts' roles. To the question – if both competition and state direction have limits, what other forces are available to co-ordinate economic affairs? – the first stab at an answer, then, appears to be some form of interest group collaboration with public policies. But we need a lot more evidence about how this phenomenon works.

## PUBLIC RESPONSIVENESS, WIDER EXAMPLES

Some years ago I set out to test the solidity of co-operative and non-co-operative phenomena at grass roots levels. I wanted to investigate what processes were at work both inside and between organizations, how distinguishable these processes were from competition and coercion, and whether any typologies of organizational response to public interests could be found. My work grew out of previous studies in business history, since historical evidence was more readily available for business enterprises (though I hoped the findings would apply to other types of sectional organization).

Studies of the British steel industry were particularly revealing. Few industries had experienced greater efforts at social control through negotiation and persuasion, long before both nationalization and the post-1945 macro-policy developments observed by Shonfield. Rich records were newly available on individual firms, industry associations and the relevant public bodies. Hence it would be possible to investigate not just the intricacies of a firm's policies towards government and the public over long periods, but also the interactions with other firms, local communities, public opinion and government objectives.

Major contrasts in co-operation and non-co-operation soon emerged. They appeared in a series of 1914–39 comparisons between two major firms, United Steel Companies (USC), and Stewarts and Lloyds (SL). USC was generally pro-active and contributive towards publicly approved efforts to reorganize the industry; SL was generally unilateralist and detached. USC was moderate in its relationships with the public authorities; SL was pushful. USC tended to conform, in the main, to the eventual regime of centrally administered prices; SL repeatedly evaded it.[9]

The contrasts between the two firms went wider. They extended to a wide range of social issues: philanthropy; pollution; worker consultation and pensions; employment maintenance in depressed areas; help to redundant workers. On all these issues certain norms were enjoined by public opinion and/or government. On all of them, one company USC, tended to be publicly responsive, whereas the other, SL, tended to be publicly *un*responsive. I should add that on most of the issues another firm in the study, Dorman Long, tended to fall between the extremes. Overall, in terms of public policies and social norms, the three firms appeared to fall into categories of 'co-operative', 'separatist', and 'intermediate' or 'conformist'.[10]

Another study looked at British business behaviour in the First World War. During the war, firms were repeatedly exhorted by government and public opinion to co-operate with public interests, well beyond the ambit of laws and formal controls: to contribute to war charities; to help with the central organization of production and supplies; to abide by price controls whose enforcement was often weak; to exercise restraint in seeking profits and personal gains. The study indicated that a minority of businessmen had 'profiteered' both deliberately and effectively; a further minority had shown significant price–profit restraint; most had probably been involved in 'partial, involuntary or intermittent profiteering'. In each trade, in varying proportions, significant minorities either resisted or actively supported price controls at the outset; a small minority evaded them once they were in place. Firms donated widely varying amounts to war charities. There was a hint that, within each industry, a few firms tended to be co-operative or non-co-operative in general ways, as with USC and SL. But most appeared to combine, in varying mixtures, socially approved and stigmatized activities.[11]

Similar contrasts occurred in time of peace, judging by a wide array of secondary sources on British business between 1880 and 1939. For example, the chemical industry giant, Imperial Chemical Industries (ICI), formed under government auspices in 1926, acted as a semi-public concern. It geared many of its investment, product and pricing decisions towards public policies and acted internationally as a UK/imperial champion. It also introduced socially approved practices on labour relations and joint consultation. Interestingly, during earlier phases, one of ICI's chief predecessor firms, Nobels Explosives Ltd, had followed a markedly different path, repeatedly showing forms of ruthlessness and deceit towards competitors, customers, government and the public. Again, however, these appeared to be polar cases; most of British business probably lay between.[12]

These contrasts complement other findings. In the USA, over long periods, multiple social deviance was shown by Standard Oil, the Ford Motor Company and the California Railroad; in marked contrast with the record of some 'corporate liberals' (for example, Mark Hanna, George W. Perkins, Gerard Swope), who pioneered improvements in business–labour–government relationships. But again, most of American business probably fell in the middle. Coming to more recent times, one investigation tells us how various American companies in the 1960s and 1970s divided between 'resistance', 'passivity', 'active negotiation' and 'pioneering' with regard to issues like pollution, racial integration and women's rights. Another study suggests that, while some modern companies in the UK avoid public involvements, others 'treat them like the weather' while yet others attempt high profiles along the various dimensions, as with Pedigree Petfood's efforts to develop a well-behaved canine population and to educate customers in the virtues of controlling dog excrement in public parks.[13]

Going wider than business, studies of trade union behaviour towards public policies in modern times have sometimes compared a given industry between different countries. As a result, we learn in broad, two-way terms that organized labour (as well as business) was 'co-operative' in, for example, the West German motor or chemical industries, with regard to reorganization and safety issues respectively, but relatively 'conflictual' over those same issues in counterpart sectors in the UK and the USA.[14]

## PUBLIC INTENTIONS AND SACRIFICES

In my studies, I sought to test public responsiveness in a searching way. I went into considerable detail in examining an organization's public intentions and any specific immediate sacrifices it made.

For example, in relation to a single company policy the question was posed, 'Hope, inefficiency or public duty? The United Steel Companies and West Cumberland, 1918–39.' Did this firm maintain large uneconomic operations because of ignorance of the losses or, more likely, of the available investment alternatives? Was it a case of mere inanition? How far did they hope for an eventual economic upturn which would make even these decrepit operations pay? I concluded that a crass inefficiency which soon, anyway, receded, could not bear the main burden of explanation. Neither accounting controls nor market perceptions were ever so bad as to disguise an obvious, indeed notorious, economic marginality. A Micawberish optimism, which retreated as the depression years took their toll, did not go far towards explaining the West Cumberland policy either. By contrast, considerations of public pressure, political repute and 'social responsibility' appeared to play a major role.[15]

In these and other cases, little weight was attached to the rhetoric of public statements or chairmen's speeches. It was the 'hard' record of external contacts, the testimony of significant outside observers, and still more the internal evidence of directors' letters, managers' reports and confidential memoranda, which proved more telling as to public sensitivities where these existed. References to 'national interests' or 'social responsibilities' counted for more in a board paper or consultants' report, or in private notes to a colleague, than in a letter to some public figure. Sometimes, an obvious public trigger for the relevant decisions sprang out from the evidence: a governmental request; a press campaign; a major public row; some public colloquy in which the firm was involved.

Complementary clues sometimes came from the decision makers' long-expressed social convictions, perhaps still more from their personal characters and ambitions. Thus, our attribution of public motives to key decisions during ICI's formative phase benefits from an appreciation not only of its chairman's, Alfred Mond's, proclaimed beliefs, but also of his close connections with politics and Whitehall, and of the psychological factor of his apparent appetite for public status. Similarly, the charismatic and autocratic attributes of Austria's national trade union leader over many years, Anton Benya, help to explain why government pleas for pay restraint found a ready response from the peak trade union body. There, they went with the grain of Benya's personal power thrusts and centralizing tendencies towards the constituent trade unions.[16]

The likely motivations for co-operating with public policies and social norms appeared to be richly diverse. They ranged from clear overlaps with commercial interest, through desires for honours and 'a good press', across to local pride, chauvinist and imperialist sentiments, and humanitarian or vaguely communitarian ideals.[17]

Perhaps the most telling check on the solidity of public responsiveness was to examine any short-run costs which organizations thereby incurred. I found that many such costs could be assessed to a greater extent than anticipated. They included time spent by leading officials in discussions with government, public agencies, or industry-wide bodies engaged in publicly approved activities; probable delays in corporate decision making as a result of considering or discussing public factors; and direct financial outlays on, for example, philanthropy, *ex gratia* payments to redundant workers, or anti-pollution measures.

It was harder to assess any profitable alternatives which might have been given up. But here again some of the data could be directly revealing. After all, some people in the organization could have been enthusiastic for the alternatives, and angry at their rejection. Thus, some managers within ICI campaigned for lighter, consumer-orientated products which would have been more profitable to the firm. These internal critics' vocal objections help us to perceive, in rough terms, the immediate sacrifices which ICI's publicly influenced production concentrations entailed.[18] Again, some trade union and business minorities in Austria argued for larger pay or price increases. Their complaints provide some measure of the immediate costs to trade unionists and firms, respectively, of successive bouts of publicly influenced pay and price restraints.

More often, direct evidence on the opportunity costs to organizations is lacking, and it is to political and economic theory that we have to turn. But unfortunately, such theory can provide major clues. For instance, elementary political analysis tells us that USC was under no legal or constitutional obligation to follow maximum prices, to disclose its costs or to adapt its investment plans. Similarly, it is clear that ICI was far from being the British government's political pawn; and that the powers of post-1945 Austrian governments, although greater than some others' at that time, had severe constitutional and operational limits. In all these cases, therefore, the political context left a lot of discretion to the economic interests in question, and greater sectional pushfulness would have been feasible.

At the same time, industrial economics indicates that the organizations possessed high degrees of market power. For example, ICI could have pitched prices in its more nearly monopolistic markets higher than it did; Austria's labour and business chieftains could have exploited more fully their labour market monopolies or pricing muscle, as also the surrounding conditions of full employment and expanding demand. Economic theory is clear that they had the ability to extract higher pay or profits in the short run, and could have jointly passed on cost increases to the consumer, instead of exercising restraint.

## THE CORE PHENOMENON – PUBLIC CO-OPERATION

What underlying patterns, if any, emerge from these findings?

In order to tease out the guiding threads, it is necessary to stand back from the detail and to make a brief excursion into some more abstract ideas. The aim should be to develop a conceptual framework or descriptive model. This will help us to make fuller sense of the

phenomena I have been discussing. It should give some coherent shape
to a field which is all too often split up by different disciplines and a
bewildering variety of notions. A unifying concept should also enable us
to place the phenomena in a wider perspective, one transcending the
historical circumstances and institutions of the western mixed
economies over the past few decades.

Three main questions have to be considered. One relates to the
freedom of choice which economic units possess on public matters;
another to the diverse norms and institutions which tell them what to do
with that freedom. The third and most important question relates to the
specific steps which economic units have to take, or the processes they
have to go through, in order to use their public discretion 'responsibly'
or 'well'.

To begin with, it is clear that firms, trade unions and other sectional
organizations inhabit a large, wide-frontier zone of public discretion.
They enjoy considerable political freedom since state discretion and the
law are far from omnipotent. They typically possess fair degrees of
market power since competition and economic pressures are far from
absolute; and this, too, gives them wide scope to promote, evade or defy
public interests.

State direction and the law have obvious limits: the constitutional
restraints on government within parliamentary systems; the indirectness
of many government controls in a market economy; the sheer
governmental 'failures' or 'control deficits'; the many areas of organizational decision making in which laws are inoperable, inappropriate or
not yet developed; the 'soft laws' whose enforcement has no teeth and
whose implementation relies heavily on civic goodwill; the fact that
many public policies are non-mandatory, more like guidelines or
exhortations, so that government itself often has to persuade and even to
plead.

The limits of competition are no less clear. It is true that if economic–
competitive pressures are extreme, there is little room for public (or
indeed any) discretion. Hypercompetitive industries have, historically,
been festering grounds for free-riding and civic neglect, for sweated
labour, dangerous accidents or commercial malpractices. However,
competition is seldom an all-purpose, all-powerful influence. It is never
complete, let alone textbook 'perfect'. It can be pursued in socially
approved or disapproved ways. The discretionary profit which it
commonly yields can be employed socially or anti-socially. Above all,
its dynamics permit, indeed encourage, leverage over markets to be
widely exercised by firms, trade unions or professional groups. The

ample role such market power leaves for public choices will emerge even more clearly as we go along.

The next question moves inwards from the boundaries of the zone of public discretion in order to consider its positive character, its distinctive geography or topography, the various categories of prescription and pressure that exist within it.

On the one hand, there are precepts or 'public interests', crudely definable for the moment as things that the public is interested in, as applicable to economic organizations. Such public interests are manifested through (1) the general social ethos, (2) dominant opinions on matters of the day, and (3) the policies of elected governments and their offshoots. Public interests include abstract values (Justice, Liberty, etc.) and related general exhortations (like 'tell the truth' and 'help the needy'). They include injunctions which are clear in broad direction, if not degree (for example, 'promote more blacks and women', 'raise productivity in return for pay rises', 'buy American' or 'European'). Occasionally, they may be highly specific ('emissions of pollutant XYZ should not exceed 7.3 units').[19]

On the other hand, the discretionary zone comprises concrete institutions as well as abstract precepts. For a typical economic unit, the territory is marked out most palpably by external groupings which represent various public interests: groupings which the unit affects and which also put pressure on it. Thus, consumer-orientated public interests are embodied by the relevant buying sectors and championed by specialist consumer bodies. Many public interests in the environment are focused by, say, Greenpeace or Friends of the Earth. Local authorities, neighbourhood groups and welfare agencies exhort responsiveness to the public interests they represent. Government departments become would-be persuasive (not only coercive) agents for public policies over, say, exports, training or anti-inflation.

It should be noted that not all the organized pressures which impinge on economic units at any time will represent public interests. Some powerful external pressures may even defy them (the Mafia? a corrupt public agency?). Conversely, some public interests, however sympathetic to the general social ethos, may not yet have, or may *never* have, organizational 'voice' or institutional muscle, thus remaining purely as socio-ethical precepts.[20]

It should also be noted that the discretionary zone's signals are highly diverse, sometimes fluid, and often rivalrous. This is true of both the precepts and the organizations. A better conceptual 'mapping' of the public interests, and their more effective institutionalization, could never abolish difficult dilemmas in decision making. Economic organizations would still have to puzzle over, and strive to balance, the diverse public interests and the (more or less public-interest-laden) external groupings. It is mechanistic and trivializing to believe that these could ever become like traffic signals or highway codes. Indeed, for an economic organization, it will always be impossible 'to please all the people all the time' – and still more impossible to satisfy fully all the public interests at stake.

This is hardly surprising. After all, economic organizations are no exception to the inescapable characteristic of ethical choice, also applying to persons and governments; that in the face of variable, frequently unpredictable situations, judgements and decisions have to be made *between* (often conflicting) 'oughts' or 'goods'.

We now approach the third, core phenomenon. Given that economic organizations have wide public discretion – but are urged to use this in diverse or even inconsistent ways – what do they have to do to behave 'virtuously', 'responsibly' or 'well'? Can the outlines of an 'ideal-type' response be discerned?

Once we examine more closely the publicly responsive phenomena which were reviewed in the last two sections, the outlines of an answer to these questions become clear. The steps which an organization 'ought' to follow in the discretionary zone emerge as reasonably specifiable. Even an overall format for 'good' organizational behaviour can be discerned without too much difficulty.

The core concept here is 'public co-operation'. What this means is that economic decision units freely collaborate with each other, and with external groups or government, in the cause of public interests. They thereby engage in processes of (1) internal forethought, (2) external colloquy and (3) operational adjustment, all of which involve (4) immediate costs to them (whatever the wider or longer-term consequences, either for themselves or others). Let us briefly consider these four processes in turn.

*Internal forethought* means that the organization takes account of public interests and that, in so doing, it brings into the reckoning both the wide implications of its actions and the diverse social groupings it affects. However, as in other areas of policy formation, the 'forethought' may often be implicit rather than explicit. It may be difficult to pin down to specific discussions or decisions inside the organization, thus needing to be inferred from behaviour.[21]

For example, suppose we are studying a trade union's public co-operativeness over a long period. We would want to know what public interests it took into account (industrial peace? anti-inflation and incomes restraint? high employment? the balance of payments?). We would be interested in the partly overlapping question of what external groupings it considered (trade unionists in supplying or consuming sectors? final consumers? the unemployed? environmental or other pressure groups? government departments?). Such a study would also question how much time and effort had been spent on information gathering, interpretation and discussion under these various headings, by whom, and in relation to what strategic decisions.

*External colloquy* occurs when economic units discuss public interests with groupings external to themselves; parallel organizations, intermediary bodies, public agencies, local authorities, central government, etc. But the focus must be on public interests. This excludes both cartel/price ring get-togethers with competitors, and the huge amount of lobbying that goes on for financial favours from government. On the other hand, external colloquy may feature in collective bargaining (as when national economic policies on inflation are discussed in pay negotiations). It may go on inside industry or employer associations, or trade union federations (where, as often happens, these bodies incorporate public interest activities as part of their normal work). Often, external colloquy is informal and ad hoc (as for example between a firm and an environmental pressure group).

*Operational adjustment* is crucial. Here the economic unit alters its internal behaviour in some publicly collaborative way. Neither forethought nor colloquy is enough; they should be crowned by operational acts. Primary activities have to be altered; for example, a firm's pricing, product, investment or employee policies, a trade union's wage claim or industrial action, the entry controls or quality standards of a professional body. 'Public relations' tend to fail this test. Gifts to charities and social causes qualify (although typically a small ratio to available resources). Examples of operational adjustment include those made by United Steel Companies and ICI during certain phases, and by Austria's trade unions and business organizations between the late 1940s and the 1970s (see pp. 59-60, 61 and 62).

*Immediate organizational costs* arise at every stage. Some resources, however small, are diverted to internal forethought. Then, external colloquy involves travel, time, perhaps specific delays in decision making. Not least, direct costs and/or losses of gainful alternatives are incurred through the making of operational adjustments, sometimes substantially so. As we have seen, to searchlight these immediate organizational costs is a useful exercise. It helps to pin public co-operation down to earth. However, this should not prejudge the larger question of public co-operation's wider or longer-term benefits, whether to the organization itself, other groupings, or the economy and society.

These, then, make up the core processes of public co-operation. Is it possible to evaluate them together, so that the public co-operativeness of organizations can be measured and compared?

Reflection suggests that no overall measure would be worth having which did not take account of two dimensions. It is important that a broad span of public interests be deferred to; but also that genuine sacrifices be made, relative to an organisation's resources. Thus, a sensible indicator needs to test both breadth, and intensity or depth. We would not be greatly impressed by an organization which incurred costs, however large, for just a single public interest. But neither would we be inclined to applaud a great display of internal talk, outside dialogue and policy adjustment, however widely spread across public interests, if only a fleabite organizational sacrifice resulted.

On this basis, the outline of a composite measure begins to appear. Where $B$ is the diversity of public factors taken into account (through internal forethought, external colloquy and operational adjustment) and $I$ is total immediate costs, then an organization's public co-operativeness, $OPC$, can be thought of as a multiple of $B$ and $I$. At least this provides a starting point for analysis and comparison.[22]

## A PERSISTENT PURSUIT

There is one implication of the above definition of public co-operation whose significance must not be overlooked. The definition necessarily abstracts from particular institutions, circumstances and historical periods. It is not limited, for example, to those post-1945 collaborative phenomena, as discussed by Shonfield and others, with which this chapter began. The core processes I have outlined may happen under a diversity of regimes, during different historical phases, and with respect to a wide variety of social issues.

Suppose that most of business came to be controlled by mega-multinationals, or small entrepreneurs, or worker co-operatives. Or suppose that trade unions expanded in power, or merged into omnibus Durkheim-style corporations, or even disappeared. There would still be wide requirements for cognizance, colloquy and publicly angled realignments between the economy's decision points. Wholesale 'privatization' would not alter this fundamental condition; nor would the supersession of many existing financial institutions by publicly owned agencies. The need for such decision units to have social antennae and networks, both mutually and towards government and public opinion, would persist.

Suppose there was a dramatic shift of politico-economic power either downwards towards regions or localities, or upwards to a supranational entity like the EEC. In both cases, the institutional topography of the discretionary zone would alter. The identity of many of public co-operation's pressure points or pivots would change, as would that of many of the actual or hoped-for co-operators. But the basic phenomenon and its pursuit would survive. A wide discretionary zone, marked out by government–legal limitations and the vagaries of market power, would remain. There would still be major social tasks for which, at any level, political direction, laws, monetary and fiscal measures and competition would be inadequate.

Major shifts in public interests would not diminish imperatives for economic organizations to interact responsively, under their aegis. No economy which continued to grow would be immune from human problems which characteristically demand 'round-table' or consensus-seeking remedies at points of stress. Whatever production or employment trends may be predicted, for example towards robotics or part-time jobs, would not change this requirement; they would merely alter its forms. Even the (perhaps unattainable) feat of a decisive conquest of 'stagflation' would leave other priorities for publicly collaborative solutions untouched. In some fields, voluntary restraints seem likely to become even more urgent, as with natural resource depletion and pollution; in other cases, if past experience is anything to go by, new demands for sectional interest restraint or public spirit would proliferate.

## A POINTER TO ECONOMIC COMMUNITY

I turn finally to the connection between public co-operation in the economy and community values. Of course, any such connection is unlikely to be universal or automatic, to say the least. It is bound to be flawed and imperfect, a matter of approximations, pale reflections or potentials. None the less, the connection emerges with increasing clarity if we reconsider, first, public co-operation's core processes one by one; next their combination; and finally, their varying levels of aggregation, from fragmented acts through micro-concentrations to an economy-wide critical mass.

The internal consideration of public factors, to start with, hovers on the threshold of economic associativeness. Even just to consider the social norms and public policies which may relate to one's activities, and to note the outside groupings likely to be affected by one's decisions, is not ethically negligible. It means, in effect, asking the economic equivalents of the questions: 'who are my neighbours?' and 'what would good relationships towards them entail'?

Of course, one may still make only a cursory nod in these directions, or even recoil from their implications, and indeed go on to defy them. But even then, things will not be quite the same as if the public factors had not been considered. That the existence of duties and neighbours has been entertained at all, and in some collective fashion, makes probable one salutary outcome at least. Some bad consciences are likely to linger; and in this field bad consciences are better than none.

Suppose, though, that a wide span of public factors is reviewed. Suppose, too, that relative priorities among the public interests are wrestled with in relation to key organizational policies. Then an important threshold has been crossed. Internal forethought has taken on some perennial attributes of an ethical forum. The people involved are expressing communal participation, if only symbolically, and sharing in a tiny way in public tasks, even in a sense in government itself, at least in its deliberative aspect. Fragments of fraternal 'common goods' already exist: an affirmation of aims or values shared with society; a socially approved 'communion' as the internal decision makers share the publicly ratified ideas, face to face.

With external colloquy, there are further possibilities for economic associativeness. But a lot depends on who is talking to whom, and about what. The bigger the contrasts between the groups involved, and the closer the discussion is to national policy, the fuller its potential towards the ideal. A meeting of pig farmers to discuss publicly decided production quotas offers little span for solidarity stretching. Much more scope is offered by a debate about national economic priorities within some forum involving business, labour, consumers, government, etc. Subject to its positioning along the two dimensions (interest group breadth and policy scope), external colloquy offers possibilities for:

1 extended fraternity – across the various gulfs, the individual persons involved may become companions and mutual educators, under the aegis of explicitly shared commitments to public interests;
2 relationships of associateship or social partnership between

the different economic and social organizations;
3  democratic participation in the 'expressive' mode just
   through joint affirmations of public interests (analogous, at
   minimum, to café gossip about public affairs, see chapter 3);
4  democratic participation in the 'shaping' mode if
   contributions are made to the formulation and/or
   implementation of national policies (as particularly occurs
   under regimes characterized by high levels of
   'corporatism').[23]

Operational adjustment offers still further scope at least for extended
fraternity. Back within the organization, interpersonal relationships may
feature companionship, mutuality and sharing in the explicit cause of
public interests. For example, suppose that, after forethought and
external colloquy, a firm decides to produce safer and less pollution-
prone widgets. Now, implementing this change may well involve a lot
of intra-organizational *camaraderie*. But in addition, scope exists for the
organizational people (executives, export and sales staff, factory
workers, etc.) to be jointly dedicated to a more clearly articulated public
aim. They can experience togetherness in helping people 'out there'
more authoritatively. They can find 'communion' *via* an economic
activity which is more clearly socially approved and meritorious.
Conviviality, mutual help and shared commitment to more assured
public goods all find a place.[24]

So much for the community potentials of each of public
co-operation's processes, considered separately. But clearly, their
mixture is more important. Even the most painstaking internal
forethought may be insular, publicly insensitive. External colloquy on
its own may be nothing more than a pacifying ritual, a 'front', a mere
display of 'public faces in public places'. Operational adjustment may
be socially maladroit without careful preconsideration and discussion
with others. It is when these things combine that positive implications
for free associativeness are likely. Then, public co-operation in a
rounded form can sustain wider communitarian values. It can contribute
to a diffusion of public tasks, as opposed to these being neglected,
centrally monopolised, or selfishly defied. It can help to prevent both
coercion and factionalism, and their perverse interaction.

Readers will note that I have been using a cautious language of
'potentials' or 'possibilities'. The reasons for this should be clear. The
connection between public co-operation and communitarian values
remains tenuous at least until the co-operativeness or organizations

attains a certain coherence. It depends a lot on a web of reciprocities through the economy, or the confidence that others will follow suit. As we shall discover, too, support from community forces elsewhere in society is important. So is an active recognition, shared through the culture, that the economy's public zone really is fraught with the relevant ethical meanings and options. Bearing these variables in mind, it is probable that so far, in practice, three broad gradations of (an always imperfect) economic associativeness have been attained.

*First*, many day-to-day acts of public co-operation already have some significance for associativeness in liberty. They help to avert sheer moral anarchy, a Hobbesian war-of-all-against-all. They put up barriers to much cheating, lying and bullying. They are far from valueless. However, such individual acts tend to be far too minute, isolated and sporadic to approach any kind of coherence. They reflect no stable or concentrated stance on the part of the organizations concerned.

*Second*, suppose that a whole organization exhibits much public co-operativeness over a long period. At an appreciable cost, through forethought, colloquy and adjustment, it consistently defers to a wide range of public factors. Here a major jump has occurred. At least the community ideal is present in miniature or embryo. But no more; for associativeness cannot be unilateral; it has to be reciprocal and the work of many hands. Even a whole sector of intensive inter-unit collaboration will tend to be flawed and/or vulnerable if the surrounding conditions are adverse.

Thus, returning to the micro-examples cited above, communitarian defects clearly flawed the public co-operativeness of an ICI or a USC. Their partnerships with labour were distinctly unequal and tinged with paternalism. Sometimes, their co-operative efforts evaporated for want of answering chords elsewhere in the industry or in wider business circles. Their public responsiveness was often geared to interwar public policies which reflected a less than representative political system and which promoted, for example, the distinctly subcommunitarian cause of British imperialism.

Looking wider, it is not difficult to find micro-cases of isolated, vulnerable public co-operativeness. For example, above-average business–labour–civic relationships might develop within certain sorts of locality. But these formed isolated enclaves in a wider context of conflict and turbulent change, and were therefore unsustainable.[25]

*Third*, as we saw early in this chapter, a whole economic system may develop some critical mass in public co-operation. Here a much bigger jump has been transacted. For the relevant processes have become entrenched across the spectrum of manufacturing, finance, distribution, organized labour, and other economic groups, or at least their leading parts. Even then, such systems tend to have marked communitarian flaws. A country's political structure may not be fully representative, thus skewing the genuine 'publicness' of the public policies signalled to economic units. Channels for democratic participation may be lacking. The background systems of education, housing, welfare and social class may still put up needless barriers to fraternity, thus weakening its pursuit in the economy as well. There may be a serious short-changing of the condition that public co-operation's community potential should be culturally exalted and celebrated.

Judged by these tests, the systems of public co-operation which developed over long periods in Austria and some other modern economies are no more than crude, limited approximations to economic community. It should be clear, none the less, that they have edged somewhat closer to that ideal.

An economy-wide critical mass in public co-operation greatly assists the cause of social control through conscience, compatibility and consent. The existence of national-level ententes, even with elitist overtones, is a decided advance on situations of sectional apartheid or factionalism where the (arguably perfidious) assumption is that all the healing, harmonizing and concerting that needs to be done can, will, or even should be done by the state. That large numbers of people should practise mutuality in certain critical fields, moderating their immediate economic demands, is a benefit to democratic community, not just the economy. That many more social adjustments reflect free collaborativeness, rather than brute coercion or narrow acquisitiveness, is even a gain for civilization and morality.

There is also a development potential. An extensive collaborative apparatus – within enterprises, between sectors and at 'the centre' – establishes habits as well as channels which can be extended to new social problems. That apparatus may well be improvable: a bridgehead towards greater fraternity and democratic participation. Of course, such a system still has limits. It does not replace competition or state direction even though it strongly qualifies them. It may be vulnerable to erosion through time. In a more fundamental sense, it is still provisional, *en route*, a continued pilgrimage.[26] There is no guarantee of economic sanctity or civic heroism; indeed, backsliding persists. People repeatedly lose out ethically by neglecting the opportunities for extended fraternity, inter-organizational associateship and public responsibility. But at least such opportunities are widely and clearly available. This makes their neglect, let alone their subversion, much less disguisable and more transparent, indeed less excusable and more palpably a *moral* failure. At least the system has come a long way up from obfuscating the growth of persons in community, let alone propagating its antithesis.

Thus, the case for an economy-wide public co-operation goes far beyond its apparent economic utility, for example for steady growth, anti-inflation and 'supply-side' efficiency measures (though these things are important). It goes wider than the welfare, environmental or anti-poverty objectives which public co-operation can help to promote. The case also related to effects on persons inside the system and their ethical growth. An economy-wide public co-operation is still far from the peaks of economic community; but it is none the less located some way up the mountain, and it is improvable. From a democratic communitarian viewpoint, then, much can be learnt from its historical achievements and failures, and its origins.

# Chapter 5

# Structures, emergencies and beliefs

We have been going at quite a rapid pace; so a brief pause may be useful in order to summarize the argument so far.

First, some rich streams of communitarian thinking have been looked at: Durkheim's libertarian 'solidarity'; the pluriform communality of Maritain and other personalist Christian democrat thinkers; political virtue according to the civic humanists. The battered, exploited, under-developed idea of community has been reassessed. Its essence has been found to lie in three fundamental and interrelated values: fraternity, complementary association and democratic participation. I have suggested that these values provide (1) a coherent summit way of thinking about society and politics, (2) a yardstick for interpreting other key values, notably liberty and equality, and (3) the basis for an ideal of economic community.

Economic community would involve an intricate, far-reaching social fabric or tissue – of recognitions, affiliations and connections – across a modern, democratic, mixed economy. This fabric would link economic organizations and the people who work in them with society, government and public interests, actively and continuously, but also elastically and consistently with decentralized choice. It would complement and qualify both competition and state direction. Although far from being an economic system's sole organizing principle, economic community would be its crowning arch.

Second, we have reviewed a wide variety of historical manifestations of sectional interests' responsiveness to public interests within twentieth-century advanced economies. We have sought to assess whether, and how far, such manifestations have approached towards the economic community ideal, however faintly and falteringly.

A central finding is that, within a zone of public discretion whose wide, though variable, boundaries are set by coercion and competitive pressure, it has been possible for economic organizations to show sensitivity towards social norms and public policies. This phenomenon, defined as public co-operation, has been broken down into its core, grass roots processes: internal forethought, external colloquy, operational adjustment, and immediate cost bearing.

I have shown that public co-operation is a reasonably measurable phenomenon in terms of processes and/or hoped-for outcomes, both at micro- and macro-levels; and that it appears to have been a considerably stronger influence in some economic systems, over long periods, than in others. I have also suggested that, for all its evident limitations, public co-operation appears to have been a significant contributor to economic and social policy objectives, and a persistent pursuit.

A central implication is clear, though many of its ramifications still have to be explored. In our efforts to understand how advanced economic systems work, and how diverse public interests are promoted, we can no longer be satisfied with the long-dominant, bipolarized models of competition and state direction. We need the concept of public co-operation as well.

Third, I have argued that there are indeed connecting threads between public co-operation, as a limited historical phenomenon, and economic community as an ideal. Different configurations of internal forethought, external colloquy, operational adjustment and immediate organizational sacrifice have complex ethical meanings; in varying degrees, they approximate to communitarian values. Capacities for contributing to extended fraternity, complementary association and democratic participation ascend in strength: from isolated acts, through single-organization concentrations, to an economy-wide co-operativeness. Modern political economies which have displayed high-level public co-operation over long periods still transgress democratic communitarian criteria. They still fall short of ideal economic community; but they have moved a fair bit closer to it.

Thus, public co-operation appears not only as a likely contributor to economic success in important ways, but also as a pointer or bridgehead to democratic communitarian pursuits.

The implications of these claims will further unravel through the rest of this book. However, the time has come to move the argument forward. We now proceed to the most important, yet most hazardous part of our enquiry, the search for explanations. What forces appear to have obstructed or encouraged public co-operation in the western advanced economies?

## TOWARDS AN EXPLANATION OF PUBLIC CO-OPERATION

In trying to explain public co-operation, several guidelines should be emphasized. Not the least important is to employ a long-term perspective.

Public co-operation may sometimes increase in short, sharp bursts across a whole economy, in time of war. Then, typically, there is a major spasm of uncoerced collaboration, not just an increase in central controls. Twice in this century, in several western democracies, business, labour and other interests were drawn by wartime exigencies into intense partnerships (not only enforced compliances) with government, and into acute sensitivities towards a public opinion hostile to 'profiteers' and insistent on all-round voluntary sacrifices.

Much can be learnt from these war experiences. The threat to survival and to fundamental values provided the impetus (whilst also throwing into sharp relief the deviant minorities). But once that impetus was removed, public co-operation in the economy could easily fall back again, as largely happened in the UK, France and the USA after 1918.[1]

Wartime spasms aside, it seems reasonable to suppose that intensities or weaknesses in public co-operation tend to persist over long periods. A short time-scale of observation, let alone a purely cross-sectional study, is likely to be grossly inadequate both for intercountry comparisons and evaluations of trends. One might be tempted to think that certain countries are ineradicably frozen in some co-operative or unco-operative stance, or even that some universal straight-line tendency is at work, a persistent trend of increase or decline. Even the whole period since 1945 is too short for reliable judgements as to possible ebbs and flows, let alone their origins. For example, one could easily exaggerate the importance, for good or ill, of the post-war reconstruction pressures, the social democratic welfare consensus of the 1950s and 1960s, or the stagflation, political polarization and 'New Right' advances of the 1970s and 1980s.

The micro-cases of intense public co-operation quoted in the previous chapter, for example those manifested by ICI and the USC in the UK, tended to last for several decades. Patterns of single-organization insensitivity or separatism, in both the UK and the USA, appear to have been equally prolonged. On a national level, Austria's critical mass in public co-operation started in the late 1940s, but it then persisted, broadly, through the 1950s, 1960s and 1970s. An economy-wide weakness in public co-operation (still to be explored) is unlikely to be shorter lived. But in both cases the possibility of a reversal or change of trend in the 'very long term' cannot be ruled out. All of this reinforces the case for a long time perspective, one extending right through the twentieth century at least.

Next, as we turn to possible explanatory theories, a familiar dilemma appears: the choice between a misleading coherence and an untidy breadth. The approach which follows will opt for breadth even though the penalty for this is diverse explanatory categories, evoking 'shops, shoes and sealing wax', so that commensurability is difficult.

For example, suppose the hypothesis is that two farmers, Jones and Robinson, do not co-operate because (1) they live many miles apart, (2) they do not believe in co-operation, and (3) there are no overwhelming reasons for co-operating such as a drought or an invasion of beetles. It is going to be difficult to assign relative weights of importance to (1), (2) and (3). In addition, there may be reason to doubt if they are really independent of one another. Further back in the chain of possible causes and effects, (1), (2) and (3) may well be intertwined.

Yet however irritating such blurred boundaries may be, this pales into insignificance beside the impoverishment which a single type of explanatory variable inflicts. There simplicity and measurability, perhaps intellectual elegance, are obtained at the cost of explanatory richness and realism. Probably, a number of contestable and not even explicit philosophical assumptions will be thrown in as well.

In the case of public co-operation, as in many other social fields, three principal explanatory approaches tend to compete. These may be broadly classified as institutional, attitudinal and conjunctural.

For the institutionalist, the dimensions of economic or social organization hold the key: such factors as organizational size, class systems, or attributes of the motley intermediary agencies which have proliferated between business, labour, government and the public. By contrast, an attitudinal approach would look to people's opinions, values or beliefs. In trying to explain public co-operation, it would emphasize the degree of consensus, nationalist, ethnic or religious ideals, or political ideology. Finally, particular categories of historical events may be identified as catalysts or conditioners: revolution, war, civic crisis, or natural disaster. A particularly broad explanation would find the biggest clues to a country's economic peace or conflict in the intensity of its original industrialization.

Each of these explanatory methods tends to crumble when pushed too far. If economic and social structures are credited with primacy, deterministic models take over, as with Marxism and certain theories of 'economic self-interest'. Decision makers are portrayed as agents of underlying forces; free will and moral choice are discounted. But attitudinal explanations risk becoming tenuous. To assert that people co-operate 'because they agree' verges on triteness. To claim that particular sorts of belief are uniquely efficacious defies the observation that even the best intentions can be negated by bad structures. Size, distance or ignorance may create a huge division between Jones and Robinson, however consonant their ideals.

As for conjunctural approaches, 'explanation' easily slides towards mere description. Categories like 'revolution' or 'economic crisis' may be too vague and far reaching. They, too, tend to downgrade ethical choice and freedom. And they abandon the hope of an element of predictability; for the alleged historical turning points tend to be rare occurrences, randomly distributed and extremely hard to forecast. Therefore, it is wise to seek some sort of *combination* of the institutional, attitudinal and conjunctural approaches.

Finally, however, such pluralism can easily become cumbrous, even amorphous. To avoid this, a lot of abstraction and selectivity is needed. It is necessary to specify fairly precisely what sort of structures, beliefs and historical catalysts are likely to have been at work, and not to have too long a list of them, and also to indicate how they may be expected to interrelate.

## THE SIX KEY FORCES INTRODUCED

In the explanatory framework developed through the next few chapters, six key forces will be singled out. Four of these fall into the 'institutional' category. They reflect the idea that public co-operation is influenced to some extent by economic and socio-political structures. These structures are thought to influence capacities for public perception, contact or empathy on the part of economic organizations. Even together, they are far from being a supreme or even a primary influence; but they are likely to be important and they have been badly neglected.[2]

The dimensions drawn upon are time, the size and number of organizations, transparency, and contiguity. Under each of these 'structural' headings the key forces which facilitate public co-operation will be identified more precisely as,

1 *threshold continuities* of economic organizations and their
   decision makers, and of the public bodies which may

influence them to co-operate, or the idea that excessive transience is an impediment;

2 *conformable size distributions*, or situations where economic organizations are not 'too small', 'too many' or 'too large' relative to the size of the country, the government, and national public opinion;

3 *organizational transparency*, or capacities for being publicly watched, as inherent in some economic sectors, statutorily imposed, or induced by social monitors;

4 *background proximities* between decision makers, pre-established through wider social structures or within the economic system itself, particularly through the agency of forums representing both sectional and public interests.

The fifth thesis is attitudinal, ideological or cultural. It is that public co-operation is particularly favoured by beliefs which connect it with the highest ethical virtues. That there is an ideal type of such beliefs, democratic communitarianism, has already been argued at some length. So the test is, how far have actual patterns of twentieth-century beliefs about public co-operation in the west approximated to this model? The extent to which they do so provides a further explanatory variable, one to which great importance is assigned. Let us call this fifth key factor *communitarian beliefs*.

Finally comes a more sombre thesis, which has been arrived at reluctantly, even ruefully. This thesis recognizes that smooth convergences between the above factors are historically unlikely. It suggests that some additional catalytic factor has tended to be useful in pushing public co-operation to a sustainable higher level; and that nation-wide shocks or emergencies have often been a positive influence, albeit in conjunction with the above conditions, especially communitarian beliefs. This sixth explanatory factor (to be specified in greater detail later) can be labelled for the time being as *catalytic emergency*.[3]

## THE LOGIC OF CO-OPERATIVE STRUCTURES

It is useful to being by reflecting on the logic of co-operative relationships in a general way. This will help to illuminate all four of the structural hypotheses mentioned above: threshold continuity, conformable size, transparency, and social proximity. Let us start with the simplest situation, a relationship between two economic decision units, A and B.

One factor which appears to favour a collaborative relationship is some past continuity in the relationship between A and B, and an expectation of further continuity. Without this, it is likely that trust will be lacking. 'Fly-by-nights', even newcomers to an otherwise stable scene, tend to be poor prospects for making agreements, let alone keeping them. Second, there is the numbers factor. It helps that only two decision units, A and B, are involved. A larger number would set up communication problems, diluting the quality of contact, even providing cover for 'free riders'. This is a commonplace in the behaviour of cartels and in industrial relations.

A further condition for co-operation between A and B is cognitive. Are their principal affairs reasonably open and transparent to each other? Ignorance and mystery will tend to create suspicion. Trust will be harder to achieve if there is an acute disparity in knowledge of each other's situations. A wider dimension of transparency is also relevant, namely the degree to which A and B are able to be observed by other people, particularly third parties, social agencies interested in whether they co-operate or not, and members of the public. A and B are more likely to co-operate for public purposes (as distinct from, say, a private cartel) in so far as these wider, more social dimensions of transparency also apply.

Finally, there is the proximity factor. In a small pre-industrial village pretty well everybody knew each other. In an advanced, specialized, highly populated economy, direct contact is the exception. But it is still relevant to ask questions about subtler forms of contact. Do A and B possess (1) a working understanding of each other's roles, even if they have not actually met, (2) previous acquaintance with somebody of their type, or (3) experience at least of the sort of conditions that the other faces? Such indirect categories of proximity are bound up with wider social systems of education and training, domicile and location, regional or ethnic differentiation, and social class. Hence their inclusion as a further structural factor.

These dimensions of continuity, number and size, transparency and social contiguity are experienced every day. Their influence is frequently taken for granted in politics and social life. Yet it is surprising how little they are considered in the context of the public behaviour of economic organizations.

Our next example is slightly more complicated for it brings in third parties and external effects. Suppose the Hydropoxic Chemical

Company is considering a decision which would affect some faraway social group, say potential pollution sufferers in Trans-Patagonia. The Hydropoxic Company has certain precepts or requests laid upon it by the common culture or public opinion: to take the Trans-Patagonians into account, to behave towards them 'responsibly', humanely or just circumspectly.

Now the Hydropoxic Company's sensitivity towards the issue of polluting the Trans-Patagonians may well be lower than otherwise if the company is very fresh to this area of operation or likely to leave it soon. In personal terms, the directors may feel less like bothering if they do not expect to be around to 'pick up the tabs' by the time the Trans-Patagonians may be suffering palpably. Again, if the Trans-Patagonians are a hotchpotch of scattered individuals, it will be easier to ignore them. In so far as the Hydropoxic is a very large company, too, relative to the resources commanded by the Trans-Patagonians, it may be inclined to defy their interests.

The transparency and proximity factors equally demand attention. Does the Hydropoxic Company feel that it is well known by the potential pollution sufferers? Are its affairs able to be scrutinized, praised or stigmatized by them? Such a sense of being 'watched' is likely to influence its behaviour. It would also seem sensible to ask whether the Hydropoxic directors ever themselves had experience of Trans-Patagonia or the Trans-Patagonians, or indeed of the sort of people generally who might be affected by pollution. The hypothesis is that this, too, other things being equal, would tend to increase their sensitivity.

The types of relationships mentioned so far arise between comparable economic units (A and B), or between economic units and third party groups (Hydropoxic and the potential pollutees). All the interests considered are sectional ones. The relevant relationships can be said to be horizontal in form. Higher authorities have not been introduced; public agencies and government are not necessarily seeking to influence the decision making. But suppose we finally introduce the criterion of responsiveness to the public bodies. Even then the structural factors under consideration do not disappear. Their existence and likely influence press in as much as ever.

For purposes of co-operation with government, it is relevant (1) whether the Hydropoxic Chemical Company is a complete newcomer or a fly-by-night, (2) whether it is atomistically small or overweeningly large (this time relatively to national government and official agencies), (3) how transparent and open its affairs are, and (4) how far its decision makers have had some acquaintanceship with public people and problems.

As for public opinion as a wider arbiter or final point of reference, yet again the same considerations are inescapable. If public opinion is to be an alert and influential senior partner to economic interests, as public co-operation requires, those interests need to be structured in certain ways. They should be reasonably stable, well proportioned, open to being watched, and endowed with preset capacities for being in touch.

## THEORETICAL CLUES, EMPIRICAL SUPPORTS

The idea of facilitative structures, as just outlined, was foreshadowed by Durkheim. In discussing the nature of 'solidary ties' between economic organizations, Durkheim referred to a 'contiguity' which 'reminded organizations of their mutual dependance', but which would suffer without 'a sufficient prolongation' or if 'some opaque environment' were 'interposed'. Later, J.M. Clark emphasized the need for 'bringing home', particularly to business organizations, the distant impacts of their decisions.[4]

Some useful light comes from sociological investigations in other fields. When looking at local, voluntary or political activities, observers have sometimes emphasized a stability in relationships which encourages trust and reciprocity; a contiguity of varying shapes and intensities; an organizational size which appears to favour both mutual recognition and sustainable agreements. Care must be taken in transplanting such dimensions into the economy. But their suitably amended transposition to the socio-political relationships of economic organizations is what our structural interpretation transacts.

A negative counterpart to the idea of co-operatively helpful structures emerges, hauntingly, in the 'prisoner's dilemma' of game theory. In this model, incommunicado, prison-like conditions not only prevent isolated decision makers (the 'prisoners') from achieving individual gains, but also entice them into making self-defeating and destructive choices. The implication is that if only the 'prisoners' could be liberated from their mutual isolation, they would all be 'better off'.[5]

Although this model is too narrow for the context of public co-operation (particularly in terms of its criteria of 'better-offness'), the 'prisoner's dilemma' is an expressive metaphor for the distorting barriers to contact. The 'prison walls' of the metaphor come out as the 'bad structures' in our theory, certain measurable factors which not only prevent different interests from recognizing each other or getting together, but which also increase the chance that if they do so, public interests may suffer: ephemerality; asymmetrical size; organizational opacity; socio-physical distance.

Turning to the influence of communitarian beliefs, we have already negotiated a critical step in the argument. I have shown that, despite much apparent confusion, beliefs about community are capably of coherent structuring into a model set of prescriptions, namely democratic communitarianism (chapters 2 and 3).[6] To this must be added a critical assumption with a long and rich intellectual descent, one which also reflects a version of 'anti-materialist' historical theory. The view is that beliefs of this or other kinds, as embedded in culture, politics and ideology, do, in fact, constitute an important and traceable explanatory factor in economic life.[7]

Social reality does not consist of a one-way passage from all-powerful external structures to merely reactive human wills. Neither persons nor organizations come to the structures with vacant minds, ready simply for capture or bending. They are not pieces of inert plastic, waiting to be moulded. Rather, they are the subtle, wilful repositories of (inherited and acquired) values or ideals, and mental interpretations; and these tend to possess a distinctive role and to wield some inherent causal power.

People's and organizations' beliefs are going to affect significantly their responses to the institutional structures. In so far as the structures are alterable, beliefs may even change them as well as qualifying their effects. Ideologically motivated reforms may have erected some of the structures in the first place. Without appropriate beliefs, many elementary acts of internal forethought, external colloquy and operational realignment would be unlikely. In so far as these acts depend on conscience, the beliefs of those involved are crucial.

Armed with this assumption, and with the democratic communitarian model, our task is to confront the beliefs about public co-operation which have prevailed over the past century. We will find that various leading groups of ideas have been hostile, ambivalent or favourable to the democratic communitarian model, in varying degrees. If my thesis is correct, we should expect to find that where the ideas closest to the model have had a strong historical influence, there high-level public co-operation also prevailed.

Indeed, the case for all of the six factors I have put forward has to rest, above all, on the historical evidence. Some first indications, related to the illustrative material in the previous chapter, do suggest that an explanatory role for them appears reasonable.

For example, in trying to explain the micro-public co-operativeness over long periods of the two large British companies, ICI and USC, most of the factors appear relevant. These companies were well past an infancy that is often pre- or anti-co-operative, and large enough to attract much public attention, but not so large as to elude national surveillance. Their operations were not particularly transparent; but their main activities were at least familiar to national government. Their top management was influenced by elements of previous or continued contiguity to the shopfloor and to Whitehall. Their leaders were personally swayed by pro-co-operative values and ideas.[8]

In the macro-case of Austria after 1945, again the available evidence is supportive. Reasonable continuities applied to the trade unions, the principal intermediary bodies for labour and business, the economic ministeries, the key national agencies. The organization of industry, commerce and labour was neither atomistically fragmented nor politically overweening in size. With respect to the transparency and social proximity factors, Austria may have been inferior to some other relatively co- operative economies, for example Sweden. However, the public transparency of its economic organizations, and a background social contiguity at least among the leading economic groups, probably excelled those in Western Europe's less co-operative systems.

As for co-operativist values and an emergency component, these definitely applied in post-1945 Austria. The former were strongly entrenched in both politics and economic life; the latter reflected the aftermath of civil war, the *Anschluss* and war devastation, along with persistent cold-war pressures.[9]

These initial indications are very provisional. Fuller empirical support for the explanatory model will emerge as we investigate each factor in turn through the next few chapters. Meantime, though, we still have to consider some possible dynamics of the model and how the factors are likely to interact.

## THE COMPLEMENTARITY OF STRUCTURES, SHOCKS AND IDEALS

Most of the explanatory factors introduced above relate to capacities, not objectives or 'needs'. Except for national emergency, emphasis is put on the varying propensities of potential collaborators, not on the economic or political requirements for public co-operation. The latter are viewed as relatively unremitting, even unremarkable; it is a system's ability to respond to them which appears to be the most critical factor, and the most puzzling one. To adopt economic terminology, demand is assumed persistently to outstrip supply. So it is the 'supply side' of public co-operation which primarily calls for explanation.[10]

A uniform method of working through to an economic system's social linkages can hardly apply to communication frameworks, system-wide shocks, and motivating ideals. For the same reason, the relative importance of these would-be explanatory factors is not readily measurable, for they are qualitively different. Yet the respective roles they are likely to play do begin to emerge once we consider how it is that, even at its most favourable, each category seems likely to fall short.

First, in terms of structures, let us suppose that the appropriate dimensions of continuity, proportionality, transparency and contiguity (still to be specified in detail) were to apply through most of an economic system. Mutual accessibilities amongst economic and public decision units would be institutionally encouraged to the fullest possible extent. The point is that even such conditions would be no more than facilitative. Public co-operation would not be guaranteed by a mere abundance of communication channels, signals and connecting devices. The horse could be brought to the water, yet still not drink. The psychological will, the conscience and the surrounding cultural ethos might still be lacking.

Next, let us imagine that the ideal type of community beliefs is widely and intensely subscribed to. People's ideals would connect public co-operation in the economic system with the highest ethical goals. The leading focuses of moral and religious life, intellectual influence and political allegiance would all resound this message. Such attitudes might cause a lot of bad structures to be swept away through legislation and policy changes. In theory, they might even be sufficient for public co-operation to attain its full flowering.

But time would be an Achilles heel. It is doubtful whether, over long periods, social idealism could motivate structural reforms or high-level public co-operation without some extra impetus. Modern history is littered with examples of idealistic, 'intentional' communities which became vulnerable to erosion over time. An intellectual movement towards democratic communitarianism might influence one or two generations, then recede. A phenomenon like the Israeli kibbutzim might eventually find its idealistic resources depleted. A leading political movement might effectively take up a lot of the requisite ideological ground but subsequently go out of government or, perhaps more likely, slide away from its original ideals.[11]

Finally, in terms of national emergency, even the most propitious of crisis or post-crisis conditions could fail to deliver or could even misfire. Assume at the very least that the country has moved beyond the disasters which constituted the 'emergency' in the first place (war, civil war, dictatorship or whatever). It would not be enough for the worst dangers or divisions to be overcome, even for the political atmosphere to be steeped in consensus. The obsession might well be with short-term management, not the building of long-term co-operation, with 'getting the economy back on its feet' rather than reforming its institutions and structures with some sort of sustainable economic community in view. Ideological blockages could supervene: obsessions with automatic markets or mechanical controls, or, more seductively, one-sided individualism, libertarianism or egalitarianism.

These considerations suggest that an 'ideal' underpinning for public co-operation would have to combine the three sets of factors, in some complementary fashion. There would have to be a mixture of facilitative frameworks, emergency, and democratic communitarian ideals. But we may still wonder what such complementarity would entail, let alone how it could – or has already sometimes – come into being. Let us conclude by briefly glancing at these issues, first in relation to an economy's grass roots, then across a whole system.

## GRASS ROOTS INTERACTIONS

It is reasonable to assume that the relevant structures, emergencies and beliefs are, in part, causally independent of one another. Some of the structural features, for example the size distribution of firms, are impermeable by the other factors. They depend a lot on extraneous factors, not included in the above explanatory model, for example, the economics of changing technology or international trade. National emergencies tend at least to be triggered by random events such as an earthquake or a Sarajevo assassination. As for beliefs, I have already rejected the notion that these are pure derivatives or epiphenomena, whether of structures or emergencies, or indeed anything else.

However, some causal interactions do seem likely between structures, emergencies and beliefs. Where the temporal, logistical or spatial impediments to communication are particularly daunting, people probably find it harder to recognize the moral virtues of public co-operation: a case of structures impacting on beliefs. In reverse sequence, a strong communitarian ethos makes more likely the ideological impetus and commitment needed for the promotion of structural reforms. Clearly, such interactions between our causal factors have to be distinguished from the many other influences on those factors, as just mentioned, which are exogenous or dictated by influences outside the model.

A first thesis is that the economic forces and exogenously influenced changes tend to be equivocal for public co-operation and cannot be relied upon to improve it.

We need to recall the boundary conditions set by extreme competitive pressure in an industry or economy (see chapter 4). Big changes in the degree of competition are likely to affect the scope for public discretion. A major increase in competitive pressure will tend to create less room for manoeuvre towards public interests; a major decrease will tend to create more. But such changes in the extent or availability of public choice do not necessarily produce proportionate swings in actual behaviour, respectively away from public co-operation or towards it. There may even be an asymmetry in so far as the levels of public co-operation are changed at all.

If an industry comes to be lashed consistently by ice-cold competitive winds, for example in connection with long-term decline, the resources available for sensitivity to others, as expressed through forethought, colloquy and adjustment, will be reduced. If the market-economic pressures are draconian, some outright damage to public co-operation can hardly be avoided.

When prosperity or market power increase, however, a reverse sequence is unlikely. More freedom and resources do not necessarily or even, perhaps, typically, bump up the ratio of public sensitivity. Voluntary restraint is no simple correlate of increased power. Getting additional resources and discretion is not likely, of itself, to make companies, trade unions or pressure groups more disposed to collaborate with each other, public opinion or government, in the cause of public interests. Such an increased propensity would surely depend on much more than accretions in bargaining power or bank balances.

Thus, while greatly sharpened competition in an industry will tend to undermine public co-operation, accretions in market power and organizational profit cannot be relied on to increase it. This asymmetry discourages any hopes of public co-operation springing from economic or market forces in themselves.

Similarly, economic and market forces repeatedly alter the structural dimensions of time, size, transparency, and proximity. But those alterations to the structures which stem from economic and market factors are not necessarily convergent. Rather, they tend to be two-edged and have an awkward habit of contradicting each other.

This applies strikingly to such familiar factors as concentration and diversification. When an industry gets concentrated into fewer hands, this reduces one type of structural impediment to public co-operation, namely fragmentation; but it may well increase another, the risk of a few large organizations becoming politically 'too big for their boots'. Diversification is similarly two-edged. Firms' strategies to diversify sometimes bring them closer to ordinary citizen–consumers. This may be expected to increase transparency, as when an oil company sets up in petrol stations. But diversification, combined with greater overall concentration in the economy, is often a potent transparency destroyer. Typically, there is 'information loss'; the total information statutorily disclosed by companies to shareholders and the public is reduced.[12]

Changing technology also produces swings-and-roundabouts effects on the relevant structures. For example, advances in information technology increase the potential for social monitoring agencies and citizens to scrutinize corporate affairs, an important aspect of transparency. But technological and market changes also make certain types of resource transfer even more opaque. There is a tendency for short-term money to be moved about the world by speculators or corporate portfolio managers in still more shadowy ways. It has been argued that, following major changes in the world financial system, 'the general effect has been gradually to extend the area of significant ignorance' in the money markets.[13]

The cross-currents may occur even within a single unit. For instance, an organization's public antennae may benefit because it is growing larger and more socially prominent, while its sub-activities become more opaque to the public because of less disclosure and greater complexity.

We are led, then, to a second thesis concerning public co-operation at industry or organizational levels. This is that sustainable improvements call for conscious, deliberate effort, involving both an ideological impetus and a reform of malleable structures.

In theory, within a grass roots corner of the economy, a sharp ideological shift could effect a turnaround on its own. A few powerful and ideologically committed individuals, even a single such individual, could push a whole organization towards some highly co-operative or non-co-operative stance over a long period. The requisite combination is rare among business leaders: not only the prolonged concentration of power but also a fervent social ideology transcending the economic sphere, together with a readiness to stand by that ideology through thick and thin.

Where this combination existed, however, it helps to explain how a particular industry, or more likely an individual firm, moved downwards or upwards in public co-operation. For example, Henry Ford I's rugged classical individualism contributed to keeping his great company notably in the rear during the New Deal period in the USA; George Cadbury's deeply held Quaker ideals pushed his firm to the forefront in the early 1900s in the UK. Historically, an exceptional impress of philosophical individualism or Manchester School liberalism on powerful economic leaders has tended at least to discourage public co-operation via external colloquy. By contrast, high-level public co-operation within a particular firm could owe a good deal to the influence of extreme nationalism, US-type 'corporate liberalism', or social Christianity.[14]

More often, as the explanatory framework implies, there has to be a combination of an emergency-type catalyst, an improvement in structures, and a change in internal attitudes. A push from behind, the simultaneous removal of several types of structural impediment, and some sort of ideological–cultural conversion: these appear to form the classic scenario for a major, subsequently sustained shift towards greater public co-operation in a corner of the economy.

Thus, a strong impetus comes from external criticism or new public policies. Along with this, some facilitative structures tend to improve. Intensified surveillance by voluntary or official bodies, the media or pressure groups, and sometimes, too, tighter statutory disclosure requirements, increase the sector's public transparency, its sense of being 'watched'. New networks for communication and consultation increase its proximity to public opinion, social agencies and government, and the co-operative dispositions which this may encourage, often in the longer term. Where the target industry is also relatively new, as is sometimes the case, it may well be simultaneously moving away from both an extreme instability of institutions and persons, and ultra-fragmentation. But the 'internal conversion' factor also has its own momentum. Leading people in the industry have both consciences and concepts which are moved by the situation or which have already changed even before the catalytic events in question.

It was by this array of means, to a considerable extent, that some of the worst excesses of labour exploitation were slowly driven back, in the early twentieth century, in sections of iron and steel, and other heavy industries, in the USA and the UK. A strong leverage was exerted in other industries, too, by internal reformism, bridge-building communications exercises, public scandals and searchlighting, and by moves towards greater continuity and conformable size. This combination played a large part in pulling sectors like life insurance and commercial advertising from their earlier skullduggeries and exploitations of the public.[15]

In more recent times the evidence is less clear. But a similar chemistry appears to account, in major part, for improvements across a range of industries over aspects of environmental pollution, product safety, worker health, and racial discrimination. In the 1970s, the processes for policy making in connection with some potentially dangerous chemicals were markedly more co-operative in West Germany than the USA. This owed much, it seems, to greater continuities of key personnel; fewer actors and a greater organizational compactness; pre-established networks for communication and consultation across the various divides; and a pro-co-operative ideology in both government and industry.[16]

In similar fashion, major economic reforms in leading parts of the West German motor industry, in response to public interests, would not have come about co-operatively and participatively had it not been for a whole array of previous structural and ideological changes: in trade union size conformability, industry–finance–labour–government communications networks, and belief patterns among both top managers and trade union leaders.[17]

As we have seen, however, micro-concentrations of high public co-operation tend to be isolated and vulnerable. Patterns of sectoral change are less important than those which can sometimes impel whole political economies upwards. Many of the grass roots changes themselves cannot be properly understood without this larger dimension.

Only at the level of a whole national political system and culture, as well as a whole economy, can the structural and ideological factors be fully assessed. At this level, too, the issues of malleability and reformability come to a head, along with the vexing, nagging question of how far improvements have to rely on emergency, with its frequently tragic attributes. To tease out the sources of economy-wide advances in public co-operation would represent far and away the biggest explanatory prize.

## DYNAMICS OF ECONOMY-WIDE ADVANCES

In a nutshell, my thesis is that a sustainable increase in public co-operation across a whole economy has typically required a sequence as follows: (1) some starting rudiments of favourable structures, (2) the representation of democratic communitarian beliefs by a significant political movement, (3) a catalytic event like defeat in war, the aftermath or fear of civil war, or a continuous external threat, and then (4) a coalitionist phase during which the communitarian political movement acts as a fulcrum. Such a phase would involve (5) both general community building and improvements in the structures favouring public co-operation in the economy, thus closing the loop and bringing us back to (1).[18]

This model of a progression towards increased public co-operation could be modified in two possible ways. One way would involve less tragedy. The transition might be more peaceful if democratic communitarian beliefs were relatively well entrenched and also, less importantly, if the political economy was relatively small, and if its structural contours were favourable. But even this would not completely dispense with some emergency factor. The contrasted, less pleasant pathway is obvious. To the extent that the economy was large, poorly structured for public co-operation, and more especially lacking in a democratic communitarian political focus, the role of emergency and crisis would be greater.

In neither of these two situations would the upward shift necessarily be sustainable indefinitely. A political economy could remain on a high level of public co-operation for a long period, but not 'for ever'. The eventual likelihood of gradual slippage or deterioration, probably of a less dramatic character, must be borne in mind. As suggested earlier in this chapter, it is probable that abundances in the supply of public co-operation come in 'long waves' or phases of several decades.

A gap in explanation remains in connection with countries which have never advanced significantly in public co-operation during the twentieth century in time of peace. In these countries, it will be argued, *none* of the relevant factors has been properly present. Such a national situation has been infertile. Large-scale public co-operation might never be attempted, or it might be tried but fruitlessly. However, before these large issues can be confronted, we need to examine the key explanatory forces one by one. It is to their detailed exploration that the next few chapters are devoted.

# Chapter 6

# Threshold continuity and conformable size

It is easy to see that extreme instability is bad for public co-operation in the economy. Sweeping industrialization, mass migration and hell-for-leather economic growth have, in general, been hostile forces. The 'first industrial revolution' in England provides a classic, perhaps *the* classic, case. Economic civility broke down; socio-ethical codes dissolved; a mixture of rank coercion and exploitation took over. In the USA, modified counterparts emerged in the successive 'frontier' experiences. Socio-economic conflict largely prevailed across semi-nomadic open spaces and in cattle towns, mining settlements and Klondykes.

But the US 'frontier' experiences also suggest that a pre- or anti-co-operative instability comes in different shapes, sizes and mixtures. For example, the farming settlements on the north-west 'frontier' were not so bad; there a stable and traditional occupation assisted towards some ethical underpinning for economic life. Relatively homogeneous ethnic and religious groupings among the settlers were also a great help. In some other areas and phases, the various categories of flux and novelty conspired to make a witches' brew. Thus, in early copper mining or oil prospecting, not only were the economic locations new; these were also new industries without established habits. In addition, they involved new settlers who had no previous relationships with each other, and who were often rootless, shiftless and footloose in their ways of life.[1]

Our awareness of these economy-wide, industrial or local types of economic 'frontier' is well developed. Over-rapid industrialization and raw-edged novelty breed familiar social problems. Until a new industry 'settles down' and gets past its 'infancy', irresponsibility tends to thrive. For example, new pharmaceutical products have sometimes featured deceptions towards the consumer, as with pain-killing drugs or contraceptives. Repeatedly, periods of some years have had to pass before the worst excesses could evaporate and before commercial behaviour got into line with social norms (not only laws), which themselves often needed time to develop in such novel fields.

However, further types of 'frontiers' exist about which we know much less. These 'frontiers' arise under 'normal' conditions, and they are more sociological or even demographic in character. They apply, first, to economic organizations and their leaders; both may exhibit particularly high degrees of flux. Second, severe discontinuities may pertain to the public agencies which seek to supervise economic organizations, and to the officials in these agencies. Third, a double asymmetry may arise *between* the sectional organizations and the public ones. Both the institutions and the people involved in efforts at public suasion may come and go more rapidly than those they are supposed to influence in the private sectors. All these discontinuity factors may be expected to have some adverse effects on public co-operation in the economy.

## ANTI-CO-OPERATIVE DISCONTINUITIES IN SECTIONAL ORGANIZATIONS

One hypothesis about the effect of time can surely be discounted: that the chances of public co-operation continue to improve indefinitely, the longer organizations survive and the longer their leading people's tenures last. This appears unlikely. It does not seem plausible that public co-operativeness should be a continuous function, even in a limited way, either of sheer institutional longevity or of top people's periods at the helm. What seems more probable, with respect to both organizations and persons, is that there are extreme anti-co-operative *dis*continuities, and that once these are overcome, time ceases to be an explanatory variable in itself. Before certain time threshold were reached, public co-operation would be impaired; afterwards, the problem would diminish but without reducing further as additional time elapsed.

Typically, the first few years of an organization's life are dominated by a struggle to survive, a cliff-hanging effort to achieve economic viability. The establishment of some kind of 'corporate personality' tends to take longer. Without this, it is hard to create patterns of predictability and responsibility in dealing with public interests, and with other economic organizations, public opinion and government. But a 'corporate personality' is often the result of a single outstanding leader's or leadership group's influence; and this often takes a decade or more to make its mark.

A further issue is whether expectations about one's own personal continuity or discontinuity affect the disposition to take account of public factors. Readers will recall that internal forethought, an important component of public co-operation, means reviewing public interests (social norms and public policies) as part of the preparation for decision making inside an organization. It also means considering, at the same stage, various external groupings which embody the public interests and which the organization already relates to, or impacts on.[2]

For purposes of internal forethought, it seems clear that the leading people should expect their organizations, at least, to be 'still around' when the long-term results of their decisions emerge. This excludes 'fly-by-night' units: the business versions of Aesop's bats, as irresponsible as they are transitory; for example, the vagrant encyclopedia salesman or the transient wartime speculator. Their very rationale is to exploit discontinuity. For them the whole point is to defy public factors by being 'here today, gone tomorrow'. But in organizations which are established and seemingly stable, the bearing of personal expectations of continuity on public co-operation is likely to be more complex.

Ideally, the decision makers would expect to be in responsible positions for long enough to be accountable to their peers, and to society, as the ripple effects of their crucial actions worked through. In business, this would mean when the results of, for example, a major long-term investment were able to be fairly evaluated not only by superiors, shareholders or employees, but also by public constituencies. In the case of trade union officials, it would mean when the impacts of major decisions worked through for their own members, neighbouring groups of workers, and more widely; for example, not only immediate pay rises in year 1, but also (perhaps partly consequential) economic difficulties in their industries in year 2, or ripple effects on others' earnings in year 3.

Fully fledged internal forethought means that important, often highly long-term 'external effects' should also be taken into account. The decision makers would then expect still to be around when those younger people whom they had trained eventually proved themselves, often in other organizations; or when the public came to appreciate social causes they had helped, buildings they had beautified, or trees they had planted. On the negative side, the decision makers would expect still to be in place when the pollution for which they bore some responsibility eventually had harmful effects on health, safety or the ecology. But this last is a heroic requirement since many such 'external effects' run to several, even many, decades ahead, and are fraught with uncertainty and forecasting problems, especially in areas of advanced technology.

The threshold expectations implied by external colloquy, the second of public co-operation's operational processes, are more realizable. According to sociologists, 'co-operative settlements are encouraged by anticipated future interactions', and interorganizational collaboration benefits from 'lasting ties'. Tournament experiments show that the players are more inclined to co-operate in so far as they foresee further dealings with one another in later rounds of the game. Habits of mutual confidence, for example between companies and trade unions, take some time to build up. Since inter-organizational colloquy depends a good deal on personal factors, the continuity of those involved in the interactions matter. Even the most long-lived organizations would find it hard to collaborate if their key people, including those at the 'interface', were constantly changing.[3]

It is hard to assign quantities to these co-operation-facilitating thresholds in economic life. The time periods required for (1) personal moral commitment, (2) a sense of social accountability, (3) organizational awareness of relevant public factors, and (4) inter-organizational trust are difficult to verify. They are even likely to be inconsistent. Moreover, the normative implications are far from clear. Many discontinuities are an unavoidable part of a growing economy, even of a free society. To try to eliminate these would be to reject not only new technology, new firms and new forms of social organization, but also the free movement of persons: it would be dictatorial as well as ossifying. Any reforming efforts would have to concentrate on grossly anti-co-operative discontinuities which were (1) uncompensated by public advantages and (2) avoidable in practice.

Several such categories appear to be targets of concern. Managers in large companies, perhaps particularly multinational ones, may be moved about so rapidly between jobs and places that it is difficult for them to put down roots, to experience external loyalties, to build up mutual trust with external constituencies. For this situation highly elaborate organizational hierarchies are considerably to blame. The periods upwardly mobile executives spend at each level are reduced; indeed, there may be a deliberate policy of rushing through high fliers so they can get to 'the top' in time to make a sustained impact there. Alternatively, the top people have very short periods in office. Nor are trade unions and other organizations exempt from these problems. Sometimes their internal election systems incorporate frequent votes and a rapid rotation of the elected officials. This, too, may be expected to hinder the organization's stances towards public factors.

All of these discontinuities are partially avoidable. Large companies, particularly multinationals, could pay regard to public factors in planning the careers, and more especially the geographical movements, of their managers. An additional argument emerges for 'flattened' hierarchies or 'matrix', 'network' types of internal organization. These are often advocated on grounds of flexibility, innovativeness and 'anti-bureaucracy'. But having fewer steps on the latter should also encourage the sort of threshold job continuities, including continuities at the very top, which consort better with people building up public commitments, adapting to external constituencies and being held to account socially. As for the over-rapid rotation of elected senior officials, particularly in trade unions, this is an area of legitimate public interest, along with such organizations' general systems of internal democracy and accountability to members. By the same token, it is a valid area for public policy and the law.

## ANTI-CO-OPERATIVE DISCONTINUITIES IN THE PUBLIC SECTOR

The case for threshold continuity does not stop short at economic organizations in the strict sense of this term. It also applies to the public and social agencies which seek to influence these organizations towards public co-operation. They, too, need thresholds of time and expectation in order to build up a lively sense of long-term moral consequences and relationships of trust, not to mention efficacy, towards the sectional constituencies they relate to. From these points of view, the actual and expected continuities of their officials may be important as well.

Indeed, there is a strong argument to the effect that the official and social agencies of public co-operation probably require *longer* continuities than the sectional organizations they interact with. At stake here is the vital norm that public organizations should be 'senior partners', that socio-political forces should be superior to sectional–economic ones. The Burke-ean view that deference attaches to the sheer age of an institution goes too far. However, it is a reasonable hypothesis that if a body is to attract the respect due to a 'senior', then among other attributes, it should last longer. More important, if the public agencies are to perform effectively their roles of surveillance and persuasion, they need to be able to accumulate experience of the economic sectors; and this, too, is partly a function of time.

It is often assumed that social or public institutions are inherently more continuous than economic ones. On the one hand, an image of rapid turnover attaches to economic, particularly business, organizations. This image is encouraged by economic theories of competition, and by metaphors like Joseph Schumpeter's 'creative destruction'. It is constantly reinforced by reports of corporate mergers and take-overs. On the other hand, there is an equally common, though less explicit, tendency to credit public organizations with longevity. This takes colour from the undoubted venerableness of traditional political institutions, of monarchies and presidencies, mayoralties, civic entities, and departments of state.

Yet both images are frequently mistaken. A good deal of evidence attests to the solid, entrenched continuities of many leading business, trade union and professional organizations. It is not less clear that large areas of flux and instability often exist on the public side. Transience and rapid turnover often characterize precisely those specialist (and often new) official agencies which are supposed to influence and interact with economic organizations.

In fact, the desirable ratios are frequently reversed. The relevant public agencies come and go more rapidly than their opposite number sectional institutions. In addition, the to'ings and fro'ings of senior civil servants, top regulators and key intermediary persons may be particularly marked. They may well exceed those of leading businessmen, trade unionists and other sectional chieftains. When both types of flux are greater on the public side of affairs, a serious asymmetry occurs.

There is evidence that, over long periods, precisely this asymmetry has applied along many of the public–private frontiers in some of the advanced mixed economies. Particularly in the UK and the USA, continuity thresholds in major parts of the public sector have for long been seriously transgressed. Indeed, in those systems it is likely that the public discontinuities have gone so far as to exceed, in many fields, those in the private sector, in terms of both institutions and persons.[4]

This is an unhealthy situation from the viewpoint of social partnership and public co-operation. To redress it should be a major long-term priority for public policy.

## CO-OPERATIVE DISPROPORTIONALITY: 'TOO BIG', 'TOO SMALL', 'TOO MANY'

In chapter 5, I introduced a further 'structural' thesis, one relating to organizational sizes and numbers. The idea was that the sizes and numbers of economic organizations would affect their ability to identify, contact and publicly co-operate both with each other and with public or social agencies. As with the time factors, the size distributions could also influence relative power as between sectional units and the state. Thus, it would be bad if an economic organization dwarfed the political authorities in size, or if sizes were grossly unequal as between the principal sectors. It would be bad, too, if an economic system were fragmented to such a degree that mutual recognition, interorganizational collaboration and public surveillance would be likely to suffer.

The probable influence of organizational sizes and numbers should not be exaggerated. Although their quantifiability makes them a seductive target for social scientists, it does not guarantee their importance. Moreover, the implications for social control are unlikely to be simple. Ideally, a structural framework for public co-operation would have to fulfil a wide variety of tests, including mutual recognizability, reasonable lines of communication, broad sectoral parities, and accessibility to, and amenability to a primary influence from, the public and social organs. All of these criteria matter; it is a mistake to concentrate on just one.

For example, Mancur Olson has presented the idea of 'encompassingness'. Olson claims that social control is helped if sectional organizations are large enough to include a wide diversity of economic interests within their memberships. The 'encompassing' organizations then have to harmonize the diverse interests and discipline them internally. Thereby, public interests are advanced; quasi-governmental functions are performed; central government 'overload' is relieved.[5] Olson's claim is reasonable as far as it goes, but it is based on only one criterion. On its own, intra-organizational 'encompassingness' is unlikely to make a decisive contribution to decentralized social control. Even just in terms of sizes and numbers, other tests surely matter, for example an avoidance of excessive organizational bigness *vis-à-vis* the state. Moreover, other structural influences altogether may well be more important, notably from transparency and proximity (see chapters 7 and 8).

Then there is the question of political relativity. 'Too large', 'too small' or 'too many' in relation to *what*? Local authorities or communities? The region? The nation state? A supranational authority?

This book's main assumptions as to political focus have already been made clear. Ethically, democratic communitarianism offers a qualified 'yes' to the nation state. The Durkheimian solidarists, the personalist

Christian democrats, and the civic humanists all made moderate claims
for the nation state as an important focus for moral effort and communal
pursuits. Pragmatically, there is a great concentration of pressures for
public co-operation at this level. National government still is, and is
likely long to remain, a major focus of power. Therefore, it is at national
levels that a large part of the case for democratic accountability arises.
Neither a major decentralization to regions and localities, nor a movement towards supranational decision making, however desirable either
or both of these may be, seems likely to alter significantly the well-
entrenched solidities, indeed solidarities, of most existing nation states.

It follows, then, that 'proportionality', or the avoidance of 'too
large', 'too small' and 'too many' economic organizations, has to be
chiefly aimed for across a whole national economy. A central
government, a national public opinion and culture, a nationally elected
parliament: these will continue to be the main touchstones for deciding
the co-operatively 'best' size configurations of business, labour and
other sectional group organizations. From this flows, in turn, the main
thesis to be considered through the rest of this chapter. Although subject
to many ramifications and some key provisos, this thesis is essentially
simple. It is best to have a national pattern of economic organizations
which is reasonably compact.

Three principal criteria point in this direction.

## (1) Intersectoral collaborativeness across the economy

Public co-operation is often called for between the main sectional
interests: industry, labour, distribution, finance, agriculture,
representatives of consumers and of the main pressure groups. Such
multilateralism may be needed for a broad national policy consensus,
for example over sectional self-disciplines on pay and market power.
But the organizations involved need to cover most of the activity within
their own fields; otherwise, not enough of the economy will be drawn
into the net. Equally, there should not be too many such organizations,
overall. For if their numbers are too great, the fewer contacts which exist
between them will reduce the chances of varied trade-offs and mutually
advantageous agreements. There will be less ability both to negotiate
multilateral agreements and to make such agreements 'stick'. There will
also be poor prospects for a generalized mutual watchfulness among the
sectional organizations. Such peer group or 'sideways' social control is
a useful supplement to both public opinion's and government's
surveillance. Excessive numbers can only help to defeat it.

Samuel Beer expresses some of these ideas pungently as part of his concept of 'pluralistic stagnation' in the UK. With large numbers of interest groups, Beer says, each is tempted to refuse decisions which impose immediate costs on it (despite recognizing that if the rest also paid these costs, all would benefit). Also, each interest group is tempted to seek decisions which provide immediate benefit for itself (despite the realization that, if the rest acted like this, too, all would suffer). Respectively, these are 'free rider' and 'prisoners' dilemma' situations, both resulting in self-defeating deadlocks. Whereas, in Beer's words, 'if there were so few participants that each could monitor the actions of the others, they could co-ordinate their actions', and, moreover, 'each would know what the others were doing and all would be aware of being watched'.[6]

Beer's formulation does not go quite far enough. It leaves out those cases where agreements are thought desirable by the state or public opinion even though they do not directly benefit the organizations concerned, and where it is arguably still desirable for such agreements to be concluded voluntarily, if possible. As with Olson's theory, too, the size–numbers factors may be credited with rather too much power. However, Beer's general argument is persuasive.

## (2) Public opinion's effective oversight

Here the issue is how well monitoring agencies and intelligent citizens are able to watch and appraise the sectional organizations. This capability is particularly desirable for national public opinion, the mass media, academe, pressure groups, the churches, various public bodies. The principal economic organizations should be identifiable at these levels, able to be pinpointed individually. But this objective will be impeded if the numbers of these organisations are too great. Public scrutiny will be defeated if too much of the economy is in the hands of units which are hidden in the crowd. Of the organizations which collectively control most activity, every one should feel that it is subject to being singled out for recognition, praise or criticism, whether by active, thoughtful citizens or by the main organs of public opinion. Again, excessive numbers will tend to defeat this.

## (3) Active junior partnership towards government

Here the most obvious consideration is that national government, too, should be able to exercise surveillance. In addition, public co-operation requires that sectional organizations should participate to some degree in public policy making. On top of which, national government and the organizations controlling most of the activity sometimes need to be able to make specific agreements.

All of these aims are likely to be obstructed, in some measure, if the number of sectional units is too great. Government is then unable to see the organizations in the round, to keep tabs on them, to appraise them fairly. Its persuasion becomes too vague, distant or merely exhortatory. At the same time, government's ear cannot be secured so well by the organizations; nor is genuine collective consultation feasible. Very large numbers also reduce the many-sidedness of the organizational–governmental relationships, again diminishing the chances of useful trade-offs and reciprocity.

Of course, the accountability of government itself demands vigilance by parliament. Indeed, parliament should be able to oversee government's own relationships with the sectional interests. But even this higher democratic objective, important as it is, will be assisted by moderate organizational numbers. If the governmental–sectional relationships are characterized by a sprawling multiplicity and atomization, parliament's eventual scrutiny can only be hindered.

Thus, we arrive by several routes at the idea that public co-operation is helped by a certain national compactness among the economic organizations. Two important riders to this have been anticipated. First, the compactness formula discounts 'smallness' as politically or economically dominant, but not its indispensability in minority roles. A nationally compact size distribution still has a 'long tail' of small economic units endowed with vital tasks. There is no implication that public co-operation at local and regional levels is unimportant. Great value may still be attached to a lot of small units exercising initiative and acting in junior partner capacities towards local and regional, rather than national, government. But such activities cannot compose more than a minority, if perhaps a substantial minority, of the total business to be covered by collaborative processes.

The second rider relates to organizational giantism. The national compactness precept does not exclude concerns about individual economic organizations becoming 'too large'. From the viewpoint of public co-operation, there is still a justified fear that businesses, trade unions or pressure groups may sometimes get 'too big for their boots', relative to national government and public opinion. The compactness formula leaves untouched the familiar argument that such politically 'oversize' sectional units probably require special monitoring or even perhaps, in some cases, breaking up.

## VILLAGE-TYPE NUMBERS AT NATIONAL LEVELS

To prescribe the general norm of national compactness is easier than to clarify its meaning for particular economic systems, let alone to decide what methods might be used to bring it about.

A useful way of bringing the concept down to earth is through the analogy of a village. Once the compactness formula has to be translated into actual numbers, this similitude emerges readily. We find that the total number of principal organizations within a national political economy would approximate to the population of a small village (or perhaps a fair-sized urban neighbourhood). This image is to be preferred to the cinema or concert hall analogies sometimes used. There, the test is whether the relevant economic units are able to 'fit inside'. But the implication that these units are to form an 'audience', as for a film or a concert, is too passive, and out of tune with public co-operation's actively participative character.

The formula of village-type numbers suggests a grand total well within the bounds of the 5,040 inhabitants prescribed for an ideal society in Plato's *Laws*. It approximates more nearly to the numbers invoked by Aristotle in discussing an optimal size for the polity. Aristotle stipulated that, ideally, all the citizens should be able to be called to arms by the shouting of a single herald in a normal voice. Similarly, the village numbers formula means hundreds of organizations not thousands. For practical purposes, it implies a rough maximum of 1,000 principal units.

This order of numbers has virtually all the relevant arguments on its side. Getting heads together is easier; so is the making of interunit agreements. Even the more diffused, non-interactive forms of public co-operation are assisted. Mutual recognition between the contrasted sectional interests is helped even when, as is often the case, they do not need to be in direct contact. Ignorance of external groups towards whom sensitivity is desirable becomes less likely. With hundreds of principal organizations, not thousands, the potential both for contributions to public policy making and for direct access to government is enhanced. Government is better able to know about the organizations and to influence them non-coercively. Its own complex dealings with them are more able to be watched by parliament. And one further barrier is removed to the exercise of public surveillance by citizens and monitoring agencies.

How far is such a situation attainable? One would-be approach to village-type numbers should be discounted. This is the idea that national compactness is best achieved by, or even impossible without, across-the-board aggregations of economic organizations. The proposal is that, ideally, 'peak' representative bodies would cover all the principal decision units. Business, labour and other sectional interests would be consolidated within large organizations (for example, the CBI or the TUC in the UK). It is those bodies, in the main, which would then fulfil the roles of advising the state and contributing to national policy making, reaching agreements with each other and with government, holding their constituent units to such agreements, and accounting for their respective sectors' behaviour to the public.

This viewpoint has some limited validity. It is true that some sectional interests demand national organization on these lines if they are to be organized at all. These interests start by being fragmented, as the 'long tail' of the distribution, and such fragmentation is unavoidable and often desirable. Hence, there is no alternative but to contrive these interests' national representation and participation – still a desirable and necessary aim – on the basis of intermediary national bodies. Examples are agriculture and, by definition, small firms and, still more markedly, individual consumers (not to mention seriously under-represented elements like the unemployed).

In some situations, too, aggregation is a desirable remedy for an anarchic pluralism among the 'peak' organizations themselves. In some countries, the employer, trade union, engineering or other professional sectors are represented by a multiplicity of national bodies. Collaborative solutions are thereby impeded even apart from any outright conflicts. So there is a case for national policy to aim at compositing the various bodies.

None the less, para-organizational aggregation is far from being the most effective pathway towards village-type numbers at national levels, and it may even prove a cul-de-sac or a diversion.

If such an approach is seriously attempted, there is a likelihood of (1) excessive centralization, or (2) ineffective public co-operation. Under (1), the 'peak' bodies tend to seek more and more power over their constituent units. They do this in order to consolidate advice to government, to possess the authority to make agreements on their members' behalf, and to make those agreements 'stick', even to the extent of being able to 'discipline' their members. By contrast, under

(2), the 'peak' bodies continue to be, in effect, no more than clearing houses or sounding boards. Given the high hopes for social control invested in them, the implications are unfortunate. Damage is done to a whole series of objectives for public co-operation, which have been premised on these agencies' effectiveness.

Of the two dangers, the first is also a threat to decentralized decision making within a market economy. It could be thought likely to deprive individual businesses, trade unions or occupational subgroups of too much responsibility and power of initiative. As for the second danger, this poses a threat to the efficacy of public co-operation itself. For under the aggregation approach, public co-operation has come to depend a good deal on the ability of the 'peak' bodies to co-ordinate, to 'commit' and to 'deliver'. Yet such an extravagant hope is bound to be cheated in so far as these bodies remain weak.

There may even be an unsettling seesaw between the two bad outcomes. First, sweeping expectations are pinned on to the idea of a very few central bodies getting together with government and concluding the economic equivalents of, say, the Congress of Vienna or disarmament agreements between the superpowers. Then, as the implications work through, there are widespread 'backlashes' against the real or implied centralization. Not just indignation, but outright deviation, build up at the grass roots. Militant shop stewards and Poujadiste businessmen increasingly run rings round the 'system'. The essentials of power swing back to the trade union or big business chieftains in the constituent organizations, if indeed they ever left them.

From these general considerations it follows that the best general route to village-type numbers is not through across-the-board aggregation or para-'encompassingness'. It makes more sense for the 'village's' population to be composed mainly of the units which possess, and are likely to go on possessing, direct economic power. What have to be counted for this purpose, then, are not the representative institutions but the directly responsible units.

So far as business and labour are concerned, most of the 'village's' inhabitants would be those corporations which cover the bulk of industry, together with banks and financial institutions which similarly command most of the financial sector, and the individual trade unions. These groupings' 'peak' agencies would be included, but with no pretence that they have wide powers to 'represent', 'commit' or 'control' their members. Such 'peak' agencies as are needed in order to cover naturally dispersed sectors like agriculture, the professions and consumers would be included, and would indeed possess due weight.

But over most of the economic system it is the idea of embracing the direct controllers of resources that would be paramount.

Finally, what are the chances of a political economy getting to this sort of situation in practice?

First, it helps if the country is reasonably small. Then the number of organizations commanding the majority of economic activity tends to be few. Provided the economy is fairly industrialized and advanced, a small overall size will tend to correlate with a high concentratedness of ownership and control. To a large extent compactness will be built in. 'Half the economy' can be represented inside the proverbial small hall or conference chamber, or even around a single table.[7] There is a major proviso. If the country is ultra-small, its economics, even its politics, may be dwarfed by a very few sectional giants, probably multinational enterprises.

A second helpful factor towards village-type numbers is obviously a high degree of already established concentration of business and organized labour. The 'top 200 companies' would typically control most of national output and employment in the private sector. On the labour side, there would be only a score, perhaps a few dozen, of individual trade unions. These factors would go a fair way towards establishing national compactness, bearing in mind that other economic interests, consumers and social groupings would require compact representative bodies (indeed, probably all the more so as a counterweight). As already emphasized, the concentratedness of the 'peak' representative agencies of labour and business is less important; but it is obviously helpful that their numbers be limited as well.

Third, it matters whether the country has a tradition of governmental intervention in organizational structuring, particularly of trade unions, business associations and representative bodies. In some of the advanced mixed economies, the convention has long been that this is a legitimate concern of the state. The long-term implications of such interventionism are not necessarily *dirigiste*; they may well be the reverse. Indeed, there is a plausible argument to the effect that, once the basic organizational 'design' has been 'improved' by central mandate, things can be more readily decentralized and central government 'overload' is likely to be reduced, not increased, if hardly in a dramatic fashion.[8]

In other countries, however, the tradition has been, and still is, different. How trade union, business and professional interests structure themselves has been overwhelmingly regarded as 'their own business'. Their numbers and sizes are still very much subject to *laissez-faire*.

Even if their structure remains unduly fragmented, and in conflict with industrial logic (as with some trade unions in the UK), it is not thought right for government to intervene. But if the argument just cited is correct, such short-term *laissez-faire* is likely to provide a further fillip towards greater government intervention in the long run.

In several West European countries, all three of the favourable conditions have been largely fulfilled. The economy is small; both business and labour concentrations are high; the pattern of interest group representation is a recognized public concern. Hence, village-type numbers are approximated. This broadly applies to the Scandinavian countries, Austria, Belgium and The Netherlands. In West Germany, although the economy is bigger, at least a high concentration has been partially achieved, notably on the trade union side, and public involvement in the representational structures has been present.

But elsewhere, village-type numbers seem very far off. For example, in the UK only part of the second condition has emerged, a fairly high level of business concentration: the rest is lacking. As for the USA, draconian obstacles are created by the overall size of the country, the extreme fragmentedness of sectional interests, and the long-entrenched traditions of governmental *laissez-faire*.

To sum up, then, conformable size is likely to be a positive, if still minor, contributor to public co-operation. Like threshold continuity, it helps to remove some palpable obstacles. But its best approximation, through village-type numbers, is only variably fulfilled and, in some western economies, seriously short-changed.

# Chapter 7

# Organizational transparency and social monitoring

The idea of social transparency has such rich and diverse applications that its relative absence from the study of modern economic systems is puzzling. It often appears in our concepts of ethics and politics, yet hardly at all in our understanding of economic institutions.

The philosophical background of the idea of transparency is venerable and exalted. It has been related to the inner sanctum of morality. Indeed, it has been seen as a precondition, even a litmus test, of 'rightness'. Thus, the 'principle of justification' asserts that if a proposition about morals is incapable of public statement and defence, a necessary (though presumably not sufficient) test of its validity is lacking. In other words, secrecy is ethically suspect. 'Esoteric morality is a contradiction in terms'.[1]

In political theory, the idea of transparency carries overtones of democratic virtue. Repudiating mystery and secrecy, it seems to favour both citizen and parliamentary participation. Echoes of it are to be found in the related concepts of 'open government' and 'accountability'. Theorists of conflict resolution have given it an important role. A number of utopian thinkers, from Plato onwards, have assigned a noble position to it. Their visions of an ideal society have accorded an honoured, even crucial, place to the idea of transparency of citizen, organizational or governmental affairs.[2]

In this chapter, I argue that public co-operation is impeded when, to use Durkheim's terminology, 'opaque environments' are 'interposed' between economic organizations, and public opinion and the state. I suggest, correspondingly, that an all-round transparency of economic organizations is an important facilitator. Such transparency will be found to depend on (1) the nature of the organizations' economic activities, (2) legal disclosure requirements, or (3) special processes of social monitoring. But I also intend to argue that the conditions for these (partly related) structures to facilitate public co-operation are highly demanding. Nearly always, the institutions for ensuring transparency are seriously defective, and stand in need of major extension and reform.

## INHERENT TRANSPARENCY

To begin with, certain parts of the economic system are relatively open and transparent by their very nature. Certain types of products and services have this characteristic inherently: for example, a staple food, a piece of furniture, a restaurant, a haircut. Similarly with certain categories of operations (say, the baking of bread), and some 'external effects' (for instance, traffic congestion, factory beautification). Such things are highly visible, physically accessible to large numbers of people, and reasonably intelligible. Within some business sectors, transparency applies both to commodities or services, and to the ways of producing and transacting them (while external or third-party effects are marginal or similarly obvious). Leading examples are an open market in simple goods, or a small owner-managed grocery shop which sells staple, everyday household products.

In complex and sophisticated modern conditions, however, such elementary transparencies soon peter out. In the majority of manufacturing business, even where the products themselves are simple and familiar, the intricate ways in which they are produced, administered and marketed are obscure to the public. Often, the product itself is opaque. An extreme case of diverse *non*-transparency is a large multi-product heavy chemical factory, or a nuclear power station. There the interlinked technological processes are highly complex and esoteric. The corporate bureaucracies and producer-related markets associated with heavy chemicals or nuclear power are impenetrable to the public gaze. So are some aspects of pollution. Various types of financial institutions and markets are similarly secreted behind multiple veils. Across wide swathes of the financial sectors, physical hiddenness, organizational density and intellectual complexity largely prevail. From public points of view, in those sectors, 'the area of significant ignorance' is often massive.[3]

These gradations of light and shade find counterparts in other types of sectional organization. A trade union will be more socially transparent if it is linked with the simpler economic activities just mentioned. On this scale, a union of shopworkers or nurses, say, comes considerably higher than one organizing chemical or engineering workers. Similarly, amongst pressure groups, exposure is automatically achieved by those which champion widespread, accessible and intelligible social causes: a lobby for pensioners, say, rather than one doing battle for isolated sub-categories of the socially deprived.

The case for associating inherent economic transparency with public co-operation is strong, although the evidence for it is highly scattered. Let us take some examples. When American public opinion raged against the 'trusts' in the early twentieth century, it appears to have been the companies dealing with familiar, simple consumer products which attracted the most indignation. When pricing restraint was publicly enjoined in wartime, it was retail food suppliers who showed the most compliance. According to a contemporary observer, this was partly because of food retailers' greater observability, and because customers had 'an interest in policing them': 'it is easy to apply social pressure to conspicuous men'. In the UK, during the anti-'profiteering' agitations of 1914–18, it was companies in retail distribution, services and consumer goods manufacturing which appealed most frequently to public opinion in their annual reports and chairmen's speeches. These categories of companies showed an above-average propensity to claim public-spirited actions of various kinds, and to report gifts to charities and war causes.[4]

We discover that 'self-regulation' in the advertising industry, in response to wide public criticisms, came earlier in its more visible sections. Reforms were quickly forthcoming with regard to huge outdoor hoardings which rampantly disfigured the landscape; but they took much longer in the case of grossly deceptive advertisements hidden away in the middle pages of magazines. We learn that retail distribution companies were particularly sensitive to the public over long periods, partly because 'their products are sold to household consumers' so that publicity became 'a more effective regulatory instrument'. Again, public sensitivity is said to have increased in the US oil industry when, among other influences, forward integration brought the major oil companies into a public arena which involved millions of citizen–consumers at gasoline stations across the whole nation.[5]

Conversely, many abuses festered behind the cloud of darkness. The fact that mining operations were hidden in far-away places, and underground, made it easier for mining companies to exploit their labour forces. The complexity of products like cables and electric lamps helped to shelter monopoly and cartel practices over long periods. The remoteness of finance and overseas companies from the public gaze doubtless contributed to their making fewer-than-average claims of public virtue in wartime: they would have felt less onus to justify themselves socially. Pharmaceuticals provide another case. For decades, the consumer persisted in being 'peculiarly helpless in his drug purchases'. Although drugs were familiar, everyday products, the industry's oligopolies were able to wield additional power over consumers through the (often exaggerated) mysteriousness attached to those products.[6]

Evidence of this sort, though piecemeal, provides some chapter and verse for the central hypothesis: that through openness both to the public and each other, organizational decision makers are subjected to the disciplines of being more easily watched, and more amenable to social appraisal, applause or criticism, and therefore that they become more desirous to please, and more averse to opprobrium.

Economic theory does a disservice in this field by dealing with 'knowledge' in a restricted way. It proposes, as a condition for fair competition in market dealings, 'parity of knowledge' between buyers and sellers. This proposition is unexceptional, but it does not go far enough. It neglects social transparency's wider dimensions, thereby impoverishing our understanding of social control.

Economic analysis ignores consumers' knowledge or ignorance in their wider capacities as citizens endowed with votes and political 'voice'. For example, consider an agricultural machinery firm which sells its equipment to farmers. Economic theory is (rightly) interested in how far farmers understand the machinery, its prices and markets, and by implication, too, something about the firm in question. Characteristically, though, it neglects the social influence and electoral power of farmers, and their numbers across a nation. Yet these factors are also likely to be important in influencing the machinery supplier's behaviour, even in the ways much analysed by economics, and towards a more restrained use of market power.[7]

Economic theory also restricts the 'knowledge' concept to buyers and sellers. It misses out on third-party beneficiaries and sufferers from external effects: local neighbours; distant but affected social groupings; public opinion as onlooker and invigilator rather than consumer; national government. Yet in so far as inherent transparencies exist, these constituencies, too, are possessed of greater or lesser abilities to observe economic organizations. Thereby their potential for social control, as a background influence towards public co-operation, is enhanced or reduced.

Inherent transparency, then, is a force to be reckoned with. Its benefits for decentralized social control have been unfairly neglected. The sectors where it is strong – broadly, retail distribution, various types of personal services, and a few parts of consumer goods manufacturing – are automatically subject to a quiet form of social discipline. Partly for this reason, no doubt, they are often models of popular capitalism or 'good' business behaviour. It is relatively easy for an unremitting (if usually unobtrusive) public surveillance to apply.

But the limitations of inherent transparency have to be recognized. The relevant sectors are no more than a minority. Over long periods, the retail and ultrasimple personal consumer sectors persist in being marginal within a whole economy. Their contribution to economic transparency is no more than an isolated beacon, throwing into relief the far more extensive fields where openness is lacking. Organizational mist and murk are far more prevalent through the economy as a whole.

## STATUTORY TRANSPARENCY

Basic transparency across the whole spectrum of economic organizations can be achieved in only one way, and that is by law. Only statutory requirements can bring the affairs of all significant economic institutions at least potentially into the public view. Only laws compelling disclosure can create a comprehensive framework for social openness. More is then known, or at any rate more can be found out. Enquirers have something to work on. Scope is provided for greater public scrutiny by investigative agencies, ordinary citizens, other organizations, and government.

Two sorts of objection may be made to the claim that there is a link between statutory transparency and public co-operation. First, there is scepticism as to the value of what legally enforced transparency discloses, both generally and for public co-operation. This objection is not lethal, but it is serious enough to warrant discussion in the next section of this chapter. It is true that legal disclosure requirements often create resistance; that they risk obstruction on the part of the organizations affected; that the resulting data may well be crude, ambiguous and incoherent, and too raw to form a reasonable basis for public surveillance. Such problems call out for special institutional treatment (see next section).

Second, there is a more ideologically based suspicion that if transparency is coerced, decentralized decision making in a market economy may suffer, even that freedom may be violated.

This objection has Orwellian overtones of an all-seeing, hyper-intrusive 'big brother'. It implies that enforced disclosure plants a time bomb for the state to coerce the disclosers in further ways. It suggests that if the public authorities get their hands on vital organizational information, free enterprise will suffer. Enforced disclosure may be accepted on the grounds that it improves 'market knowledge' in the restricted sense proposed by standard economic theory (see p. 113). But its wider utility for public co-operation may be denied. It may even be thought to defy the very nature of public co-operation as free and uncoerced.

But this objection is misconceived, for several reasons. First, central government is certainly a significant user of the information resulting from enforced transparency; indeed, it directly commandeers quite a lot for its own purposes. But the information is usually aggregated, with anonymity preserved. In non-centrally planned, relatively liberal economies, government tends to employ the resulting data largely for statistical purposes and to help towards more informed public policies. It also widely disseminates much of the data back to economic decision units and the public.

Then, the information produced by statutory disclosure also spreads 'cross-ways', or horizontally, directly from company and organizational reports to a wide spectrum of external constituencies. Large quantities of organization-specific data become available to customers, share-holders, pressure groups, journalists, TV sleuths, diverse monitoring agencies, the public at large. If these observers then approve or disapprove the 'opened-up' organizations; if they adjust their targets for pressure; if they move their adherences or transfer their resources – that is not part of the political economy of direction. It is primarily grist to the mill of informal social control (and of the market mechanism, too, if investment funds are switched).

Third, in so far as the behaviour of economic units is affected, as often appears to be the case, this similarly happens in decentralized ways. If the organizations become more responsive to public factors as a result of being more transparent, they still do so as free agents and in diffused fashion. If they step up their processes of internal forethought, external colloquy and operational adjustment, in this case with a view to winning repute or avoiding 'a bad press', that mainly connects with public co-operation, not state direction.

These points have been assumed by a long line of twentieth-century advocates of enforced 'publicity'. For example, J.M. Keynes suggested that 'the collection and dissemination on a large scale of data relating to the business situation . . . by law if necessary', would reduce instability, increase efficiency and also improve the quality of public policy; but (and this is the crucial point here) it 'would leave private initiative and enterprise unhindered'. For other advocates, the primary aim of statutory disclosure was to uncover 'sins', to prevent 'extortion' or to promote 'honesty' and 'public service', working on 'the desire to keep a good name' and to 'avoid scandal'. But again, the behavioural implications were envisaged as consistent with both economic enterprise and political liberty.[8]

By one attractive image it is suggested that transparency creates a 'goldfish bowl' within which the decision makers are more likely to become 'good fish'. The goldfish bowl's translucency is to be morally invigorating, but without undue constraints being imposed on those inside. The organizational 'fish' are to have a further spur to being 'good' whilst also remaining substantially free to be enterprising 'swimmers'.[9] Yet the goldfish bowl has to be *inclusive*; and in complex, advanced economies, this is not possible without a comprehensive framework of constraints.

In this field, then, public co-operation and the law are complementary, not opposed. It is for public co-operation's benefit and along decentralized pathways, in the main, that the effects of organizational transparency work through; but centrally imposed statute is a necessary precondition for it. There is a paradox here but no contradiction. Coercion is needed for a framework which then produces routine, largely free form results. Compulsory disclosure provides an economic equivalent to laws on public health: its public good attributes are similar to those of laws on, say, sanitation and non-pollution, but for the results to be beneficial, everybody has to contribute.

Extensive statutory disclosure is needed as part of the groundwork for decision units to co-operate freely in a way that is mutually informed and understanding, and 'fair'. It is required so that the public can get some idea of what is going on. Without a base line of enforced disclosure, running across the economy's main sectors, public opinion, parliament and government would be deprived of a major source of influence and leverage, and the basis for more detailed social surveillance of sectional interests would be lacking.

But at any point of time, the framework of statutory disclosure is almost certain to be patchy and flawed. Some sectors will be imperfectly covered: many others will be omitted. Nearly always, major reinforcements and expansions in the framework will be required. In any coherent strategy for increased public co-operation, a case for improvements along these fronts is likely to loom large.

## TRANSPARENCY THROUGH SOCIAL MONITORING

Economic organizations may become publicly open in a further, partly complementary way, through the agency of social monitors. These are bodies which evaluate, praise or criticize sectional units from the outside. Often they start out from legally disclosed data, as just discussed. The social monitors may be cultural, commercial or governmental. They include consumer, environmental and other pressure groups, academe, religious organizations, the media and, in terms of some of their work, public regulatory agencies. Monitoring by these bodies appears likely, in general, to increase the sum of public co-operation; but the conditions for it to do this are far from smooth. Indeed, they are particularly problematic.

It is essential that the monitors be detached from, and independent of, the organizations they appraise. At once this marks them off from both professional codes and 'self-regulation'. Monitors do not have to specialize in this work; many of them have other activities. They should be able to approve as well as stigmatize. Their work should be open and public so that a wider public opinion is informed and focused, and brought to bear. Further, as with the legal transparency provisions discussed above, the ambit of social monitoring should be comprehensive in terms of both economic sectors and organizations.

Ideally, social monitors would have four main roles. (1) They would filter and process those organizational data which result from statutory transparency (see previous section); otherwise, such data would often be too raw or even confusing. (2) They would focus and represent a public opinion which would otherwise tend to be amorphous. (3) They would be capable of the forceful probing which is needed to break down typical institutional secrecies or even obstructions. And (4) they would play an evaluative role since it has to be borne in mind that the 'facts' about sectional organizations are no less ambiguous than others relating to the social world. Selection and interpretation are required; hence value judgements; and hence, very importantly, *debate*; and for this purpose, too, focusing agents are needed.

It is plain that in almost any conceivable advanced mixed economy actual monitoring practice is going to fall seriously short of these ideals. Most systems are very far from possessing surveillance systems of such probity, fairness, efficiency and scope. Yet the process already operates in rudimentary, often unobtrusive fashion.

To start with a polar case: a detailed study examined 'major publicity crises' since 1960, which affected seventeen large multinational companies in the USA and Australasia. Nine of these companies were guilty of serious offences against safety or health, ranging from unsafe car engines, through dangerous chemical wastes, to explosions and air crashes. Three of the companies had engaged in extensive bribery of politicians or public officials. The remaining cases involved violations of anti-trust or labour laws; political interference in Chile; and deceptive advertising.

These companies were invariably pursued by the press, sometimes by television, often by legislative enquiries and/or legal actions, in some cases by church or pressure group protests, occasionally by a published exposé, a shareholder action or a consumer boycott. In consequence, many experienced reduced sales, legal or other costs, lower stock market prices. More important, though, according to both the researchers and the companies, was the 'loss of prestige in the community for top management, trauma for executives in facing cross-examination about the scandal, distraction of top management from normal duties, and decline in employee morale'. The study claimed that in every company some reforms had resulted: 'major' or 'minor' steps had been taken to remedy policies and standards, sometimes to change personnel. The wider effects included tougher legislation and, within the realm of public co-operation, there were signs of other businesses voluntarily emphasizing the relevant public factors to a greater extent than before.[10]

This is a polar case, of course, since many of the offences were technically illegal or criminal, and more likely than average to attract searchlighting by monitors. For reliable inferences as to the benefits of social monitoring for public co-operation, we would need evidence on wider, less glaring and more complex categories of behaviour. We would need this over longer periods, too, and less prominent economic organizations would have to be looked at.

The historical evidence we do have is fragmented. Much of it refers to situations earlier in the century. For example, we read about the influence of the churches on labour–employer conciliation. We learn about specific victories won by environmental groups against pollution, by 'muck-raking' publicists against labour exploitation, by consumer lobbies against deceptive advertising. We find that when certain industries moved towards reforms at various times, for example insurance, retailing, iron and steel, it is pressures from social monitoring which appear to have played a major part. Information is sometimes available on social monitoring carried out from within the public sector, often by agencies with wider roles, like the US Federal Trade

Commission from the 1920s, or the British official inquiries in the early 1900s which searchlighted 'sweated labour' and the 'dangerous trades'.[11]

None the less, all this is only the tip of the iceberg. Obscurity still largely applies to the day-to-day influence on organizational behaviour of social monitoring, or the fear of such monitoring.

There is bound to be an area of hidden successes. You cannot have diverse social monitors operating over long periods without their power often being taken into account. Yet much of this taking into account will lie below the surface. Diffuse objectives of 'keeping a good name' or 'avoiding a bad press' will be more frequent than having a particular social monitor's praise or criticism explicitly in view. Typically, there is no specific, or at least recorded, decision. This is very much the case with the significant category of 'unthinkable' or 'unmentionable' actions. If a link is traceable, it is with a 'policy', often incorporated in rules of thumb, and with long-entrenched value assumptions and social attitudes.

It seems reasonable to credit social monitoring, in part, with a large number of nasty things *not* done: deceits; bribes; defacements; safety risks; ruthless lock-outs or strikes; arbitrary sackings; ruinations of small competitors. In such cases, it seems safe to assume that the desire to keep a good name and the fear of being 'found out' probably loomed large.

Yet even if considerably more scholarly work is done in teasing out the linkages, a large part of social monitoring's success is likely to remain hidden. This would also apply to its failures: the many deviances which persisted despite continued excoriation by monitors. Only the most blatant cases of failure have attracted attention: the occasional putative social monitoring agency which got aborted or driven off the field, or vivid objections to the very principle, like Henry Vanderbilt's 'the public be damned'.

The thesis that social monitoring helps public co-operation seems to have a lot going for it. But this thesis needs testing against the ideal benchmarks outlined above. It requires to be interpreted in the light of the many shortfalls in social monitoring which those criteria uncover.

## GAPS AND SHORTFALLS IN SOCIAL MONITORING

Some public interests have no social monitors to watch out for them. They do not have probing champions or institutional 'voice'. The business sector is characteristically covered in the most haphazard and arbitrary fashion. For example, what regular, open, non-esoteric social monitoring is applied to banks, insurance companies or pension funds, not to mention foreign exchange markets, merger broking, or the portfolio investments of large financial institutions and multinational companies? Coverage of the professions is normally patchy. In most countries, who bothers to invigilate lawyers, architects, teachers, engineers, accountants? Many trade union practices (if not the trade unions themselves) equally escape the net. Ironically, an important social monitor, the press, is itself largely unmonitored, as if its behaviour, too, did not merit searching public scrutiny.

Some established institutions which arguably should be on the monitoring scene are frequently absentees from it. For example, in the UK, neither the universities nor the churches have notably brought within their evaluative capacities the sectional institutions of a modern advanced economy. High tables and convocations, lecture rostrums and pulpits, typically exhibit a lofty detachment. To a large extent, this reflects a prolonged historical split, even something of a schism, between economic institutions and the higher institutions of national culture.

The charge of 'negative bias' is often levelled, with some justification, particularly at the mass media. It is obvious that the exposure of sin is preferred to the extolment of virtue. Disproportional displays of such negative bias are sometimes found, as for example in treatments of trade unions by the press. Whatever the deeper reasons, serious implications arise for public co-operation. It is likely that sectional organizations are deprived of a positive stimulus; that overdefensive reactions are encouraged; that the public is tempted towards automatically jaundiced or cynical attitudes; that a largely confrontational and adversarial atmosphere results.

This brings us to the final and perhaps most subtle defect of most existing systems of social monitoring, their conflictual fragmentation.

A diversity of social monitors is unavoidable in advanced mixed economies and liberal societies. More, it is defensible in the interests of both wide participation and evaluative debate. Yet something important is missing if all that happens is a multiplicity of mutually isolated social monitors telling sectional organizations to do often contradictory things. The monitors themselves are then in competitive conflict. Each makes extravagant or excessive demands, oblivious of the others and of alternative pressures. The sectional organizations are faced with precepts so confusing and rivalrous that even the objects of social monitoring may suffer.

Although a cacophony of social monitors is partly unavoidable, it threatens an element of unfairness. Sectional decision makers are left with no picture of the overall guidelines society would like them to follow. They are entitled to that, if only in broad terms, but do not get it. Moreover, if social monitoring becomes too atomized and contradictory, the pressure tend to cancel each other out. The organizations are enabled to hide behind the resulting confusion; they are let off the hook too easily; they can play the critics off against each other. Public relations, or the effort to 'explain oneself', may get more emphasis than actual improvements in behaviour. Not least, an adversarial atmosphere is encouraged. This particularly occurs in political economies where a pluralistic–competitive monitoring system combines with a great dependence on the law. There, social monitoring too often slides towards the ad hoc exposé or the courtroom; its leading agents become muck-raking journalists and lawyers.[12]

There is an influential viewpoint which refuses to get exercised about such dangers. According to this viewpoint, society will automatically throw up monitoring forces. These forces will somehow be adequate, at least in the long run, and moreover their conflict, both mutually and with the sectional organizations, will be harmless or even salutary: an echo of the 'spontaneous order' concept. It is a view similar to Galbraith's earlier notion of 'countervailing power'.[13]

Yet like all models of self-correcting social processes, this idea is too complacent. It neglects a host of monitoring gaps and defects: where important public interests have no monitors to care for them; where large economic sectors consistently escape monitoring; where the monitors themselves are exempt from checking; where public opinion remains apathetic; where there is no attempt at overall umpiring or pace-setting; where no single agency is able to acknowledge the existence of the conflicts and uncertainties which consequently affect the monitored organizations, let alone to elaborate the implications of these and, perhaps, to indicate ways of living with them better.

Judged by the test of encouraging public co-operation, then, a sheer proliferation of monitoring agencies is an ambiguous, perhaps misleading, measure. Still less valid is a decibel yardstick, an assessment which sees virtue in the mere volume of criticism of economic institutions. For much of this criticism would not arise, along with the abuses in question, if a more balanced, effective and pro-co-operative form of social monitoring had existed in the first place. It would be ironical, even contradictory, if aspects of the structural apparatus which public co-operation requires turned out to be *anti*-co-operative.

I conclude with two further thoughts which arise from the above.

*First*, there is the priority to monitor the social monitoring process itself. Not only its existing or potential role in assisting public co-operation, but also its persistent limitations and the risks of abuse justify continuous review. The para-monitoring would pinpoint any major public interests unrepresented and what economic sectors were left out. It would also evaluate how far the process met the criteria of detachment, balance and fairness, and how well it performed the functions of filtering, investigation and interpretation.

In the long run, such a para-monitoring process would work in the enlightened interests of the economic organizations themselves. True, those sectors presently untouched might have initial cause for fear. Any who had so far escaped the net of social monitoring (let alone statutory transparency) would feel a cold wind to begin with. But the para-scrutiny would also show up elements of unfair selectivity, excessive 'negative bias' or even mendacity on the part of the monitors. The combined impact of all the pressures on the economic organizations' decision problems would be illuminated, as also the impossibility of all the public interests and external constituencies being satisfied. The extravagant pressures of some social monitors would come to appear less defensible. It would be less easy for society to set up endless hurdles and constantly to blow whistles without even hinting at the overall nature of the game and its rules.

*Second*, there is the bigger desideratum of an educated public opinion. Much of my argument through this chapter and previous ones implies that this consideration has to be at the forefront.

In the previous chapter, citizen surveillance emerged as a key criterion for both threshold continuity and conformable size. It was partly so that citizens would be able to identify and assess the main economic organizations that these structures were needed. But a reasonable starting level of citizen interest was assumed. The considerations raised in the present chapter depend still more critically on this assumption. If transparency is to do its work, a large number of interested, concerned civic observers must be present. The filtering, articulating and interpreting work of social monitors is needed as a complement to this, not a substitute, and does not dispense with the priority for public opinion to be an active force.

The question is how to pursue this priority. 'Economic education' in the usual sense is both too wide and too narrow. A smattering of the laws of supply and demand does not address the issues of public co-operation, whatever its other uses; nor does an awareness of the neo-classical, Keynesian or monetarist models of economic control. 'Consumer education' is quite inadequate. Rather, the imperative is key information on the major decision-making institutions of a modern economy, how their actions relate to public interests, and what criteria and methods can be employed to evaluate them in the light of those interests.

This is not a heroic requirement. Such knowledge does not have to be complex and esoteric. It should not be beyond the ability of educators, the media and modern technology to provide it. Nor does it have to extend to the majority of citizens. Even a sizeable minority of non-expert but interested observers of business, trade union and other sectional affairs would be a great help.

To sum up, then, both the philosophy and the methodology of public co-operation accord a high place to transparency. This institutional condition is not to be subordinate or an afterthought, as in the theories of 'perfect' or 'workable' competition. It is not to be limited to buyers and sellers, as in conventional economic analysis, nor identified with 'upward' information to a central planning mechanism, as *dirigiste* theory implies. As we have seen, public openness is only marginally fulfilled by the category of inherent visibility identified in this chapter. Rather, the claim is that transparency in the political economy is to be a major policy objective. And it is to be comprehensive, requiring both statutory disclosure and effective social surveillance, equally across the board.

As an aid to public co-operation, organizational transparency cannot be a matter of laissez-faire, as pluralist and equilibrium theories suggest. Instead, the analysis of this chapter suggests that, for purposes of public co-operation, much transparency would have to be engineered with great care, scrutinized constantly, even viewed with suspicion in view of the risks of abuse. The same applies to the institutions for social monitoring. These would not be evaluated on narrowly conflictual or adversarial criteria. Typically, a variety of reforms would be needed for social monitoring to work pro-co-operatively. Finally, a high quality of education, including some civic–economic education, is a key part of the whole. Indeed, public co-operation and a reasonably well educated society appear to be inseparable.

# Chapter 8

# Social proximity and forums

The proximity thesis is more basic than the ideas of threshold continuity, conformable size, and transparency. Like them, it is widely subscribed to in social and political fields. But it is even less discussed, at any rate systematically, in relation to a modern economy. Broadly, what the thesis says is that some form of 'closeness' to the people who are affected by one's behaviour tends to encourage 'good' behaviour towards them. This is tantamount to a denial of the cynical adage, 'familiarity breeds contempt'. It amounts to a vote of confidence in the ethical utility, in general, of being 'in touch' with significant others, and of having the effects of one's actions 'brought home' in particularly human ways.

Thus, it is said that individuals are more likely to make gifts to charities when they are acquainted with the recipients. It is suggested that a purchaser, on discovering that he has received excess change, is more likely to return this to a shopkeeper than if it has spewed out from a ticket machine. The proximity thesis may take bolder forms. There is even a related claim to the effect that seeing human targets face to face provides some sort of safeguard against indiscriminate brutality in war.[1]

To be helpful, though, proximity does not necessarily have to be direct. A charitable gift to, say, cancer research or overseas aid may be more likely if the potential giver is, or has been, in touch with any cancer sufferer or any starving person overseas. To encourage philanthropy, the actual recipients do not have to be known. In the 'excess change' case, a personal relationship with the shopkeeper is not essential in order to feel a sense of obligation which a totally impersonal commercial transaction lacks. As for war, if proximity to human targets does have some power to restrain cruelty, this would be through the agency of a general sense of shared humanity.

Transposing these ideas about proximity to a modern economy seems to be daunting. We are influenced by the thought that the industrial revolution crushed an earlier 'face-to-faceness', making this 'a world we have lost'. We are swayed by the impersonal models proposed by economic theories. So often, 'the personal touch' seems to be destroyed by mammoth-sized economic institutions, labyrinthine bureaucracies and anonymous market processes. Behind all this lies the image of an ideal economic relationship distorted, even of a noble dream betrayed. It is the image of direct personal closeness. To be forced to come to terms with intermediate possibilities is a sad let-down and may even be painful.

The direct proximity idea is far and away the most obvious and attractive, in economic life as elsewhere. If interpersonal sympathy has the ability to encourage honest market transactions, it is almost banal to predict this effect when Jones and Brown meet together to conclude the deal; all the more so if they already know each other. In advanced economic systems, however, people's and organizations' decisions are generally far more diffuse and hard to pin down, and tend to have ripple effects far beyond the decision makers or transactors, indeed far beyond any immediate circles of people they know. It is tempting to assume, therefore, that all is lost.

None the less, this reaction is mistaken, along with various (usually unspoken) premises that lie behind it. In this chapter, I am going to apply the proximity thesis, particularly in its extended form, to a modern economic system. I am going to suggest that extended proximity is a positive influence for public co-operation in our complex systems, even across their apparently worst divides; and, furthermore, that it is an *improvable* influence, subject to close analysis and due profiting from past mistakes.

My thesis is that frameworks already exist which generate ties of memory, loyalty and sharing between economic sectors, public opinion and the state; that some of these frameworks are malleable; and that improvements in them have been, and still are, highly pertinent to public co-operation's pursuit.

## CATEGORIES OF EXTENDED SOCIAL PROXIMITY

The first point that has to be made is that extended proximity often works through the agency of memory: the ability of early contacts to influence later behaviour.

The biographies and autobiographies of economic decision makers often suggest causal links between mainstream organizational decisions and social experiences in childhood, adolescence or early working life. If anything, the decision makers' eventual stances towards public factors are likely to be even more influenced by their personal social histories. Public choices tend to elicit gut reactions with particularly distant origins. Not even casual or accidental encounters can be excluded: a conversation with some stranger; a momentary observation of some human drama; an intense shared experience which perhaps occurs but once in a lifetime.

Next, extended proximity commonly involves contacts between ordinary members of different social groups, or what may be called 'cross-cutting linkages'. These experiences are often fragmented, casual or spasmodic (even where their contexts are contrived). They tend to occur between members of contrasted social classes, regions, ethnic or religious groups, or occupational categories. Again, such experiences may be important for existing or future decision makers.

Another form of extended proximity involves contact between the formal representatives of different groups. Such people are explicitly mandated to convey information, feelings and opinions from one section to another, perhaps also to symbolize or personify their constituencies in continuous and quasi- ambassadorial ways. Obvious examples are trade union officials, trade association executives, public relations people, and pressure group leaders. But similar representational roles are carried, sometimes, by any organizational person who belongs to a cross-sectional committee or other mixed body. Contacts with, and between, all such categories, and in such contexts, constitute 'cross-representing linkages'.

Finally, both cross-cutting and cross-representing linkages sometimes take a special form, best described as a 'social microcosm'. There, particularly wide varieties of interactions occur simultaneously. This may happen casually or accidentally, as when great varieties of people are 'thrown together' on holiday expeditions or in public celebrations, and in emergency or war. But 'microcosmic' features may be deliberately sought in multilateral economic negotiations, and in some sorts of committees or mixed bodies. Occasionally, the contrived microcosm even symbolizes a system-wide diversity. It represents or simulates a huge variety of socio-economic interdependences, even a miniature replica of a whole political economy or society.

## EXTENDED PROXIMITY AS A HELPFUL FORCE

Now the general argument for linking background contacts of these kinds with public co-operation has already been introduced. In a hypothetical case, I claimed that the directors of the Hydropoxic Chemical Company would be less likely to pollute Trans-Patagonia if they had some experience of Trans-Patagonia or the Trans-Patagonians, or of pollution. In the historical case of post-1945 Austria, the government, labour and business leaders had found it easier to co-operate, it appeared, partly because a set of continuous institutions for contact, this time within the political economy itself, had helped to pre-socialize them.[2]

The personal social histories of businessmen who became above-average public co-operators in their industries have some relevance. A helpful factor, it seems, was often some experience of members of widely different social groups, probably early in life. Thus, the future socially conscious businessman Frederick Marquis (later, Lord Woolton), whilst living as a young man in a poor district of Liverpool, observed a refined, emaciated lady in a local shop who died of starvation soon afterwards: 'I believe that few things have affected my life more surely than this "incident".'[3]

Other examples of this genre can be cited, from biographies and other studies (as well as memoirs) of businessmen who clearly established themselves as publicly responsive through their careers. Thus, we learn of early formative experiences in a volunteer fire department, or in the chaos and smell of a chemical town, or in a slum settlement. We read of travelling daily on public streetcars as a goad to civic action; of 'the experience of long hours, taken at an impressionable age', as a source of later empathy with employees; of 'unusual proximities to the men in the pits' as a clue to a leading industrialist's pursuit of habitable surroundings and 'community' in the workplace, many years later; of 'grit and smoke' from a family-owned ironworks 'drifting in through the windows', as a repeated reminder of interdependence and mutual obligations with both workers and neighbours.[4]

However, little is known about the comparable experiences (or lack of them) of the much larger numbers of publicly middling or deviant businessmen. So this category of data is only a starting point.

Rather more weight attaches to those cross-cutting and cross-representing experiences which occurred in time of war, often 'inside government'. For example, the First World War helped to school business leaders like Alfred Mond and Lord Ashfield in the UK, and Bernard Baruch in the USA, towards later major exploits in public co-operation in time of peace. The Second World War had similar effects in facilitating the development of some trade union leaders and para-business diplomats into 'public men'. A polar case was Norman Kipping, later the main architect of the (British) FBI's 'responsible' strategies towards government and public factors between 1945 and 1965. It is said that the Second World War so changed Kipping that, later, 'he resembled much more closely the civil servants with whom he preferred to deal than either the industrialists or the politicians'.[5]

The linkage is not restricted to war. More significantly, there are grounds for seeing a link between extended social proximities in peacetime, where these existed, and later acts of public co-operation over a wide range of issues.

Contiguities to workers, or distances from them, appear to have had some influence. According to some labour historians, voluntary (publicly exhorted) action to improve factory health and welfare, where this emerged, probably owed something to the factor of employers working or living close to their workers and factories, or getting to see these for themselves. Correspondingly, chronic neglect of decent industrial relations or human safety has sometimes been blamed, in part, on absentee ownership or management, and on the extreme physical isolatedness of certain types of work. Here coal mining and the shipping industry have been particularly cited. Even a company with a generally fair labour record could harbour gross exploitation in remote enclaves which were 'out of sight, out of mind'. In an extreme case, in Colorado, USA, it took actual bloodshed to highlight the real, semi- or pretended ignorance of the ultimate boss figure, John D. Rockefeller I. Rockefeller was trebly divorced from his browbeaten dependants: by their underground work, multiple layers of middlemen, and hundreds of miles of distance (in addition to his massive personal wealth).[6]

Absenteeism took on further dimensions of public abstention or even abdication as the employing and managerial classes 'moved out'. Migration to suburbs and the country, and the suction effects of metropolises, have been blamed in large measure for declining civic service by business leaders. So has a far-distant schooling of their children, particularly in the British public schools, with their cultural separatism and their socially standardizing, anti-regional effects. Business 'absenteeism' could be merely uninvolved. In the USA, large firms with distant headquarters and far-away shareholders tended to contribute less to local charities and civic causes. But 'absenteeism' could have sinister overtones, too. In West Virginia, virtually a 'colonial economy' up to the interwar period, the extreme absenteeism of economic proprietors combined with a restless mobility among local satraps and hangers-on.

It went alongside rank exploitation, evictions, spying, mine wars, and political corruption.[7]

Such evidence relates to early parts of the century, grass roots experiences, and public factors connected with labour, local contexts, and philanthropy. However, material exists for more recent times and wider aspects, even though the inferences we are able to draw from it become less firm.

A much cited, though restricted, case of macro-public co-operation was 'indicative planning' in France through the 1950s and 1960s. Its nub was a collaboration between civil servants and big business managers. This owed much, it seems, to their common educational backgrounds in the *Grandes Ecoles*. The cross-representing contacts provided by the UK's more limited National Economic Development Organisation (NEDO) have been credited with 'broadening' the socio-economic and public policy understanding of some trade union and business leaders. The more intensive example of post-1945 Austria has already been quoted. There, intricate cross-representing institutions enabled labour leaders, businessmen, civil servants and politicians to develop habits of intermingling, understanding and, often, personal acquaintanceship, which seem to have paid off in encouraging streams of publicly collaborative acts.[8]

A final category of support for the extended proximity thesis is more ambitious. High levels of public co-operation are seen to have occurred, over fairly long periods, within a whole economic system. The existence of widespread cross-cutting linkages in the country's educational and training systems, its domiciliary and neighbourhood patterns, and its civic activities, is also found. It is predictable, then, that a causal flow should be suggested from the general social mixing to the economic co-operation. Such a virtuous link has been particularly attributed, for example, to Sweden and Norway.[9]

The 'system-wide' argument can be stated quite simply. It is that a multitude of free-flowing linkages (cross-cutting or cross-representing, and sometimes microcosmic) helps to predispose existing or future economic decision makers towards public collaboration. By this means, it is thought, a more inclusive and vivid sense of 'the community' is provided. Class divisions are softened. There is exposure to members of less privileged groups. The experience of sharp contrasts helps to prepare for contact and consensus with decision makers in very different types of organizations or sectors. The 'culture shock' of confronting these people later is reduced.

This thesis has radical implications for our thinking about the background structures for public co-operation and their improvement. We will return to these later. But first, it is necessary to look at some further manifestations of extended proximity which exist specifically within economic life and which may similarly have pro-co-operative effects: para-intermediaries and, more especially, forums.

## THE ROLE OF PARA-INTERMEDIARIES

Para-intermediaries operate along the borders between sectional organizations, public opinion and government. They are particularly capable individuals who, from this vantage point, exercise leadership by perceiving needs and opportunities for public co-operation, influencing sectional organizations towards it, innovating methods for achieving it, and organizing it operationally. These elements come in different mixtures, depending on the individual.

An arch-exemplar or doyen of para-intermediaries was Jean Monnet. Although Monnet is chiefly known for his work on the European Common Market, I am referring here to his key role in constructing tripartite indicative planning in post-1945 France, a system which was to develop significant, if partial, elements of public co-operation over a long period.

For this achievement Monnet's long career 'in the interstices of politics, administration and business' had been an apt preparation. A provincial family business: public sector experience in inter-allied economic organizations in the First World War; subsequent roles in the League of Nations, international finance and, again, the family business; contributions to Franco–British–American co-operation both before and during the Second World War – according to Monnet himself, all of these contributed to a lifelong passion for 'unity' in conditions of freedom, pursued primarily through economic organization. They also helped to develop great diplomatic abilities and a keen sense of socio-economic interdependences.[10]

Shorn of the international overtones and the exceptional brilliance, the Monnet syndrome finds many echoes. Like Monnet, para-intermediaries tend to start within a particular business, trade union or industry. Then they broaden out, usually to other sectors, always towards public factors and government, sometimes to the extent of temporary public employment. As with Monnet, too, the vantage points from which they exercise their influence are interstitial: a trade association, a 'peak' employer or trade union body, a quasi- or semi-public agency, or a freelance or advisory status along the borders.

Para-intermediaries are far from being pure lobbyists or sectional spokespersons. Their public orientation equally distinguishes them from the general run of officials in 'peak' representative or intermediary bodies, who tend to be more sectionally minded. Yet the para-intermediaries' 'publicness' is different from that of either a leading monitoring personality (see previous chapter) or a public official. Their sectional interest connections make for a bridge-building, negotiating or orchestrating role, not one as judge, critic or moralist. Their 'publicness' is typically more enterprising, and less rule bound, than the civil servant's. These are persons who, during influential phases of their lives, personify and promote the blending of sectional understanding with pursuits of public interests.

Here are some examples. An advisory figure to government acts as a merger broker in a nationally important industry; this in pursuit of a public policy he himself helped to formulate. The leaders of a trade association act as 'intellectual brokers between the government (and society) and the businessmen'. They persuade their business colleagues to make concessions to government on labour relations issues, in return for state backing for measures against excessive competition in the industry.

The head of an industrial organization vested with some public duties protects the industry from direct, day-to-day political interference. But he also influences its ruling oligopoly towards public co-operation with respect to pricing, investment, and collective action *vis-à-vis* international competitors. The head of a trade union or employers' peak body sways its members towards accepting government policies for pay, price or dividend restraint whilst also contributing to, and often moderating, those very policies.[11]

The significance of para-intermediaries should be clear. An economy that depends on active intersectoral collaboration cannot do without them, particularly in situations where public interests have to be interpreted in subtle, flexible and changing ways. The para-intermediaries' distinctive role deserves more attention. So does the question of whether there is a sufficiency of such people for public co-operation in advanced mixed economies, and of whether their supply could, or should, be improved.

## THE FORUM

I come to the institution which has raised the most explicit discussion, the greatest misconceptions and disappointments, and the liveliest hopes. It is an institution which, in its most advanced forms, embodies many of the central principles of public co-operation.

Forums are representative bodies, operating at organizational, sectoral or national levels, within which decision makers or envoys from different sections of the economy and society, sometimes also from government, discuss and work together on public interests. They constitute a systematic and continuous way of organizing cross-representing.

For a particular economic organization, forums constitute one vehicle, among others, for external colloquy (see chapter 4); but their character is such that the colloquy tends to involve both a wide public policy scope and an extensive spread of groupings external to the organization.

The publicness of forum implies (1) official recognition and ratification, usually through statute; (2) a substantial part of activity, at least, addressed to public policies or social norms; (3) governmental access and/or direct representation; and (4) public accountability in wider ways.

Forums have to be both multilateral and 'representative'. Several types of sectional interest must be included. Mere opportunities for peers or market competitors to get together miss the point: even publicly approved cartels are disqualified. Convocations purely of a single industry's producer groups, as in the classic 'management–labour' duo, represent an impoverished category of forum. It is better for neighbouring industries and occupations to be included as well, and, better still, consumers, third parties and wider social interests. As with criteria for the 'village policy community', it is the effective decision units which should be included. The forums' members should be elected or designated representatives of core sectors, major interest groups or resource-controlling organizations; often, too, they will be key decision makers within those units.

These demanding attributes cut like a knife through the bewildering variety of intermediary institutions which have proliferated in the advanced mixed economies.

A large part of the institutional jungle which has grown up along the various frontiers comes nowhere near to forum status. Not only cartels, but also sectional interest lobbies, normally exclude themselves: these lack both the public and the cross-sectional attributes. Trade associations, managers' or employers' organizations, and many industry-wide bodies, do not qualify even when invested with wide public roles: again, a lack of cross-representingness rules them out.

Many quangos or advisory committees to government fail the same test, because of their interest group restrictedness; sometimes, too, because their members lack elective, representative or organizational weight. Many familiar institutions have forum-like façades, but otherwise belie the criteria. Others, though, turn out to be genuine forums in spite of misleading titles or formal functions. Indeed, nowhere is confusing language in our field more rife.

Thus, vague composite terms like 'consultation', 'negotiation', 'advice' and 'information' have to be unpacked. Issue-related labels like 'growth', 'stabilization', 'productivity' or 'incomes policy' often do less than justice to the economic and social functions performed. The terms 'regulation', 'supervision' and, still more, 'planning', frequently overstate, confuse or provoke.

Cross-country or cross-cultural variations add a further twist. Some genuine forums are described too grandiosely, notably the UK's National Economic Development Organisation (NEDO). Formal titles may refer to a forum's composition rather than its activities, as with Parity Commissions in Austria and Belgium. A narrow organizational *locus* sometimes masks a wide cross-representingness. The supervisory board of a large industrial company in West Germany has legal status and public tasks, and it includes representatives of managers, workers, trade unions, institutional shareholders, related sectors, and, sometimes, government. It is thus definitely a forum, although its formal designation hardly suggests this. Sometimes, a forum does more *and* less than its bare title indicates, like Sweden's Labour Market Board.[12]

## FORUMS AS CO-OPERATIVE TRAINING GROUNDS

In interpreting forums, far and away the most attention has been given to their immediate economic objectives. The limelight has been taken by their real or supposed dedication to specific economic tasks. Given the conventional wisdom, and the ideological and historical origins of most forums, this is hardly surprising.

The widely discussed economic roles of forums comprise:

1 *information transfer* for purposes of pooling forecasts and
  targets, forming stable expectations, and facilitating
  'indicative planning' (as exemplified, at their best, by the
  industry Planning Commissions in France);
2 *consultation* about impending decisions, at enterprise,
  intermediate or national levels, on the assumption that this

will improve the decisions or make them more acceptable or implementable (very much the designated aim of big company supervisory boards in West Germany, as for a time of that country's national-level machinery for *Konzierterte Aktion*);

3 *collective research* into economic problems, often geared to forecasting efforts (as with NEDO in the UK);

4 *multilateral interest group bargaining*, where organizations discuss, negotiate and mutually adjust their claims on, or bids for, scarce resources (pay, subsidies, etc.). This process differs from ordinary market bargaining, partly on account of the various dimensions of publicness. Under this public aegis, non-bargaining types of interaction are also going on between the parties. In addition, the bargaining tends to be global, background setting or tentative; final agreements tend to be arrived at elsewhere.

The orthodox assumption is that, because forums exist in 'the economy', it is by the conventional criteria of economics that they must be judged. Yet even in terms of economic performance, the realities of forums are bound to be more complex. Those realities may even confound and contradict the conventional bias. Indeed, it is possibly the case that the quieter, more diffuse and less discussed attributes of forums are precisely the things which best distinguish them and in which they most excel, to public co-operation's (and eventually, the economy's and society's) benefit.

One unnoticed, subtle, but potentially helpful characteristic of forums is *mutual social surveillance*. After all, the different parties inside the forum are closely observing and appraising each other.

More is involved in this than peer group control, as usually defined. In so far as the forums achieve a wide cross-representingness, the (usually implicit) process of justifying oneself inside them, as it were, 'sideways', becomes more diverse and testing. One has observers who are concerned because of interactions with their interests, but who are more detached than immediate neighbours, let alone own-sector rivals or peers. These semi-detached evaluators may be particularly well equipped to see through pretences and evasions, sometimes more so than government.

A second and perhaps more important, but also neglected process is *socio-economic learning*. Within a forum, wider relationships and implications emerge; others' roles become clearer; interdependence becomes more manifest. In a sense, a seminar in economics is being taken, or a lesson in civics or sociology. But significantly, the learning is primarily informal, active and interpersonal; it is also horizontal and participative, not merely received from 'on high'.

Instruction in X, Y or Z sectors of the economy is taking place; but mainly through the agency of people from those sectors who have an atmosphere to convey, a story to tell, a drama to relate or predict, or perhaps a drama to *re-* or even *pre*-enact. One may learn to understand X, Y or Z better not so much through factual data or intellectual ratiocination as through a lively, palpable sense of the persons who work inside them, and of the sort of problems those persons face.

Major public policy issues are 'taken on board' in a similar way, through the medium of personal contact, in this case with the persons who are directly wrestling with the issues: the public officials or government representatives who may be present. Further, the public policy issues take on extra intelligibility and applicability, and, sometimes, content, through cross-sectional discussion and debate. At least figuratively, they are confronted or 'experienced'. There may be some symbolic or simulated sharing in the difficult choices involved. Analogies can be drawn with case study methods, group dynamics and 'action learning', as employed in adult, post- experience education.

Two widespread shibboleths make it difficult to recognize the socio-economic learning attributes of forums. One is the assumption that sectional representatives are obsessed with preset, immutable and completely parochial objectives. Thus, forums would have no alternative but to be yet another arena for narrow interest-pushing, attempted public policy 'captures', quasi-market 'deals', or at best, information swapping. Then there is a misunderstanding of education itself; its identification with an intake of measurable, privately appropriable 'pieces of information', and with quick results. Yet the educational case for forums rests on the much wider concept of education as capacity extending, insight developing and thought provoking. It reflects the deeper view of learning as primarily open-ended, achieved through collective participation, and long term in its results.

This brings us to a third stealthy attribute of forums, their potential for *morally extending their members*. This thesis has been amply pre-pared for. If public co-operation is a route to personal growth through free communality, a testing ground for extended fraternity and demo-cratic participation, then this ethical benefit comes about partly through external colloquy. Drawn from their organizational enclaves, people in industry, finance, trade unions, pressure groups, etc. engage in dialogue about public interests. Special possibilities then open up for the exercise of civic virtue, solidarity across social gulfs, and common-good experiences.[13]

But forums are specially good for this purpose: better, in particular, than lesser mediums for external colloquy such as intra-industry bodies or trade associations, collective bargaining, or ad hoc discussion with pressure groups or government. Apart from forums, where else in economic life is it possible for colloquy to be both publicly orientated and widely cross-sectional? Other than in existing or improved forums, how can economic decision makers be brought face to face, systematically, with public interests, near and far neighbours, and widely contrasted organs of society?

Mutual surveillance, socio-economic learning, gulf-bridging between sectors and classes, personal moral growth: these are significant variations on core communitarian themes. But from the viewpoint of public co-operation even more is at stake.

An implication of all the above is that forums have a role as trainers or preconditioners for *later* acts of public co-operation. Within forums, people can develop conducive understandings, acquaintanceships and habits, often over long periods. They can undergo socialization and exposure to public factors, cumulatively and step by step. They become more likely, therefore, to incline towards public collaboration through later phases. Thus, forums represent another form of long-term investment in public co-operation.

It should be emphasized, though, that forums do not provide a quick, obvious 'return' on such investment. They do not necessarily manufacture a palpable stream of publicly collaborative 'decisions' or 'outputs'. In any case, much public co-operation does not require specific inter-organizational contact at the time it occurs. The crunch often comes not within the forum itself, but through forethought and adjustment, back in the respective decision units and semi-independently. To impute the entire cycle to forums is to exaggerate the 'decision-making' capacities of wide collectivities, much as Communists did with the Soviets. Equally, it is to denigrate the potential for decentralized, but still socially minded, choice.

The point is that, for all their necessary and even desirable spread-aboutness, the decisions are more likely to be publicly co-operative if forums have set the tone and prepared the way. In producing the whole garment of public co-operation, it is still up to individual units to do much, if not most, of the final knitting. But forums help to assemble and match the threads.

## STRATEGIES FOR ENHANCING PROXIMITY

Let us conclude by reviewing the main considerations which, on the basis of the foregoing analysis, strategies for proximity should observe, but all too probably have not.

(1) *Strategies for proximity should be linked with other structural reforms.* A reform programme addressed to social contiguity alone, disregarding the other factors, is inadequate.

To understand this point, let us imagine a forum possessed of all the correct formal attributes but surrounded by unstable, fragmented and opaque structures. Such a forum's members would be unable to rely on each others' presence for long enough for meaningful collaboration to be worthwhile or prudent. The organizations which needed to be included in the forum would be too numerous, leading to exclusions and biased memberships, or a pseudo-representation by 'peak' agencies. In terms of transparency, the forum's members would be wearers of masks, holders of organizational secrets on matters of public import. They would be 'significantly ignorant' about each others' affairs; also, the state of knowledge between them would be likely to be unequal.

The moral is clear. Forum building in particular, and proximity fostering in general, need to be accompanied by strategies for threshold continuity, conformable size and organizational transparency, as outlined in the previous two chapters.

(2) *Effort should be balanced as between the economic and the wider social institutions for contact.* Even the best sort of background social fabric could not cope with the many interdependences which arise in a specialized, fast-changing, often unpredictable economy. To help with these, a great variety of (usually cross-representing) networks are desirable within the economy itself. On the other hand, it is precisely these obvious networks for colloquy which are more likely to be promoted. To co-operatively minded pragmatists bent on quick results and schooled by conventional wisdom, it must seem that the biggest priority is to bring together the 'key people', the 'top decision makers', those who already wield major power.

But by then it may be too late. For the people in question have not been prepared for public co-operation with widely differing groups.

Indeed they may have been habituated *not* to co-operate.

Suppose that these decision makers grew up in single-class neighbourhoods, attended single-class schools, and lacked early experience of different regions, races or social groups. Their working lives have been moulded by economic specialization and corporate hierarchy. Their careers, even their social lives, have been sector bound, perhaps even quasi- extensions of school or university, the professional coterie or the working men's club. At no point have the overarching complementaries and interdependences of a modern political economy been made palpable to them. These people have never settled into a long haul of civic and public pursuits with other sectional groups. Nor have they shared, however indirectly or symbolically, in the choice problems of public officials (as opposed to ceremonial, lobbying or bilateral meetings with them).

However sophisticated as sectional chieftains, in the public realm these people are childlike or adolescent, civically immature. It is not surprising if they regard membership of the forum as some mixture of a public relations exercise, a forced enlistment and a token political ritual; if their main success criteria for it are severely economic-utilitarian and short term, leading to disappointment at the lack of quick, crunchy decisions and quantifiable results; if their contacts within the forum tend to be superficial or constrained.

Again, the moral is clear. A strategy for proximity must attend not only to the intra-economic institutions but also to wider social structures and networks. This has major implications for thinking about school, social welfare and domiciliary patterns, and for training systems.

(3) *Forums should be properly constituted and located.* Where forums are seen as mere pieces of ad hoc economic machinery, the thought given to their constitution has suffered. Where 'public' and 'private', 'government' and 'business', 'politics' and 'the economy', have been split asunder conceptually, forum building has stultified. Still more widespread, in the absence of a comprehensive view of public co-operation, there has been a tendency to proliferate half-baked, mislocated forums. Such forums have often concentrated around (a) narrowly defined, sometimes ephemeral policy issues, and (b) tight clusters of immediately adjacent sectional interests.

Enthusiasms for forums have suffered from lags in understanding. They have long been fixated on 'the industry'. A great emphasis on industry-based forums has persisted despite the destruction of many industry frontiers by technological and market changes, business diversification across industries, and the many 'contagious happenings' which make industry boundaries still more arcane. Equally, enthusiasts have concentrated on labour–management relations as if this were the only significant gap to be bridged in a modern economy. Thus, too many forums have been cast into the mould of industry-by-industry 'bipartism' or 'tripartism'. This has contributed to producer bias, neglect of consumers, and exclusion of third parties (not to mention a failure to extend forums to sectional interests unclassifiable as 'industries' or immune from labour relations problems).

Historically, those involved in such ad hocery should not be harshly judged. Nearly always, they faced highly variegated immediate issues which appeared to demand instant forum-type expedients. These pragmatists lacked the philosophical confidence to stand aside in the interests of a grand design. They did not possess a theory of free associativeness as an overarching common good, of public co-operation as a generic need, or of networks for long-term connectedness as essential to both.

Given that theory, the need for both publicness and cross-representingness would have been apparent. It would have been easier to build forums for multiple, open-ended, often unforseeable policy issues, and to design them for durability and breadth. It would also have been easier to insist on positioning them so as to be close to the principal focuses of both economic decision making and democratic social accountability.

Where, then, are the best places for stable, multi-purpose forums in an advanced mixed economy? A number of critical locations emerge with flying qualifications here. Three key frontiers particularly stand out.

The first frontier lies between each main sectional organization and the rest of society. Ideally, each substantial organization, be it a business, a trade union, a professional organization or a major pressure group, would have attached to it some forum. There the organization's leaders and representatives would sit alongside envoys from its near and far neighbours. Second, all the important local communities and regions would have forums representing the principal sectional interests in their territories. Third, at the peak, there would be a national forum, a super-microcosm. There the effort to bring interdependences home to the main participants would come to a head. Indeed, a national forum would be the principal preparatory scene for public co-operation. In a deeper sense, it would be the main theatre and testing ground for pursuits of fraternity, complementary association and democratic participation in the economy.

I repeat, then, social proximity can be a helpful influence towards public co-operation, mostly in subtle, long-term, unobtrusive ways. Its benefits work through when a country's civic, social, educational and training systems are favourable, and (within the economy itself) through external colloquy, para-intermediaries and, not least, forums. But in order to understand how these connections function badly or well, we need to put them in the perspective of the other facilitative structures, the whole theory of public co-operation, and indeed the wider communitarian viewpoint. Such a wider understanding is required all the more if what we want to do is to improve the existing institutions or to create new ones. We will return to these themes later.

# Chapter 9

# Ideological barriers
and supports

In our efforts to explain public co-operation, it is essential to direct a major focus on to ideas and beliefs. If anything, these are likely to be more important than structures and institutions.

I have already lodged a claim as to what sort of ideas and beliefs are likely to be most favourable; they are democratic communitarian ones. My thesis is that for economic co-operation to prosper fully, the surrounding culture would need to accord paramountcy to the development of persons through free community, to the quality of interpersonal and intergroup relationships, to the values of fraternity, complementary association and democratic participation.

Clearly, an ideal pattern of democratic communitarian principles (as outlined in chapter 3) has found no exact or homogeneous representation in the twentieth-century advanced political economies of the west. All we can discover are imperfect, fitful, isolated approximations. But these have to be examined if we are to understand public co-operation's mutations over long periods, and its contrasts between countries.

We need to review favourable movements of thought which declined or vanished, and more persistent ones which spread democratic communitarian and co-operativist ideas implicitly or indirectly. Tangential or ambivalent ideological currents must be included, not just explicitly congenial ones, unintentional allies and half-friends as well as outright adherents. But first we need to look a bit more closely at the enormous historical, cultural and intellectual obstacles these more or less sympathetic movements faced.

## IDEOLOGICAL OBSTACLES

Through much of the period we are concerned with, other (indirectly relevant) issues tended to claim the foreground of attention. Many of the barest threshold conditions which are necessary before democratic community can be seriously attempted were defied. In the early twentieth century, many millions still suffered from gross insecurity and exploitation, and still lacked the vote. Later, fundamental human values, along with freedom and democracy, were violated under totalitarian systems. During the interwar period, large-scale unemployment cried out for redress; but its cure urgently demanded large doses of *dirigisme*, not public co-operation (the latter's role in efforts to combine high employment, growth and counter-inflation only became evident later).

As long as the advanced political economies were immediately threatened by totalitarian aggressors, and as long as vast numbers of their citizens suffered from chronic destitution or political exclusion, the more advanced ingredients of democratic communitarianism could not necessarily take priority.

After 1945, more of the threshold conditions were in being, or at least in sight. Political democracy (at least of a minimal kind) was more widespread and more secure; labour was more fully enfranchised, economically as well as politically; mass unemployment had retreated. As these improvements took place, so it would have been feasible to move over to an attack on the more direct obstacles to fraternity, complementary association and participation.

In addition, the post-war regime of Keynesianism, full employment and state welfare-ism was creating new pressures for public co-operation. Sectional self-disciplines seemed to be increasingly necessary if inflation was to be avoided and steady growth maintained, if industry was to adapt to changing conditions, if the less fortunate were to be assisted, and if the state was not to be overloaded. By the 1960s, 1970s and 1980s, increased concerns about the environment threw up yet a further priority for civic responsibility and restraints.

Yet the principal cultural influences were still antipathetic or, more often, agnostic or uninterested. Three mighty sets of assumptions were as obstructive as ever. These assumptions were pre-political, pre-ideological and, for many people, even pre-conscious, a largely buried substratum from which everyday premises and implicit postulates flowed continuously to the surface. They constituted the dominant interpretations of social reality, indeed of the human personality itself. People could disagree radically, even furiously, about other things, yet still cling unitedly to them.

First, the objective of an indefinite accumulation of economic resources still enjoyed supremacy; not for its own sake, but because so much human welfare and fulfilment was felt to hinge upon it. Around this banner, motley enthusiasms could gather: pursuits of inventiveness, scientific progress and business enterprise; desires to destroy squalor and social deprivation; the belief in a virtuous link between economic growth and an egalitarian redistribution.

Even the still-flickering hopes of increased fraternity were often associated with economic growth. The old dream that prosperity held the key to social harmony was far from dead. J.M. Keynes voiced a widespread opinion when, writing in 1926, he imputed to a future state of material abundance, to be enjoyed by 'our grandchildren', the power to elicit nobler and more brotherly forms of human behaviour.[1]

The second huge assumption was that public ends could be largely achieved through the agency of quasi-mechanical means. The favourite models for implementing economic policies were those most credited with a push-button responsiveness, a quasi-scientific precision. The dominant theories of economic management were as would-be technical and impersonal as they had been in the nineteenth century (despite being hitched to more humane causes). This applied as much to the new doctrines of Keynesian demand management, and to the Left's fondness for 'central planning', as it did to the classical or neo-classical models of competitive markets and, later, the cult of monetarism.

Although these concepts had varying degrees of validity, the unspoken postulate behind all of them was exaggerated. The importance of negotiation, persuasion and political processes for economic co-ordination was elbowed aside. A technocratic absorption in price systems, laws and macro-economic controls, and their relative merits, crowded out systematic study of anything else. A massive intellectual concentration on the mechanisms of markets and state direction discouraged serious enquiry into the role, structures and institutions of public co-operation.

Third, the period saw a continued ascendancy of the values centring round liberty, equality and individualism. Of course, fervent disagreements about liberty and equality continued, particularly between 'right' and 'left'. But they co-existed with a common acceptance that it was the trade-offs between liberty and equality which, more than anything else, defined what social values were about.

Libertarianism and egalitarianism implicitly colluded in an even more fundamental assumption: that 'individuals', not relationships, were the fundamental unit both for interpreting and for improving social affairs. This mighty, if usually stealthy, philosophical sleight of hand produced momentous results. It imposed a massive relegation of ideas of responsibility and mutuality, and of the quality of interpersonal and intergroup relationships as primary. These ideas lay fallow or went by default. Despite their ostentatious differences, libertarianism and egalitarianism were at one in concentrating almost exclusively on 'individuals'', rights or choices, and on their actual, or would-be, separate possessions.

It was this powerful (and highly internally consistent) paradigm which continued to impregnate the debates of socialists, conservatives and liberals, indeed of so-called 'non- political' people and pragmatists.

The anti-dogma, 'end of ideology' current of the 1950s and 1960s did not loosen these doctrines' hold. Positivists and empiricists might suggest that social values equated to subjective feelings, and were suitable only for linguistic, logical or historical analysis, and unfit for philosophical exploration in their own right. But 'anti-ideology' did not dent the long ingrained habit of viewing individualism (as the premise for prosperity, liberty or equality seeking) as a self-evident truth. The pragmatic, would-be 'value-free' mood among intellectuals, though, did have one distinctly conservative success. It weakened the incentive to fundamental rethinking, whether of the reigning paradigm or of communitarian alternatives to it.

By the late 1960s and the 1970s, romantic, 'small is beautiful' versions of liberty, equality and individualism were emerging. While rejecting crude 'growthmanship', they posed no systematic challenge to the reigning paradigm. The increasingly significant 'green' movement also lacked a systematic social philosophy and analysis. The 'green' tendency stood in special need of a communitarian framework, to think through its extensive appeals for economic restraint and responsibility. Without this, it would be tempted towards a romantic, quasi-rustic slant or, alternatively, too much reliance on draconian enforcements.

Then the old market-orientated, acquisitive version of the paradigm increasingly got back into business in the shape of the 'New Right'. Particularly in the UK and the USA, this gave a sharp extra twist to the polarization between liberty and equality. The 'New Right' revived what has been, historically, the most formidable set of contradictions to the values of fraternity, complementary association and participation in the west.

Meantime, the post-war ideological consensus, which focused around Keynesianism, welfare-ism and political 'centrism', was increasingly stuck in a groove. After 1945, this consensus had achieved much by way of technical economic management, benign statism and mild redistribution within a liberal political framework. But the

Keynesian–'centrist' consensus had never developed an ideological backbone or a distinctive social philosophy. This left it peculiarly helpless, indeed almost numb, in the face of increasingly aggressive and influential assaults especially from the 'New Right'. It had become complacent and ideologically conservative, incapable of questioning the philosophical paradigm from which it, too, had sprung.[2]

These were formidable obstacles to a democratic communitarian movement of thought. Where, then, if anywhere, could such a movement find allies and supporters, let alone protagonists?[3]

## THE ECONOMIC APPROACH TO PUBLIC CO-OPERATION

In France, in 1917–18, the brilliant Minister of Commerce, Etienne Clémentel, was hustling through the final stages of national economic organization in war. Armed with the insights gained from war, Clémentel enunciated a vision which was to resound for decades. He declared that economic individualism was outdated and inadequate not only for war purposes, but also for times of peace. Clémentel advocated, instead, publicly supervised cartels, strong national organizations of business and labour, and a partnership at the peak between the central bureaucracy, big business and big labour. For this whole prospectus the guiding rationale was national economic success.[4]

Clémentel's vision lived on in France. It was adopted by proto-Keynesian supporters of 'economic planning' in the 1930s. It overlapped a lot with the ideas of the 'corporatists', both those who were democrats and the authoritarians who experimented with semi-Fascist types of 'corporatism' under Vichy. The economic version of the idea of national co-operation reached an apogee in the influential concepts of planification and an *économie concertée* advanced by Jean Monnet and others after 1945. According to those concepts, good economic performance demanded an organized, extensive, if often informal, network of negotiation and mutual influence, which would 'concert' the actions of the principal economic units, under the state's general presidency (but not its detailed diktat).[5]

These ideas had some less weighty counterparts in the USA. They surfaced through a strain of thinking in early 1900s progressivism; an enthusiastic spurt during the First Word War; a brief, if largely abortive, climax in the initial phase of the New Deal in 1932–3; and various isolated forays after 1945. In the UK, the same ideas were more widespread and persistent, if not necessarily more successful.[6]

Certain themes repeatedly sounded. Efficiency, big organization and social co-operation were regarded as virtual correlates. The idea was that criteria of national power and modernization demanded large-scale economic units; that social co-ordination of such units would be necessary; but that given their size, this would be easier to achieve through contact and persuasion. Close links between government and big business were sought in the interests of foreign trade, investment and colonial policies. Industry-wide, state-assisted co-operation was pursued in the cause of restructuring decrepit industries.

After 1945 came the argument that steady economic growth and efficient markets would benefit from the pooling of information, ideas and forecasts between government and all the main sectors. There was the claim that trade union and worker participation in consultative exercises would encourage labour's agreement to modernization of occupational, training and trade union structures. And there was the emphasis on co-operation as the key to restraint in pay and prices in order to beat inflation and secure steady growth.

However, the adherence of economic utilitarians to public co-operation was essentially pragmatic and ad hoc. They would be inclined to desert it when the going got rough, returning to their habitual reliance on classical market models, Keynesianism, monetarism or *dirigisme*. Also, the economic co-operativists tended to be elitist and 'technocratic'. Co-operation was to be an affair for top decision makers, professionals or 'experts'. A pure economic rationale should not be intruded upon by amateurs or laypersons; nor, for that matter, by politicians or ideologists.

It is not surprising that the economic argument for public co-operation excited no popular enthusiasm. No heart-felt mass adherence welled forth in its favour. In the UK, for example, advocacy of 'consensus' and 'co-operation' in the interests of growth, productivity and anti-inflation tended to be a 'top-down' affair. It was largely restricted to academics, senior administrators, industrial leaders and, sometimes, politicians. Repeatedly, it formed part of the standard rhetoric of managerial appeals, elite newspaper editorials, ministerial speeches. It reached a high point in the 1960s and 1970s in the 'white heat' mystique evoked by Harold Wilson, and in the technocratic managerial style of Edward Heath. But, as Samuel Beer points out, this theme 'failed to catch on with the voters', and it could not be expected to provide a new and positive basis for legitimate authority.[7]

Underlying all this, at the heart of the economic rationale, there have been certain limitations of philosophy and ethos from a democratic communitarian standpoint. These limitations would greatly impair its ability to inspire and sustain public co- operation in practice.

## INADEQUACIES OF THE ECONOMIC RATIONALE

The economic utilitarian starts by regarding the process of public co-operation wholly as a burden, sacrifice or cost. As explained earlier, public co-operation necessarily involves work or the giving of time and effort; in the economist's view, always an unwelcome chore. It also involves parting with money or other valued resources, and often the foregoing of opportunities for more of these, sacrifices which the economist's premises equally insist must necessarily be distasteful. That the processes of public co-operation may be enjoyable or beneficial in themselves is a possibility which economic concepts ignore.

As for the benefits, the economist typically concentrates on those which are both measurable and individually or corporately appropriable: in particular, higher wages, more jobs, extra profits, a larger gross national product. Such collective benefits as clean air and a noble environment fit uneasily into economic analysis; the concept of 'externalities' is much less central to it. Other categories of benefits are neglected: public repute or immunity from social stigma; an easier conscience; the satisfaction of seeing one's country do well. In theory, a loose concept of 'utility' may be stretched to accommodate such things, but only vacuously. As for the overarching ideals of fraternity, associativeness and participation, the moral growth of persons in community, and the common good precisely as *non*-appropriable, for an economic rationale these do not figure.[8]

Then, with respect to its own favoured categories of co-operative gains, economic utilitarianism tends to be blinkered. It overrates their attractiveness and neglects their tenuousness.

At best, such future gains are subject to risk; they can be viewed as no more than probable. More typically, they are merely uncertain. For example, a brittle delicacy applies to the causal chain which is assumed to lead from a sectional group's co-operative restraint in year 1 to wage or profit-related advantages for itself or others in years 3 and 4. That sequence can be so readily shattered by a world oil crisis, a technological disaster or a sheer political blunder.

Then there is the potential disappointingness of the (economically conceived) eventual gains. The initial 'losers' and 'gainers' from public co-operation are not necessarily the same people. Indeed, it is sometimes the express intention that they should be different; as for example, where pay restraint by the strong is sought partly in order to assist the weak and to reduce unemployment. Even where gains finally accrue to the original 'sacrificers', they tend to lack palpability. Such gains may be randomly distributed, even assuming that they can be clearly distinguished as gains from public co-operation as such.

But worse is to come. For most people, the appropriable economic gains from public co-operation are also marginal: just a few per cent on profits or the pay packet. Economic analysis exaggerates the pleasingness of such marginal gains by assuming that people's attitudes will remain the same. The (usually implicit) premise is that, if Jones desires certain gains in year 1, he will feel a corresponding satisfaction from receiving those gains in years 3 or 4. The probability that, by then, Jones's expectations will have increased again, making the realized gains less interesting to him, is ignored.

Yet a further problem arises from the fact that Jones is not Robinson Crusoe but a highly social being. When he finds, on top of everything else, that his individual gains are paralleled by Brown's and Robinson's, this again may well be a source of disappointment to him. Yet economic reasoning usually ignores social influences and comparisons with neighbours ('interdependent preferences'). So it has not prepared Jones for this category of disenchantment either. Thus, for all its coherence, the economic rationale's support for public co-operation turns out to be weak. Immediate costs to the co-operators are highlighted. Certain crucial benefits from the process, both inherent and consequential, are ignored. Other (and for a democratic communitarian, less paramount) categories of individual and social gains are *over*sold, and their frailty is *under*rated.

There have been some helpful overlaps. Economic analysis and theory have greatly added to our grasp of social interdependences in modern economies. Economic proponents of public co-operation have, at various times, advocated some of the appropriate structures, if only as bits of economic machinery. This applies to intermediation and forums, a national compactness among economic organizations, and limited aspects of transparency (stressed by both Keynes and Monnet). Some economic pragmatists have supported limited improvements in social proximity, at least within economic life. Echoing Clémentel's attack on 'the watertight compartments that separate parliament, the administration, commerce, and industry', they have argued for greater mixing and circulation, if only between existing decision makers.[9]

However, both theory and experience suggest that the economic rationale for public co-operation has serious limitations, intellectually, philosophically and in terms of popular morale. If economic success depends to a major degree on public co-operation, it appears to be a poor motivator for the latter. As an ideological, emotional and moral support to public co-operation, economic motivations cannot stand alone. They badly need to be enfolded within a bigger synthesis.


## FRAGMENTED COMMUNITARIAN TENDENCIES

If economic ideas have tended to be tangential or diversionary, and half-friendly at best, a further group of tendencies have exhibited positive support but in highly fragmented ways.

For example, a series of communitarian theories which emerged in the late nineteenth-century and the early 1900s were philosophical or quasi-scientific, often mechanistic, and usually sweepingly optimistic. They included theories of interdependence and 'social indebtedness' as ineluctable social trends; of 'mutual aid' as a biological force underlying universal progress; of 'the fraternal destiny of mankind' and an evolution upwards to 'universal solidarity'. Behind such theories lie the now largely forgotten names of their exponents: Duguit, Bourgeois, Kropotkin, Cooley.[10]

A few communitarian tendencies were more policy orientated but biased towards some communitarian values to the neglect of others. A leading example was 'solidarism' in late nineteenth-century France. With its great ambitions for a co-operative social and economic order, 'solidarism' was much inspired by some of the theories just mentioned. Apart from Emile Durkheim's special contribution, no clear and enduring movement of thought resulted from it.[11]

'Solidarism' had affinities with social Toryism in 1930s Britain, as expounded by Harold Macmillan and others. The social Tories urged social co-operation, 'economic democracy', a private enterprise committed to joint consultation, profit sharing and 'national service'. They advocated works and industrial councils, an economic parliament, and a variety of intermediary bodies in the interests of qualifying both economic fragmentation and class antipathies. They suggested greater statutory transparency. In terms of social proximity, Macmillan argued for socially integrated schooling, and for increased contacts between the prosperous south and the less privileged north.[12]

Yet despite its many relevant prescriptions, social Toryism had major philosophical gaps. The dominant values of individualism, prosperity, liberty and equality were not seriously challenged. Medium-range policies were stressed, not fundamental rethinking. Redistributive intentions were relatively tepid. More than the 'solidarists', the social Tories were somewhat isolated politically.

However, fragmentation was not mainly a product of philosophical abstraction, ethical one-sidedness or even a preference for policy over fundamental ideas. More typically, it was a case of piecemeal or parochial communitarianism. Fraternity, associativeness and participation were embraced, more or less explicitly, but only in relation to the economic system or even just parts of that system.

Thus, guild socialism in the UK, a minority which petered out by the 1920s, framed blueprints for participation and industrial democracy, from the workplace, through 'the industry', to national economic levels. In various European countries, some idealistic supporters of economic community took up a democratic version of 'corporatism'. Yet another communitarian fragment was the idea of 'business social responsibility'. Often linked with religious beliefs, this had a long series of twentieth-century manifestations in the USA and Western Europe. In the UK its archetypal figures included George Cadbury and Joseph Rowntree. Its focus was on business organizations as social partners or 'good citizens', contributors to public interests, and seekers after good relationships with external groupings.[13]

The trouble was, all these tendencies offered only partial or sector-bound versions of economic community. Pursuits of fraternity and participation could not be fully justified, nor made effective, merely through small sub-units, or *via* guild or 'corporatist' institutions, or in terms of a 'social responsibility' attempted only by business interests or even by business and labour combined. Nor was it feasible to promote 'good relationships' just in the economy, regardless of the wider society. A much wider social ethos was needed. So were commitments to related reforms in other fields.

Despite these limitations, the communitarian fragments were not without influence. They tended to improve the ideological conditions for public co-operation, if often indirectly or in minor ways.

French 'solidarism' helped to inspire, in the late nineteenth century, a series of (indirectly helpful) legislative reforms favouring family security, mutual aid societies, co-operative social welfare. Guild socialism helped to keep alive the concept of a decentralized form of economic community. The social Tories helped British Conservatism to adapt to a more democratic, 'mixed' economic system after 1945. Ideas of democratic 'corporatism' influenced various national economic regimes both before and after the Second World War. The 'social responsibility' ethos played a major part in promoting oases of intensive public co-operation at individual firm or industry levels.

## THE AMBIVALENCES OF DEMOCRATIC SOCIALISM

With democratic socialism, we come to the first large and long-established political movement whose ideological stance towards democratic communitarianism has been highly ambivalent. We also come to what is perhaps the most poignant part of the story of semi-related ideals. I call this poignant because there is much in the (admittedly vague) doctrines of democratic socialism that is, or ought to be, sympathetic. But with some notable exceptions, this affinity has become marginalized and overcast.

Much of the progressive disconnection I am about to discuss has been unintended. Yet it has also been built in from the start and goes back to the roots. Even the greatest historical strength of democratic socialism, its protest and reformism on behalf of the least privileged, contained the seeds of that dissociation. In what follows I concentrate on the mainstream trend: some significant exceptions will be considered later.

Logically, there have been five steps in the disconnection between socialist ideas and democratic communitarian values. These steps only partially correspond to an historical progression: they mainly constitute a conceptual sequence of interdependent parts.

(1) *Fraternity is abstractly exalted.* If the devotion of many nineteenth-century socialists to this ideal is beyond doubt, it is also clear that they tended to elevate fraternity beyond the reach of analysis, investigation or reasoned debate. For this they had good reasons. Here, they thought, was a social principle which cried out for simple, passionate reassertion, as against the rampant selfishness of nineteenth-century capitalism and industrialism. It seemed more urgent to get on with fighting injustices than to spend a lot of time on theory. Even those humanistic, non-Marxist socialists who were most interested in communitarian or co-operativist concepts (for example, Robert Owen, the British Christian socialists, and in France Proudhon and, later, Jaurès) did not develop these concepts systematically.

Fraternity was an idealistic aim inside many trade union lodges, labour chapels and co-operative societies. It was repeatedly enshrined in organizational constitutions, symbols and rituals through the various labour movements.[14] But although democratic socialism was typically strong on the mystique of community concepts, from the first it was weak in thinking them through.

(2) *Fraternity is seen as a total substitute.* The original vision was sweepingly utopian, again an understandable reaction to the evils of the system. Society was to be completely transformed from acquisitive selfishness to co-operation and concord. This vision of a social metamorphosis, even of moral rebirth, continued to inspire socialist hearts and minds for many decades. As a background ideal, it tended to persist through the various twentieth-century manifestations of moderate socialism: Fabianism, 'Lib–Lab' reformism and Labourism in the UK; neo- or anti-Marxist forms of 'revisionism' in various West European countries; the humanistic socialism of a Jaurès or a Blum in France.

The intellectual and practical effects of this quasi-religious vision were highly ambiguous, to say the least. It encouraged a form of split thinking. It obscured the perception that imperfect approximations to fraternity existed even under 'capitalism', and that much could be learnt from, or indeed built on, these. Still more seriously, it excluded any substantive, worked-through recognition that acquisitiveness would surely persist under 'socialism'.[15]

The idea of fraternity as a total substitute both reflected and reinforced the lack of a distinctive philosophy of human nature and social relationships. Given such a philosophy, socialist thinkers could have related fraternity to the human person not just as producer, but also as family member, neighbour, citizen, consumer, believer and enjoyer. They could have studied the historical and contemporary influences on fraternity in more empirical fashion, instead of being a-historical, futuristic or even perfectionist about it. Certain tough-grained, probably ineradicable, features of political economy could have been integrated more harmoniously into reformist socialist thinking at an earlier stage: markets, competition, private enterprise, private property. The tragedy could have been partially averted whereby these things had to be swallowed later, unwillingly, ungracefully and often unconvincingly, like a harsh, alien medicine.

(3) *A mechanical and unbalanced replacement strategy becomes part of the gospel.* Sweeping social progress, including greater fraternity, came to be equated, simplistically, with certain highly specific changes in the economic system. The desired macro-magic was expected to depend, above all, on (a) the agency of the organized industrial working class, (b) public ownership at least of basic industries or 'the commanding heights', (c) central state action, and (d) a systematic redistribution of incomes and wealth. These became the

central pillars of democratic socialism, although their relative prominence varied between different national parties (partly depending on the extent to which Marxist influences persisted).

According to democratic communitarian principles, some validity attached to all of these ideas particularly during the pre-1939 periods of massive exploitation, unemployment and primary poverty. The trade union, public ownership and *dirigiste* components then had much to be said for them. As we have seen, too, the redistribution priority continues to have strong links, on certain conditions, with democratic communitarian values.[16]

None the less, in the light of those values, too much was invested in the doctrines of class, nationalization and central control, especially after 1945. These doctrines reinforced the idea of community as a mechanical outcome of institutional changes over a narrow front. They overemphasised the central state. They concentrated on changes which were likely to have only marginal communitarian effects. They diverted attention from other, often bigger obstacles: those to be found, for example, in more variegated economic and class divisions, in residential and mobility patterns, in electoral and political systems, and not least in the area of culture and beliefs.

(4) *Fraternity seeking is postponed.* All three elements so far mentioned contributed to this further step. If fraternity was only a vague moral aspiration, requiring a complete transformation of existing reality, it could not be an immediate guide. Its day-to-day pursuit might even have to be shelved for the time being. The same inference followed from a situation in which the specific socialist strategies just mentioned proved to be infeasible or highly delayed in their effects. Democratic socialists repeatedly found giant barriers in the path of labour organization, nationalization, central planning, and redistribution. Repeatedly, these things had to be postponed as a result of electoral weakness, sheer expense or organizational cumbrousness, often under pressure of crisis in government. Sometimes they were implemented, but with disappointing results.[17]

Thus, the improvements which socialists predicated as crucial for fraternity themselves repeatedly receded. Fraternity's own position on socialist platforms and banners could only recede along with them. Its consignment to far-distant horizons could only be confirmed.

(5) *Allergic or antipathetic forces are increasingly taken on board.* As a result of all the above, a large ideological void opened up. Among democratic socialist theorists, Hendrik de Man and Evan Durbin in the 1930s, and Gunnar Myrdal in the 1950s, were exceptional in giving

serious attention to co-operativist themes. No strong communitarian challenge was made to individualistic and acquisitive interpretations of equality. Nor was such a challenge available to counterweigh the sectionalist-competitive or even quasi-capitalist streak in trade union militancy.[18]

Predictably, then, the vacuum in communitarian ideas got filled up, pervasively, with intellectual imports from the dominant paradigm. Socialist thinking became vulnerable to pragmatic, agnostic, 'end-of-ideology' currents in the 1950s and 1960s. Repeatedly, it showed an over-susceptibility to conventional wisdoms in the field of political economy: elements of classical economics at various times; more markedly, Keynesianism from the late 1930s onwards; and above all, the 'technocratic' theme of central planning for economic accumulation.

The way was now prepared for fraternity and community to be relegated, if not finally laid to rest. Their invocation tended to be rhetorical. Sometimes they resurfaced but in traditional class-bound or collectivist clothing. When the 'revisionists' got to work from the late 1940s onwards, egalitarian and libertarian themes were paramount. In Italy, Giuseppe Saragat's motto was 'liberty above all'. In Britain, Hugh Gaitskell apotheosized equality and liberty; a pragmatic, moderate concept of 'mixed economy' followed some way behind. The theorist Douglas Jay was not untypical in describing co-operation, almost in passing, simply as an instrument towards equality. Later, Willy Brandt, the German social democrat leader, put 'greater justice' and 'more true freedom' at the peak of modern socialist aspirations.[19]

The demotion of communitarian ideas reached an advanced point in Anthony Crosland's substantial *The Future of Socialism* (1956). This demotion was the more formidable because, unlike other 'revisionists', Crosland dealt explicitly with aspects of the subject. Moreover, he did so with great lucidity, and his book was highly influential. So it is worth considering in some detail.

## THE FINAL DEMOTION: CROSLAND'S *FUTURE OF SOCIALISM*

From the start, Crosland narrowed the field by avoiding discussion of fundamental assumptions about human nature, interpersonal and inter-group relationships, and social ethics. This followed a long a- or even anti-philosophical tradition among moderate socialists, reinforced by the current positivist, pragmatist currents, and by the post-war 'revisionists'' distrust of 'dogma' and 'big ideas'. Crosland did not discuss fraternity, associativeness and participation in their own right; and many of his own fundamental and largely different assumptions, which derived from the dominant paradigm, were never unravelled.

Crosland concentrated on 'the objective of substituting for unrestricted competition ... some more social organisation and set of motives', in industry and the individual enterprise. He professed a mild liking for the value of 'fellowship and social solidarity': 'few will quarrel with this ethical aspiration'. As to its modern application, Crosland declared himself an agnostic, even a sceptic. Too little was known about the appropriate institutional framework or how groups could be organized 'to make people more contented, fraternal or amiable'. It was not difficult to form industrial or professional groups; but these were often internally oppressive and selfish towards other groups. 'Whether joint participation does or does not create a co-operative atmosphere depends on social forces on the exact nature of which industrial experts are not agreed – at any rate to the extent that any clear national policy emerges.'[20]

Crosland was doubtful as to whether 'the co-operative ideal', thus interpreted, was unequivocally desirable in any case. Business competition in the UK had grown milder: its excesses had been 'significantly moderated'. In wider terms, there was already, perhaps, 'a strong trend towards sociability': the implication was that co-operativeness did not need deliberate nurture. In the private sector, there was a pressing economic need for more competition, not less, along with a greater stress on 'risk' and 'individual exertion'. A major push towards co-operation might lead to 'serious losses in other directions, such as privacy, individuality, personal independence, equality of opportunity, or the standard of living'.[21]

These views were sharpened by Crosland's passionate adherence to a particular concept of equality: 'a distribution of rewards, status and privileges egalitarian enough to minimise social resentment, to secure justice between individuals, and to equalise opportunity'. With typical candour, Crosland accepted that this brand of egalitarianism differed from, or even conflicted with, associativeness. 'The more successful the left is in equalising opportunities, the more all-pervasive mutual competition (for jobs, promotion, social prestige) becomes – whether or not the organisation of industry is formally competitive.' Indeed, by this means, 'the extensive frontier of competition' was being, or would be, widened by socialist reform itself.[22]

Not only was co-operativism less important than (individualistic) equality in cases where the two collided; according to Crosland, even the objective of worker participation, long associated with co-operativism, should now be transferred across to the (individualistic) egalitarian banner. The case for workers to have more power did not relate to 'fraternity' or 'social contentment'. Rather, it was a matter of 'social justice' and 'the rights of workers', and to be 'subsumed under the aspiration towards social equality'.[23]

Crosland's conclusions, then, were politely but firmly dismissive. Although 'the co-operative ideal' had been much espoused by socialists, he found himself unable to include it as 'part of the goal'. It lacked 'the perfectly clear relevance' enjoyed by 'the Welfare and Equality aspirations'. Yet even Crosland was not quite ready to pronounce its epitaph. A wider associativeness might eventually re-emerge, he suggested, through a popular appreciation of civilization and beauty. At some future time, when economic objectives had grown less pressing, 'the social rather than purely individual or sectional interest' in such cultural pursuits might revive; and J.M. Keynes was quoted approvingly on the communal potential of 'the age of abundance'.[24]

*The Future of Socialism* was optimistic about indefinite economic growth; still more, as to its benign effects on redistribution and 'social contentment'. The book exuded an equally ample confidence in the capacities of competitive and *dirigiste* methods to deliver these and other aims. Crosland was an enthusiast for the consensus view that social co-ordination could be left, essentially, to a judicious mixture of Keynesian demand management, legal regulation, and price systems; to this could be added a rationalization of economic institutions on which management, workers and government would surely sensibly agree. Thus, public co-operation in the economy was marginal or could be taken for granted; it did not need specific investigation.

A parallel optimism about politics helps to explain Crosland's equally striking neglect of the political dimensions of fraternity, associativeness and participation. A fair degree of political consensus had emerged in the UK by the mid-1950s: this Crosland expected to continue. He took for granted strong elements of civility, national unity and public responsibility. Even the existing restricted levels of political democracy did not cause him serious disquiet.

Democratic participation in itself was not a cardinal value for Crosland. Like economic co-operation, it fell into the category of something vaguely good, not pressing, and hard to analyse, let alone prescribe for. It was tainted by the puritanical moralism of some earlier socialists. Ideas of 'duty' or 'moral responsibility' were even more alien. Crosland's thought was distant from Durkheim, personalist

Christian democracy and even civic humanism, with their ancient antecedents and their largely West European manifestations.

Ultimately, Crosland's concept of social democracy reflected, in addition to a passionate concern for the underdog, his own philosophical roots. These lay in Benthamite and economic utilitarianism, the British individualistic tradition, and the tenets of rational planning and scientific progress. Such influences made it easier for Crosland to turn a blind eye to democratic communitarian values and public co-operation. They help to account both for the internal consistency of Crosland's thinking and for its great appeal to those who similarly subscribed to the reigning paradigm which he expressed so well.

## SOME SOCIAL DEMOCRATIC EXCEPTIONS

The tendencies just described did not prevent some socialist parties from contributing to advances in public co-operation in practice. After all, ideology was not the only factor at work. Other precipitants might produce coalitions with political groups whose relevant ideological commitments were greater. Frequently, economic pressures catapulted socialist leaders, when in office, into extensive efforts at public co-operation, albeit purely on economic grounds, and with inadequate preparation and highly mixed results. More pertinently to this chapter, the socialist disconnection from communitarian ideas was not universal.

The social democrats in Scandinavia were less constrained by utopianism or irrelevant doctrine. During the interwar period, they edged closer both to communitarian concepts and to some related reforming ideas, with major implications for public co-operation.

The most discussed case is Sweden. According to a leading historian of Swedish social democracy, when a residual Marxism largely vanished, co-operativism tended to take over. By the 1930s,

in the ideological debate socialisation had been replaced by the general welfare, class conflict by 'the people's home', democracy as a tactical method by democracy as the highest principle, the total conquest of power by compromise, agreement and collaboration with others.

The social democratic prime minister of the time, Per Albin Hansson, pictured society, 'an organism', as 'the good home of the citizens'. He saw equality and redistribution largely as solidarity enhancers. Social and economic barriers were to be broken down essentially so that the various groups would be 'nearer to each other'.[25]

Swedish social democracy adopted a fair number of democratic communitarian prescriptions while ignoring the basic axioms. It did not clarify the underlying doctrines of human nature and social ethics (as witness such primitively collectivist concepts as 'national family' or 'people's home'). Even with respect to the more concrete structural factors, the Swedish social democrats produced little theory (despite simultaneous sophisticated theorizings about macro-economic policy issues). None the less, in practice, they promoted important aspects of continuity, compactness, transparency and proximity. Their welfare and educational reforms had positive implications for preparatory cross-cutting contacts in social life. Their (lower case) communitarianism contributed to high-level public co-operation in the Swedish economy well into the post-1945 years.[26]

Thus, in the admittedly special conditions of Scandinavia, Swedish social democracy showed that it was possible to buck the trends. Almost everywhere else, the main tendency was diversionary, if not obstructive, and it would be hard to break. Democratic socialism was painfully strapped between three factors: (1) a utopian and immature concept of fraternity; (2) a heavy load of (increasingly unhelpful) class, trade union and statist ideological baggage; and (3) a 'revisionism' which tended to be eclectic and derivative, reflective of the conventional paradigm, ideologically shapeless, even morally tepid. In the last few decades of the twentieth century it looked as if the biggest problem would be here, in a philosophically anodyne pragmatism.

## CHRISTIAN DEMOCRACY: HIGH TIDES AND RECESSION

We come finally to a striking story of major affinity followed by decline. A large proportion of democratic communitarian ideas found a political focus which was influential and widespread. A fuller articulation of the ethos correlated with widespread social action, mass memberships and major parliamentary representation, for a time.

In some parts of Western Europe this combination never emerged. In some countries, the conjunction appeared before 1939; in others it was delayed until after 1945. More serious was a general tendency for high principle and political potency to drift apart. Eventually, in the main, the communitarian idealism receded even where the political institutions remained strong. None the less, where positive correlations did occur, they were sufficiently potent and long lasting to provide substantial assistance to public co-operation raising.

In chapter 2 I explained how personalist Christian democratic thinking started out from the paramountcy of human persons and their moral growth through diverse forms of free communality. Its primary emphasis was associative and participative. It advocated many of the relevant reforms: from family policy and social welfare, through politics and constitutional issues, to ideas for greater social responsibility and democracy in the economy.

Unlike mainstream democratic socialism, personalist Christian democracy was not utopian about fraternity for it possessed a sharp sense of human failings. It was not restricted to a vision of man as producer (having an equal eye for other associative dimensions). Nor was it encumbered by the historic socialist cults of labourism, nationalization and central statism. At least in theory, then, its communitarian philosophy was more balanced, and tougher grained.

In practice, the adoption of democratic communitarian ideas was patchy. Early in the century and before 1939, these ideas were promoted particularly by the Italian *Partito Popolare* under Don Luigi Sturzo, and by some Christian democratic groupings in France, Belgium and The Netherlands. Then, during the immediate post-1945 period, most of the (new or reconstructed) Christian democratic parties gave a prominent place to personalist communitarian ideals in their policy programmes. The ideas exhorted by Maritain and others reached a high point.[27]

To quote one example, the 1945 manifesto of the *Parti Social Chrétien* (PSC) in Belgium. This demonstrated a model realism about the defects of both competitive individualism and statism. It urged worker participation, social control of 'trusts', diffused, socially responsible enterprise, moderate national planning. Among its failings were excessive hopes invested in forums, especially intra-industry ones (a common trait among Christian democrats); little attention to cross-representing by other means, or remedial transparency, or general pre-socialization; a less than coherent commitment to redistribution. However, here was a clear recognition that an organized associative nexus, crowning the still-necessary forces of competition and direction, was not only economically indispensable, but also morally right and an important part of the whole communitarian design.[28]

A further favourable factor was organizational and sociological, although it partly reflected ideology. From the late nineteenth century, the Christian democratic movements tended to create varied forms of co-operative, mutual and syndical organization, involving farmers, peasants, industrial workers, etc., followed somewhat later by distinct, often sizeable Christian trade unions. Thus, the Christian democrat parties came to represent federal coalitions across the spectrum of labour, agriculture, business and the professions. This provided them with a political equivalent of 'encompassingness'.[29] It gave them practice in mediating internally between diverse economic groups and social classes; it enhanced their credentials for promoting public co-operation at national levels when the chance to do so arose; over a fairly long period, it made them the natural practitioners, in government, of economic 'partnership', *concertation* or 'social dialogue'.

Finally, the Christian democratic parties were repeatedly drawn towards various forms of communitarian politics, partly because of their political 'centrism', partly from conviction.

The Christian democrats tended to occupy a position somewhat in 'the centre' (or as their ideologists often preferred to imply, at a tangent) as between socialists on 'the left', and conservatives or classical liberals on 'the right'. This made them more likely partners in governmental coalitions. Repeatedly, governments could not be formed without them, particularly where proportional representation combined with party political statemates to make coalitions essential.

Some Christian democratic principles, too, pointed towards the desirability of coalitionism or consensus; a mediating or harmonizing role in politics; partnership with other democratic parties. Together with political pressure and personal ambition, this helped to propel the Christian democrats into key (senior or junior) roles in governmental coalitions, first in The Netherlands and Belgium during the interwar period, and then after 1945, in Italy, Austria and France.

From the 1950s, personalist Christian democracy experienced a marked downturn, politically. There were no philosophers or theorists to match the earlier ones. Apart from issues of family policy, political pluralism and European integration, where the original pulse still beat strongly, the Christian democratic parties tended, in varying degrees, to drift away from the earlier ideals. A few of the parties moved explicitly towards a moderate conservatism (notably the CDU); the rest continued to be 'centrist' but with less reformism than before. For this retreat the explanations included the pressures of a defensive stance against militant Communism in the post-war years; the wear and tear of long periods in government; a lack of new thinking; and, by the 1960s, a decline in socio-economic 'encompassingness', with the departure of many trade union and working-class voters. Not surprisingly, eager apostles of personalist–communitarian ideals often chose alternative vehicles for action.[30]

A further factor is harder to interpret. There was a long-term tendency for the Christian democratic parties' linkages with organized religion to recede. The underlying forces here were subtle, complex, hard to unravel. Whatever the reasons, the implications were ambivalent, culturally and ideologically. Increased secularization brought a wider appeal to non-believers. At the same time, it further diminished the parties' ability to tap into some popular networks at the grass roots, and it weakened their distinctive ethos.

The importance of pulpits, cassocks and processions retreated, along with the cells of social activists and the co-operative and syndical organizations. As a result, age-old historical suspicions of an ecclesiastically dominated laager decreased. But there were also marked reductions in philosophical coherence, ideological distinctness and a sense of social mission. Ironically, the social teachings of church leaders continued to be, in general and in abstract terms, strongly personalist–communitarian, and reformist.[31] An increased distance from, or even indifference to, these sources of inspiration could not fail to impose some costs.

## FINAL COMMENTS

In reviewing the ideological context of public co-operation, as I have said, one is struck by the subtle constraints which pressed in from every side, but also by a certain resilience of democratic communitarian ideals.

Ambivalence, ambiguity and tangentiality posed a major problem. In some ways, these were more of a hazard to democratic communitarianism than its outright opponents of extreme individualism, collectivism and utilitarianism. Two powerful tendencies appeared in the guise of would-be patrons or benefactors. Economic concepts crowded in on public co-operation, supporting it spasmodically, but reducing it to a sub-category of purely economic pursuits. Democratic socialism claimed a special title to the high ground of community values, invoking both history and piety. But it did not develop those values; indeed, it frequently obfuscated them.

Both tendencies' claims were widely accepted, with largely diversionary results. A spurious assumption that community and co-operation were already catered for, intellectually and ideologically, was encouraged. Attention was diverted from the need for further intense effort on principles, historical perspectives and policy prescriptions.

All three of the basic and interrelated principles, fraternity, complementary association and democratic participation, deserved affirmation and development in their own right. An integration was required of philosophical social ethics, sociology and policy thinking, relating ideals, contemporary trends and preferred remedies to the political and social as well as economic fields.

Instead, what emerged were more or less partial selections of all of these. Extreme fragmentation emerged in those turn-of-the-century theories which sketched out an abstract, disembodied fraternity, one divorced from empirical observation, and often confusing the normative and the descriptive. More often, fraternity and participation were related only to industry and the economy or sectors thereof, with no philosophical foundation or wider socio-political framework, as in guild socialism, democratic corporatism and the 'social responsibility' focus. At least a greater sectoral breadth was achieved by the solidarists, the 1930s social Tories, and the Swedish (and some other) social democrats. Only one substantial movement came within reasonable distance of the whole, Christian democracy at its ephemeral best.

All the favourable tendencies were vulnerable to erosion over time. Some made their impact within a single generation, tapering off after one or two decades. A few broke through this barrier by enlisting relatively enduring cultural forces. Democratic communitarian tendencies in Scandinavia were able to reflect and build on strong national traditions of democracy and civic responsibility. Christian democracy's communitarianism got additional staying power from its religious affiliations and popular networks.

Even then, longer-term erosions seemed unavoidable. Wider cyclical reactions against solidarity seeking might infiltrate inside the camp; religious influences might decline. Long periods in government tended to weaken the office holders' ideals while disillusioning their reformist supporters. The 'centrist' movements which often harboured democratic communitarians tended to fall prey to polarizing tendencies between 'left' and 'right'. These drained away their adherents, divided them internally or even pushed them aside.

Despite all this, the picture was not wholly gloomy. The combination of ambivalence, fragmentation and time erosion was far from lethal. Democratic communitarian ideas seldom lacked some dedicated proponents. Their deep-rooted antecedents in western culture were never entirely overlaid. Even the ephemeral communitarian movements were not without some wider influence. It is a tribute to the enduring quality of the values of fraternity, associativeness and participation that they turned up repeatedly, often in unexpected places.

Where democratic communitarianism reached some enduring mass, at least for a time, the relevant movements constituted a powerful potential resource. On their own, even then, they were incapable of securing a decisive switch in the political economy of any national system. But they could provide an influential political focus, an extensive source of enthusiasm and, not least, a timely reservoir of reforming proposals: all highly relevant during particular phases of public co-operation building. The specific ways in which these communitarian tendencies combined with other forces were crucial, as we shall see.

# Chapter 10

# Western Europe, the USA and the UK

I have already committed myself to a 'long-wave' theory; that is, to the view that high or low levels of public co-operation in an economy probably continue for several decades, perhaps even longer. This reflects the nature of the explanatory forces we have been discussing. Their complexity is such that they tend to checkmate each other in the short run. The thesis is that only occasionally would they move together to create a major shift. Then the new level would tend to be sustained for a long period.[1]

I have also committed myself to the view that there is a strong link between such 'long-waves' and economic performance. My claim is that sustained high levels of public co-operation tend to correlate with balanced economic success in the long run. Let us first reconsider what lies behind this claim.

## PUBLIC CO-OPERATION AND LONG-TERM ECONOMIC SUCCESS

Advanced mixed economies tend to be persistently caught in the toils of a conflict between competition and state direction. Nowhere in this book has the importance and remarkable resilience of these two giant tendencies been doubted. Yet it is important to recognize the economic as well as social dangers posed by their interaction.

Competition and state direction represent polarized tendencies, thesis and antithesis, thrust and counterthrust. When their interplay completely dominates, additional instability is injected into the course of the economy. Thrusting market forces and acquisitiveness, once unleashed, do not proceed unchallenged. Sooner or later, they call forth retribution, first from those they grossly disadvantage, then from state coercion and the law. *Dirigisme*, in turn provokes evasion or defiance from a host of buccaneering elements. Economic–libertarian and free market forces spring back into action at the grass roots. And so the drama goes on.

Competition and state direction are locked into an unremitting war of attrition. Both are permanently in business; neither ever gets the upper hand completely; each repeatedly bounces back. There is even a cyclical or seesaw pattern between them. Indeed, competition and direction tend to reinforce and feed on each other.[2]

However, if public co-operation reaches a position of sustained macro-strength in an economy, these dynamics alter. There are mediating as well as displacing effects. The importance of both competition and state direction is reduced (though neither is replaced). As a synthesizing force, public co-operation becomes a pivot or flywheel, smoothing their cyclical flows, softening the abrasive dialectic of competitive thrust and coercive antithrust.

A first reason why high-level public co-operation favours good economic performance, then, is that it greatly reduces harsh conflicts and unsettling jerks between free market forces and punitive controls. One good result, among others, is greater stability for long-run planning, investment and risk taking in both the private and the public sectors.

Of course, 'good economic performance' is ambiguous and demands some clarification. As already implied, I take it to be multi-faceted. There should be some combination of (1) steady growth, (2) high employment, (3) restraint of inflation, and (4) avoidance of extreme balance of payments surpluses or deficits. To these conventional aims should be added at least two further ones: (5) the enhancement of a nation's capital assets, including its environment, and (6) a resource distribution which improves for the poorest members of society or at least does not worsen against them.

There are strong grounds for associating intensive public co-operation with high degrees of harmonization between the above criteria. Indeed, certain forms of reconciliation of these aims are already implied by the 'macro' measures we have used to define intensive, system-wide public co-operation in the first place.[3]

One such measure, organized participation in national policy making by business, labour and other interests, including consumers and third parties, is very germane. This will tend to increase the number of objectives from the above list which are taken seriously. Each main participant grouping will emphasize a particular set. For example, manufacturing interests will tend to support (1), organized labour (2), consumer and financial interests (3). In so far as they are incorporated, environmental and third parties will clamour for (5), maybe also (6).

Thus, high-level public co-operation is a safeguard against tunnel vision national policies; for example, a mere 'magic triangle' of economic policy objectives, let alone a mono-obsession with, say, 'zero inflation'. It is more likely to go along with a 'magic quadrangle', a 'pentagon' or a 'magic sextet', as just outlined, or with even greater policy pluralism.

When it comes to implementation, the participative mode also has advantages. True, the processes of policy formation may take longer (a national cumulation of the 'lost-time/delay' elements of immediate micro-costs referred to in chapter 4). Economies more reliant upon pure competition and/or pure central direction probably have speedier decision processes. However, the longer-term pay-offs should be considerable. A greater consensus between the principal interests should favour stable expectations and, again, a steadier flow of new investment. Collaborative practices should assist productivity and structural adaptation. Not least, a strong participative nexus should reduce the dangers of later disaffection or rebellion at the grass roots as the policies work through, dangers to which more purely competitive or centralized systems tend to be particularly prone.

Still more pertinent is a further 'macro' indicator of public co-operation, namely sectional restraints on pay. Such restraints have to be not so much coerced by law or economic fear as induced through a climate of peacekeeping, mutuality and civic responsibility. Their benefits are far reaching. In so far as non-enforced pay restraints are achieved, the chances greatly improve at least for reconciling aims (1), (2) and (3), and probably also (4), from the above list; in addition, a deterioration on (6) may be avoided.

Voluntary incomes policies make it more likely that policies for economic growth and high employment, once embarked upon, can be sustained. They reduce the risks of these policies being knocked on the head by inflationary and balance-of-payments crises which, as experience shows with sickening repetitiveness, compel governments to resort to the brutal and wasteful quasi-medicine of deflation.[4]

Yet the qualifications as to 'balanced success' and 'the long run' are important. With narrower criteria and shorter time-scales, more striking successes may come from rip-roaring free enterprise, or from command-type government controls, Keynesianism or monetarist techniques. An intense spurt of growth may be better delivered by 'big bang' deregulation or buccaneering acquisitiveness. A lower inflation rate may be secured, classically, by a recession *plus* monetarist curbs and draconian public spending cuts. Employment and growth may be boosted, equally classically, by lavish public spending and budget deficits.

Such competitive or directive sleights of hand may well produce brilliant, if narrow, successes for a time. The economies in question may steal a quick march on their more publicly co-operative competitors. Their immediate specialized gains may even tempt the latter to lose their nerve, to jettison public co-operation, and to follow suit with neo-classical, monetarist or *dirigiste* 'quick fixes'.

The catch is that such single-track successes tend to be pyrrhic and short-lived. Often, they are of a once-for-all character; nearly always, they lead to eventual reactions or counter-swings. They tend to be highly socially divisive. Yet they do counsel caution as to the invariable economic superiority of intense public co-operation. That superiority essentially relates to both the long haul and the adoption of a balanced portfolio of aims.

The other qualification, 'in general', opens up a counter-possibility of stable prosperity combined with low-level public co-operation. Suppose a country is very large, abundant in natural resources, internationally powerful, and open to persistent influxes of capable, job-seeking immigrants. In such a country, tiger-in-the tank sectionalism would be less likely to lead either to a social explosion or to economic crisis. Competition might be seen more widely as opportunity promoting rather than unfair. Unpleasant spillovers could be spread across wide spaces or disregarded as new frontiers opened out. They could be concentrated on the newcomers, or even shifted on to less fortunate parts of the world.

Of course, many dangers lie in wait for such a mutation, not least a probable unsustainability in the much longer term. The potential for a prolonged synthesis between rapid growth, high employment and relative price stability – along with extensive economic opportunity for citizens – would be partly the mirror image of other countries' misfortune, partly the result of luck. Such a country's ability to ride to prolonged success on the back of massive competition and (probably) a good deal of regulation – with low levels of public co-operation – would be exceptional, and non-transferable.


## EMERGENCY AS THE FINAL CATALYST, MORE OR LESS

Although the combination of structures and beliefs is powerful, it is still not quite enough to explain why some countries have moved decisively upwards in public co-operation while others have not. The missing factor which comes to our aid here, much as we may regret it, is national emergency.[5]

Without this factor, it is hard to see how a major upward shift would come about. As we have seen, major reforms are typically needed in structures and institutions, reforms greatly depending on communitarian beliefs. But the vagaries of those beliefs were a frequent refrain in the last chapter. How would a communitarian tendency come to be represented in a major way in parliament, let alone government? Suppose its leaders, having achieved office, did push through extensive reforms in the co-operative infrastructure; could the spirit needed for the new institutions to work come from social idealism alone?

At every stage, reluctantly, we are driven to the hypothesis that some sort of catalytic emergency would also be needed: some danger or anxiety to throw people and diverse economic sectors together; a push or catapulting from behind.

It seems that there would have to be a widespread feeling that national survival, civilization and other primary values were gravely threatened. A classic example would be the fear of a civil war, or perhaps the aftermath of a civil war, when the desire for reconciliation and healing would be uppermost. Another classic case would be a phase of post-war construction within a nation previously defeated or occupied or largely in ruins. More subtle would be a David and Goliath sort of 'emergency', where a small country felt itself continuously threatened by a giant neighbour. The former would be impelled towards a lot of communal actions, including economic co-operativism, in the interests of morale boosting, defiance or sheer self-preservation.

There is no need to emphasize the awfulness of these sorts of emergency when, as so often, the other conditions are absent. Examples are not hard to find. They include Italy on the brink of Mussolini's march on Rome in 1923; Austria on the eve of civil war in 1932–3; the last years of the Weimar Republic.

Other emergency situations were merely disappointing. On the test of delivering a sustained upward movement in public co-operation in the economy, they simply fell short. France and Italy in the years after 1945 are cases in point. The recent traumas of dictatorship, occupation and defeat, combined with the urgency of post-war reconstruction, created the conditions for potentially helpful emergency. Yet in neither country did public co-operation reach critical mass on a sustained basis through the decades after 1945.[6]

From the analysis of structures in chapters 6–8, we can see how useful, at such a juncture, might be a nation's inherited institutional resources. It would be helpful to have already in place, for example, comprehensive peak organizations of labour and business; well-organized social monitors of economic interests; some previous experiences of forum-type institutions.

Structurally, a smaller country would be rather better placed in these respects. Compact sized distributions of business, labour and the rest would be more likely. Increases in statutory and monitored transparency, the promotion of institutions for social mixing, and the setting up of properly cross-sectional forums, all this would tend to be more manageable in an economy of modest size.

Probably more important, the analysis of chapter 9 suggests that if emergencies are not to be disappointing or even disastrous, a strong communitarian movement has to be ready in the wings. Such a movement would be the main inspiration of a political party (or parties) which occupied a focal position in parliament and which was capable of forming a government or playing a leading part in a coalition at the critical time. Historically, we observed two principal candidates for this role in Western Europe: Nordic social democracy from the 1930s onwards, and personalist Christian democracy at its initial, short-lived best; both assisted by a long-standing national ethos of democracy and political civility in certain countries.

Thus, the suggested historical ingredients for decisive upward shifts finally fall into shape. What we have to examine, from one country to another, are the ratios of influence among structures (partly related to country size), communitarian influences (both civic and party political), and potentially helpful emergencies. If my theory holds, various combinations of these would produce, in concentrated formative phases, major increases in public co-operation which were then sustained, while all-round deficiencies in them would prevent the achievement of critical mass.

Two further questions are also important. They relate to the costs, respectively, of transacting an upward shift and staying at a low level. How serious were the attendant emergencies in the successful cases, the long-run economic penalties in the unsuccessful ones?

In addressing these issues I propose to concentrate on seven countries. Five of these were relatively successful in public co-operation over long periods: Sweden, Belgium, The Netherlands, Austria, West Germany. Two countries were not: the USA and the UK.[7] If we examine the twentieth-century experience of these seven countries in the light of the complete explanatory model, four development formats emerge. I characterize these as (1) rapid promotion, (2) propulsion, (3) avoidance and (4) stultification.

## RAPID PROMOTION (THE NETHERLANDS, BELGIUM, SWEDEN)

In this first and theoretically 'best' case, there is a relatively peaceful ascent. Emergency factors, although present, play a minor role. Success largely follows from initially favourable structures, partly related to a small size, and, probably more important, from the impetus of communitarian political focuses at the appropriate time. The term 'rapid promotion' captures the relative speed of the ascent and its mainly sunny character. It suggests an element of passivity in so far as inherited structures provided a good start, but also a lot of (ideologically motivated) deliberateness and design.

In The Netherlands, Belgium and Sweden major increases in public co-operation occurred before 1939, alongside wider community building. The increases occurred during quite short highly formative phases, and they were subsequently resumed or sustained over long periods.

In all three cases, a small size of country and economy was helpful. Smallness encouraged village-type organizational numbers at national levels, and it facilitated both intermediation and forums. A modest size also made it easier for government, business, labour and other interests to find threshold continuities in their relationships, to watch each other, and to develop background contacts through the social system as well as economic institutions set up for the purpose. But smallness was far from being the only or even the main contributor.

The Netherlands experienced a rapid promotion in 1917–19. During that 'watershed', a series of long-standing political and religious conflicts were largely settled: in politics through the introduction of universal suffrage and proportional representation; in religion through the provision of proportional subsidies for Protestant and Catholic schools. During this period, too, public co-operation in the economy took a decided upward tilt. Formal 'tripartism' was established through a series of Industry Boards and a High Council of Labour. Many of the foundations were laid for The Netherlands' subsequent long record of industrial peace and economic co-operation.[8]

In terms of structures, The Netherlands' cupboard was far from bare when the rapid promotion started in 1917. For example, fairly well-developed peak organizations of trade unions, employers and agricultural interests had been in place since the turn of the century.

In terms of a communitarian political focus, two large religious parties, Calvinist and Catholic, played a crucial role in 1917–19. Despite deep historical differences, the Calvinists and Catholics had developed common interests in preserving religious institutions and in defeating what they saw as secularist, radical and Marxist dangers. Both parties possessed ideas of social harmony and industrial peace, alongside multi-class memberships and deferential rank and files. The Catholic Party already exhibited mild proto-Christian democratic interests in worker involvement and democratic corporatism as well as in a communitarian brand of politics. These features were to make it something of a centrist 'axis' in Dutch politics through the interwar period and beyond.[9]

The communitarian streak in party ideologies found allies in folk memory and history, and in the Dutch political culture. In the background, helpfully, were a centuries-old ethos of self-determination; a concept of collaboration symbolized by the common fight for land against the sea; and a mild cult of *pacificatie*, ' peaceful co-existence at high levels', or summit diplomacy between interest groups, which had been something of a feature since the late nineteenth century.[10]

Even in The Netherlands, emergency conditions played some part. In the years immediately before 1914, much pressure had built up over the religious, political and industrial relations conflicts. The war itself acted as a unifying force. By 1918, the urgency of post-war reconstruction provided a further impetus. But although these emergency features were doubtless invaluable in helping to set the scene, they were considerably milder than elsewhere, as we shall see.

The dynamics were similar in neighbouring Belgium. There, too, the upward shift appears to have reflected various inbuilt structural advantages partly related to size; a pertinent ideology whose political embodiment was both culturally evocative and nicely timed; and relatively non-traumatic emergency conditions.

In Belgium, peacetime economic co-operation took a first leap forward in 1918 and soon thereafter, as part of a major spasm of political, industrial and economic reforms. A mild form of 'liberal corporatism' started to emerge through a series of national industry employer–trade union consultative bodies, the *Commissions Paritaires*. Later, in the mid- to late 1930s, this framework was consolidated during a more intense phase of economic as well as political coalitionism. Patterns of economy-wide consultation and mediation developed, which were to persist through the years after 1945.[11]

As in The Netherlands, the background civic culture provided some helpful symbols. Belgium's very existence since 1830 had largely hinged on ideals of moderate constitutionalism and a historic compromise between previously divided elements. The viability of the national culture had depended on intricate compromise between highly diverse cultural and ethnic groups. Belgium's 'classic response' to crisis was to form party political coalitions, symbolically labelled *unions sacrées*. Yet none of this could have triggered an upward shift towards economic community on its own. The intervention of a more directly relevant and politically pivotal communitarianism would be needed.

Fortunately, this was available both in 1918–19 and 1935–9. As in The Netherlands, proto-Christian democrats were important contributors. The Belgian Catholic party, similarly economically 'encompassing', also contained large numbers of farmers, bourgeois and trade unionists, whom it mixed and mediated between partly as a matter of principle. By 1935, partly influenced by papal teachings, this party had become more interested in relevant social reforms and a vague democratic corporatism. By 1935, there were some answering chords in the Belgian socialist party. An ideology of economic co-operativism had some influence there, too, helping towards participation with the Catholics in both government and economic community building.[12]

Again, emergency conditions were far from absent. The urgency of post-war reconstruction contributed in 1918–19. By 1934–5, following severe deflation and recession, Belgium faced worsening unemployment, financial crises, and the threat of serious strikes. A Fascist movement, the Rexists, gathered major support in certain areas and at one point captured over 11 per cent of the total vote. Without these factors, it is hard to see how the other conditions could have got to work as they did. But again the crisis elements were less than cataclysmic. Again, there is a strong case for assigning greater explanatory weight to the country's size, and still more to communitarian influences.

The Netherlands and Belgium, then, provide solid (and insufficiently studied) examples of rapid promotion to greater public co-operation. A better known case, one exuding considerable glamour, is Sweden in the 1930s. Sweden's community building extended well beyond its widely admired measures for anti-poverty, full employment and family welfare. A rich variety of institutions for community in industry and the economy also emerged during this phase.

Emergency contributed in Sweden, too. In 1931 a series of crises, in farming, industry, employment and parliamentary politics, fused into a general anxiety. There was even a touch of bloodshed, traumatic for public opinion, as police shot dead unemployed marchers in Adalen in early 1931. All of this helped to bring the social democrats to power and to start the *quantum* shift of the 1930s.

But if anything, the emergency factor was milder than in the Low Countries. There were some favourable cultural inheritances: 'a legacy of peaceful transition to democracy'; a tradition of international neutrality which 'underscored the necessity for conciliatory attitudes'; 'consensus norms of moderation and compromise'.[13] As for a timely political focus, this had been well prepared. When emergency struck, it was ready and waiting. The emergence of co-operativist, partially communitarian currents in the Swedish Social Democratic Party at this time was referred to in chapter 9.

Despite marked communitarian defects, the three countries I have referred to went on to become pilot practitioners of public co-operation. Economically, they combined reasonable growth, high employment, payments stability and inflationary restraint over long periods. Qualitatively, these countries hardly scaled the summit of ideal economic community, but they moved some way towards it.

To transact such a major jump relatively peacefully was an enviable feat. Some other countries were to achieve as much or nearly as much; but they were less fortunate in the dynamics of the shift.

## PROPULSION (AUSTRIA, WEST GERMANY)

Post-war Austria's achievements in public co-operation have been favourably cited several times in this book. But their antecedents included major elements of tragedy. Although the structural and ideological factors were far from absent, emergency played a larger role.

Austria emerged from the Second World War with a ruined economy to be rebuilt and an urgent desire to overcome the tragedies of her history through the 1930s and early 1940s: civil war; authoritarianism; the *Anschluss*; war. To these inherited emergency factors was soon added the David and Goliath syndrome of being a small, neutral, vulnerable country next door to the Communist bloc. This created a further pressure for civic co-operation, and a persistent one. The very survival of Austria's newly recovered national identity and democratic system was felt to depend upon it.

Structural–institutional legacies played some part in Austria's upward shift towards economic co-operativism. There were the advantages of smallness; a tradition of national participation by sectional interests; Chambers of Trade and Labour, established respectively in 1850 and 1918, which had long embodied public service principles. There were some communitarian tendencies, evident in Austria's celebrated government coalitions, which began in 1945 and continued long thereafter. The two leading political parties were highly conciliatory, if not markedly communitarian ideologically.[14] None the less, a bigger and more persistent role appears to have been played by the dark shadows I have referred to: traumatic memories; national rebuilding priorities; pressures from the cold war.

It was in West Germany, however, that the propulsion format emerged most clearly. The post-war record of West Germany is clearly more significant because of its greater size and politico-economic weight. Yet much of the character of its political economy from the 1950s onwards has been misunderstood.

West Germany's achievements in public co-operation have played a larger part in her economic success than is often recognized. These achievements provide yet another example of the absurdity of economic system classifications restricted to state direction and competition. They must heavily qualify those stereotypes which attribute West Germany's success mainly to (often covert) *dirigiste* features, or to the amorphous concept of a 'social market economy', or, more commonly, simply to 'free enterprise'.

West Germany's record in economic co-operation included 'lower social and class conflict than in many other parts of Europe', 'a surprisingly long period of social and industrial peace', and 'a strongly consensual wage determination system'.[15] Various features of this record have been singled out: 'greater cohesion', 'collective purpose', and 'discipline' among German businessmen; the German trade unions as 'powerful' but also 'rational', 'modernizing' and 'co-operative'; 'an economic and industrial policy community which . . . transcends public and private sectors'; 'non-rigid triangular consultations'; 'medium corporatism'.[16]

Although West Germany's co-operative attainments were no more distinguished than the other countries', in some respects less so, they were substantial, and a major contributor to economic success. Their historical emergence, though, was a remarkable, if sombre, tribute to the power of emergency, only secondarily abetted by favourable structural– institutional legacies and communitarian ideas.

The extreme gravity of the emergency factors stands out starkly. After 1945, a stricken society and economy had to be recreated; the traumas from Weimar, Hitler, Nazism and colossal defeat had to be got over. There was a widely held determination not to 'rock the boat' lest such horrors be repeated. A continuing sense of insecurity partly reflected the cold war and the division of Germany. There was a powerful sense that the neighbouring Communist bloc had to be defended against, morally defied, and economically excelled. There was, too, a yearning for new legitimacy and respectability within western Europe.

West Germany's passage to intensive public co-operation was more spun out than elsewhere. Marked indications emerged through the 1950s; but a wider spread of labour participation was delayed until the 1970s, as was a more explicit, if still qualified, form of 'corporatism'. The country's size made for more complexity. Organized labour's markedly junior status took time to improve.[17] A vaguely communitarian brand of national politics developed slowly. For a long time the (relatively conservative) Christian democrats dominated West German governments. The social democrats did not abandon a traditional ideological–cultural laager with Marxist undertones until the late 1950s and did not enter government until 1966. The small but often focal free democrats did not retreat from right-wing economic liberalism until the 1970s, and then rather uncertainly.

As in Austria, there were some useful institutional legacies: influential, partly publicly orientated trade associations or *Verbande*; private banks with 'public prefect' dispositions dating a long way back; a number of collaborative practices inherited from the Nazi period or much earlier.[18] Significantly, another structural advantage largely arose from the emergency factor of allied occupation. This was a drastically overhauled trade union movement with relatively few unions, and those well arranged industrially, well resourced, and internally centralized: a great help to forums and intermediaries as well as threshold continuities and organizational compactness.

As in Austria, communitarian currents of thought were far from absent. They existed in the Christian Democratic Party in the early post-war period, particularly in its 'Christian socialist' and trade union wings, helping 'co-determination' to make a start. Enthusiastic communitarianism, though, soon petered out in the CDU as that party moved rapidly towards moderate conservatism. The social democrats did not adopt democratic communitarianism, despite their vigorous 'revisionism' from 1956 onwards and the consensus politics practised with some success by their Chancellors, Brandt and Schmidt, in the 1970s.[19] As elsewhere, it was easier for the social democrats to turn towards a pragmatism of 'the centre' than to undergo a major ideological and cultural rebirth.

Thus, we are repeatedly driven back to an emergency-led inter-pretation of West Germany's co-operative ascent. The legacies of Weimar, Hitler and allied victory and occupation, followed by partition and the cold war, appear to tower over the other factors. In so far as favourable structures depend on small country size, clearly this advantage was not available. Communitarian influences from civic and political sources were more patchy and protracted than in the countries mentioned above. A combination of crisis-related factors appears to have been especially important.

## AVOIDANCE (THE USA)

So far the explanatory model has served us quite well. It has helped us to interpret the 'long waves' of relative success in public co-operation achieved in different ways by five countries in Western Europe. Clearly, though, we need to be able to apply the model to further cases. In particular, we have to see whether it can survive the transatlantic test.

As we turn to the experience of the USA, doubts arise. Is it reasonable to classify the USA as a relative failure in public co-operation? If so, will explanatory factors which work for Western Europe equally apply? Can the USA's prolonged economic success be reconciled with my suggested long-run correlation between balanced economic performance and intensive public co-operation?

As to the continuous shortfall in public co-operation there can be little doubt. The signs have long been evident. The USA's system of business–government relations intensely features both quasi-market bargaining and legal enforcement. Marked degrees of regulation and adversarial confrontation co-exist with fragmented pipelines to government and a spaghetti junction of lobbies and bilateral linkages. Organized labour has remained distinctly junior to business; it has not been integrated into enterprise, let alone national-level decision making. Industrial relations have followed a strongly market-competitive path. 'Corporatism' has been peripheral. Voluntary incomes policies have hardly featured.

Overall, the American political economy assigns a higher-than-usual importance to competition, followed fairly closely (though in less acknowledged ways) by government involvement and legal regulation.

As to whether this underdeveloped public co-operation reflects deficiencies in structures, beliefs and emergencies, I suggest that the answer is 'yes'. A more perplexing question relates to the considerable economic success which the USA achieved, none the less. I call this 'perplexing' even though part of the answer was hinted at earlier when I referred to a possible exception to the suggested linkage between public co-operation and balanced economic success, but one which would be largely non-imitable. I suggest that the USA fits into this form of exceptionality very well.

The analysis of public co-operation we have been pursuing shows that the requisite structures, ideological stimuli and emergencies have indeed been greatly deficient in the USA. Yet, partly in parallel, that analysis *also* helps to explain (1) why bad economic consequences did not result and (2) why the American experience could not be readily repeated elsewhere.

Careful account must be taken of the USA's sheer size, linked with its abundant natural resources, its ability to receive successive waves of immigrants, and the mobility of its people. These factors help us to understand not only why less public co-operation has been achieved, but also why less has been attempted or even *needed*.

Historians have repeatedly emphasized the importance of vast spaces, rich endowments and mass movements to the USA. Thus, Boorstin writes of the enormous scope these gave for competition, variety and fluidity to flourish; but to flourish in ways which, although often unpleasant, were relatively non-destructive or at least disguised. Another leading historian, Wiebe, emphasizes that the USA's sheer size and human mobility made national organization not just difficult but less urgent. With so much elasticity in resources, conflict could be more readily accommodated. If people disliked their contexts, they moved away to form new settlements. Economic abrasiveness and exploitation could be diluted, spread out, or lost to sight as new frontiers repeatedly opened out. Fresh resources of land, wealth and opportunity kept things on the move, relieving the pressure for negotiated or associated solutions. 'Differences were spread across space rather than managed within it.'[20]

The USA's structural context has been largely adverse to public co-operation in the economy. Threshold continuity has been widely transgressed. Public officials and regulators concerned with economic institutions have tended to be particularly ephemeral; so, often, have their agencies. The country's huge size has contributed to a whole series of co-operative disproportionalities: a relatively unconcentrated business system; atomized labour and pressure group organizations; logistical as well as psychological obstacles to achieving unified national representation; and a highly pluralistic, fragmented governmental system.

The institutional incompatibilities extend to the mechanisms for both social surveillance and public colloquy. Social monitoring is highly adversarial and even competitive in the sense discussed in chapter 7. It is greatly influenced by punitive legal probes; by mushrooming, often buccaneering pressure groups; by the commercial criteria of the mass media. As for forums, these have been singularly lacking at national levels.

It is not that economic institutions in the USA are isolated from public opinion or government. Myriads of informal pathways, bilateral pipelines and shifting coalitions exist. But there is little place for these sectional–public interactions in the public ethos or the central constitutional arena. Sectional interests have no central focus to help to define their responsibilities; no sanctioned national places in which to consort, to converge or to contribute civically. Instead, the teeming public–private interactions tend to relapse into covert, quasi-market or litigious forms. There is an alienness about the concept of a relatedness which is to be legitimized, stable, open and multilateral, and within a distinctive public space.

As for communitarian ideals, their low national status is evident in the entrenched, even judicial hallowing of economic competition as a cult; in the pragmatic or tangential emphases of the two main political parties; in a nation-wide ideological supremacy of liberty and individualism, followed by equality of opportunity, private property and prosperity.

For the USA as a whole, as distinct from many of its sub-elements, one central tendency is for diluted community concepts to march obediently behind the national flag. Equally, these concepts tend to melt in the direction of a consensus as to 'a common game', a tolerance of diversity or separateness, even just a general agreement 'to compete within the law'. The wonder is that micro-forms of fraternity, associativeness and participation still richly flourish. They are still vigorously evident, after all, in many ethnic, local and religious subcultures, and in some notable manifestations of business 'social responsibility'.[21]

Finally, there has been a lack of the sort of emergencies that have typically helped to trigger concentrated pursuits of public co-operation elsewhere. Civil wars ceased after 1865; there was victory in two world wars; the country was never occupied by a foreign power. Industrial disputes were often bitter, but localized; class conflicts generally failed to polarize, let alone ignite; even a prolonged interwar depression brought no cataclysmic strife.

Given this relatively smooth development, spasms of national public co-operation building in the economy have been rare, half-baked and short-lived. Little was achieved, or even attempted, along this line by 1900s progressivism, or the early New Deal, or sporadic attempts at national economic consultation or voluntary incomes policies since 1945.

That the USA has so far achieved considerable degrees of economic success, none the less, can be explained by many of the same factors which have impeded public co-operation, as just discussed. But the more these influences are examined, the more special they appear.

We can see many communitarian faults in this system. Over recent years, American reinterpreters of their own half-buried 'civic and biblical republican traditions' have eloquently pointed out these faults.[22] We can also venture a cautious prediction. With such factors as diminishing returns to scale, increasing environmental interdependences internally, and intensified international pressures, both the needs and the demands for public co-operation may well grow. Its neglect is unlikely to be sustainable, after all.

What stands out is the predominant non-exportability of the American system. The American amalgam of high performance and underdeveloped public co-operation owes a vast amount to one-off factors. It has required a perhaps unique combination of size, space and natural endowments, business, labour and public pluralism, libertarian–competitive ideology, and freedom from emergency. This combination is relatively (and probably increasingly) unavailable elsewhere.

Even apart from the ethical ambivalences, sweeping imitations of the American model tend to defy realities, particularly in countries which are smaller and more densely crowded, and which have greatly different histories and cultures. For these reasons alone, if no other, it is particularly inappropriate to seek the wholesale transplantation of the American model to the conditions of Europe.

## STULTIFICATION (THE UK)

I have deliberately left the UK's experience to the last. By this stage in the book the main features of a communitarian–co-operativist critique of the UK's political economy should be clear. This critique overlaps on some points with more familiar diagnoses of the 'British disease', but it also departs quite radically from them.

There is a shared concern about the UK's long-evident economic weakness: its prolonged shortfalls in investment and training, new technology and export competitiveness; its persistent inability to combine high growth and employment with anti-inflation. But there the similarity ends. As readers will appreciate from my general argument, major divergences arise with regard to much of the long historical explanation of this weakness, what steps might be taken to rectify it, and the social philosophy that should guide a turnaround.

I have applied the term 'stultification' to the UK. By this I do not simply mean that the UK has long occupied the 'downstairs' regions of public co-operation. Nor is it only a matter of pointing to this shortfall as a major contributor to the UK's long-standing economic malaise. There is a further historical dimension which the term 'stultification' seeks to capture, that of frustrated co-operative effort. In terms of political economy, the UK has fallen between all the stools. Over the past century, she has been unable and unwilling, for defensible reasons, to venture robustly along the polarized pathways of either free market competition or centralized control. She has experienced in a marked form the attrition and cyclicality between these two sets of forces referred to earlier in this chapter. Yet in a partly related fashion, the UK has also failed to achieve much public co-operation in the economy, despite frequent desires for it.

Successive searches for a more publicly co-operative system form an important part of the background of the UK's predicament. They included late Victorian and Edwardian pursuits of industrial peace; isolated forays towards national forums in 1911, 1919 and 1929; the vicissitudes of 'voluntarism' and 'corporatism' in the 1930s; the 'indicative planning' experiments of 1961–7; the various attempts at voluntary incomes policies from the late 1940s through to the 'social contract' phase in the late 1970s. Yet most of this story is of half-baked successes and blighted hopes.[23]

To start with the background structures, how could public co-operation flourish in the teeth of so much organizational instability, particularly among the public and semi-public bodies dealing with sectional interests? Particularly since 1945, the to'ing and fro'ing of both agencies and persons has been extreme, indeed almost frivolous, by the general standards of the democratic mixed economies (with the probable exception of the USA, as just discussed).

How could public co-operation prosper in a fairly large-scale economic system which has exhibited much fragmentation, duplication and 'overcrowding' among the organizations that needed to collaborate, especially trade unions, peak business bodies and pressure groups? Would not a further obstacle be created by the marked opacities of many of the UK's economic institutions, for example those of big finance and the 'City', and by the severe inadequacies of her systems of statutory transparency?

Many of the institutional stimuli of public co-operation have been lacking. Actual or potential social monitors (mass media, supervisory bodies, academe, the churches) have typically been narrowly focused and prejudiced against one or other, or often all, economic interests. For these biases and neglects deep historical causes can be adduced, often under the heading of a 'split' between economic–business life and the higher institutions of the national culture. In addition, there has been a chronic lack of forums in the strict sense, particularly in large organizations, in and around boardrooms, and at the national level.

Among other structural factors, the UK's 'class system' has much to answer for, although not mainly in the ways usually singled out. Similar inequalities in income, wealth and status could, and did, exist elsewhere but without the same yawning gaps between classes and sectors. Some of the co-operatively successful countries discussed above were no less unequal on the conventional measures; but they were, or became, far more capable of social mixing and economic gulf-bridging. Then there has been the lack of a potentially helpful emergency. In this context tragically, if in other ways happily, neither defeat in war, nor civil war, nor any profound social, economic or political trauma has appeared in the UK over the past century, of the sort that might have helped to catalyse peacetime community building on a major scale, including community building in the economy.

As for beliefs, in no country has the political economy debate polarized more crudely in terms of 'free enterprise' *versus* 'the state', 'private' *versus* 'public'. There has been little emphasis on the economic system as a focus for socio-ethical ideals, civic co-operation, or the growths of persons in community. The successive efforts at public co-operation in the economy have not only fallen foul of structural obstacles, they have also suffered from a self-inflicted wound: that of being soaked in economic pragmatism or instrumentalism, with all its conceptual and motivational defects.[24]

The roots of these ideological categories lie deep. They may be traced back to the Industrial Revolution, the liberal enlightenment, the Whig parliamentary victories of the seventeenth and eighteenth centuries, the Reformation, even earlier. It was in the UK, after all, that critical mass gathered around the ideas of possessive individualism, 'maximising', an 'invisible hand', utilitarianism, neo-classical economics.

The Conservative Party has adopted, at best, a vague 'one-nation' ethos with hierarchical, non-participative overtones. Even this has been outweighed by individualistic, privatizing and market cults, particularly in more recent times. The Labour Party has presented a marked example of the communitarian–co-operativist shortfalls of mainstream democratic socialist ideology, as discussed in chapter 9. The smaller parties, although more ideologically sympathetic at times, have failed to address the communitarian heights. Generally, class influences have loomed large; so have (individualistically interpreted) notions of liberty, equality and prosperity.

Community concepts have far from disappeared, of course, but they have shrunk, or retreated, or merely marked time. Bursts of chauvinism or 'Dunkirk spirit' manifest their elemental forms. Certain local or minority subcultures still preserve them. Grass roots revivals of 'community politics' or civic action witness to their continued microvitality. Some historical reverence is still accorded to religious, ceremonial and literary traditions which incorporate a more associative ethos. For the rest, the concept of a wide community is underdeveloped. At best, it denotes not much more than live and let live, a tolerance of separate elements, a mild patience with adversity. This is amiable and well worth having, but democratic community would require much more.

# Chapter 11

# Implications and prospects

Suppose the values of fraternity, complementary association and democratic participation are accorded primacy in our social thinking. Suppose public co-operation is recognized as a flawed, faltering approach to those values, as well as a key to balanced economic success. Suppose, finally, that the interpretation of this book is accepted as to why public co-operation generally languishes, but occasionally prospers in some countries over long periods (while competition and state direction's cyclicality continues unremittingly, respectively, to a greater or lesser extent). Clearly, the next step would be to seek appropriate improvements.

What would a normative approach based on economic communitarianism entail? What sort of reforms does it advocate? How would it be promoted, and what are the intellectual, cultural and political prospects for its success?

## THE DANGERS OF CONTINUING AS BEFORE

It is difficult to think of a major objective in the advanced mixed economies which will not call, over the coming few decades, for a lot of public co-operation. This applies to sustainable economic growth; the adoption of technological change and still more its humane application; environmental protection; pursuits of anti-squalor and anti-poverty. None of these priorities can rely solely on price systems, central controls, taxes and laws. All of them require public networks for persuasion, negotiation and consent. As for many quality-of-life issues, let alone participatory democracy, there public co-operation itself largely defines the objective.

To recast training systems for the new technologies requires an intricate co-operative nexus among government, educational agencies, industry and trade unions. To revitalize derelict inner cities necessitates not just public spending and market forces but co-operation between local authorities, private enterprise and social organizations, along with voluntary civic action by many individuals. To frame anti-pollution laws effectively, while reducing risks to human life and the ecology in the meantime, requires a vigilant public opinion, a pooling of resources of scarce, often secreted knowledge, and massive forbearance on the part of the potential polluters.

Many of the co-operative needs come to a head over the problem of anti-inflationary incomes policy. An uncoerced restraint on incomes constitutes an economy-wide measure of public co-operation (chapter 4). Incomes restraint is a key condition for improving employment and growth while avoiding repeated crises from inflation. It is crucial if a country like the UK is to escape from the treadmill of stagflation. If ever there was a policy area which called for virtually the whole panoply of public co-operation and its institutional methodologies, it is this one!

To begin with, it is a multilateral problem. Not just trade union elements are involved but also companies whose market power enables them to push pay rises on to prices, top earners who help themselves surreptitiously to huge rewards, lobbyists for subsidies or tax concessions who cumulatively highjack the public coffers. All of these stand in need of virtually the whole range of treatments discussed in this book.

The (usually unwitting) agents of inflation need to be influenced by more stable public agencies. They need to be grouped into more identifiable power formations, made more observable both to each other and to public opinion, subjected to greater scrutiny by social monitors. They need to be convoked into forums: there, they need to explain themselves and to be appraised; to mingle with those who will lose out if they grab at quick advantages; to undergo slow, subtle processes of social learning. In some economic systems, trade union numbers would be consolidated. Corporate secrecies about profits would be broken down. There would be a closing of the background social chasms which mean that decision makers start by being virtual strangers to each others' predicaments.

Such changes are justified by much more than just incomes policies, important though these are. In fact, no single policy area taken in isolation would make worthwhile the wide array of measures just outlined. Certainly, no single priority for public co-operation can be sensibly thought through on its own. Yet at present not even the first steps have been taken towards thinking about public co-operation as a whole. It is the minor intricacies of competition, tax, monetary and legal remedies that are exclusively and endlessly debated. Although there is often a rhetorical acceptance of the need for more public co-operation, there is no coherent analysis and no system-wide evaluation.

A number of dangers can be predicted as a result of this neglect if, as seems likely, increased public co-operation is widely sought in the next two or three decades.

First, excessive hopes would be pinned on to just one method, the colloquy. Existing intermediary agencies would have big new tasks hurriedly thrust upon them. The peak bodies of business and labour would be loaded with unwonted responsibilities to influence, perhaps even discipline, their members. Both ad hoc and would-be permanent institutions for consultation would proliferate, not properly constituted forums. No careful planning would have prepared for these changes. The results would be deeply disappointing, as often before.

Second, public co-operation would be pursued in a piecemeal fashion as between policy areas. As a result, there would be greater risks of duplication; missed opportunities for pooling costly organizational resources; reduced chances for diverse trade-offs and reciprocities among the key organizations, and between these and government. There would be little or no systematic provision for wider habits of public co-operativeness to develop, of the sort that could also cope with unpredictable further problems.

Third, only institutional stimuli would be attempted, with background structures ignored. But even the best equipped of social monitors are undermined if the organizations they have to evaluate are fly by night, or atomistic, or cloaked by an inherent opacity untempered by statutory disclosure. Even the most gifted of para-intermediaries will be stymied by an organizational landscape which features extreme fluidity, fragmentation, secrecy, and built-in social divisions. As for meeting places, if people are used to being radically split apart in their wider social habitats, their interaction through economic forums and other devices is likely to have severe limitations.

Fourth, the assumption would persist that public co-operation is equally attainable, even in the short run, as between different sectors. This posits a constant ratio of dependence on public co-operation, relative to other control methods. Absurdly, it takes for granted that its supply conditions are uniform when, as I have shown, they are *not*.

In parts of industry and commerce, it would not be too difficult to increase degrees of concentratedness, transparency and contiguity, nor to build on existing (primitive) forms of surveillance, nor to reform communication channels with government and other sections of society which are already present in embryo. The same applies to trade unions and major pressure groups. There, in addition, the theoretical alternative of relying massively on market-competitive or economically punitive routes to social control is inappropriate for other reasons.[1]

But in other sectors intensive public co-operation could only be a long-term goal at best. At national level, it cannot fully solve the problems of control of the multinational enterprises. For them supranational political suasion is also needed, reinforced by legal regulation at the same level and sometimes, perhaps, deconcentration. Many financial institutions are too fluid, fragmented and opaque to be good candidates for a major reliance on public co-operation even in the medium term. In the UK, for example, it would take much time to remedy the 'City's' social remoteness, its relative neglect by the monitors, and its lack of a legacy of public forums, as distinct from private self-regulating bodies and cartels.

For all these reasons, a scenario of seriously botched or bungled public co-operation appears probable. Linked with this, a persistent, sharp-bending cyclicality between competition and state direction is all too likely to continue.

In those countries which have endured the excesses of the 'New Right', the most probable sequel would be a massive reaction towards regulation. Abrasive privatization and commercialization eventually provoke a counter-lurch towards legal constraints and state controls; they may necessitate this even in the short run. Such a replay of an old, old story does not have to be explicitly sought and may even be disliked. History suggests that the backlash would accumulate not through coherent design, let alone ideological proclamation, but quietly and ad hoc. Each of a host of anomalies and evils would be seen as remediable only by central fiat or legislation. Often they would be, but by no means always. The excessive reaction towards controls would hinder many facets of enterprise. It, too, would be unstable and likely to provoke yet a further counter-swing, possibly at an early stage.[2]

Far from offering a release from this perverse interaction, some contemporary nostrums may worsen it, by abetting sectionalism and acquisitiveness. The exaggerated cult of 'individual effort' or 'the entrepreneur' is only one version of economic parochialism; among others must be numbered the elevation into supreme goals of industrial democracy or 'workers' control' or 'smallness'.

The enthronement of a 'sovereign consumer' has a more plausibly universal ring, let alone the fashionable rhetoric of a paramount 'chooser'. After all, virtually everybody is a 'consumer', a 'client' or a 'user of public facilities'. Yet even here the 'sovereignty' notion is mistaken: an offence against economic as well as political community's breadth. This emphasis, too, abstracts from our other social and economic roles, many of which would suffer. It exaggerates the pleasingness of the relevant acts of consumption; above all, it is crudely individualistic and one-sidedly rights-obsessed, and it ignores the importance of relationships, responsibilities and reciprocities.

## ECONOMIC COMMUNITARIANISM AS AN ALTERNATIVE

As a guide to policy thinking, economic communitarianism is quite radical. It calls on us to revise certain deeply entrenched cultural and intellectual habits. Instead of always thinking first and foremost of economic or welfare policies, then of co-operative instruments, we would have to spend a lot of trouble doing the reverse. We would have to be at least as committed and systematic about the co-operative 'processes' as about their conventionally perceived 'outcomes'. We would have to salute as a key subject in its own right, even as an over-arching priority, the quality of sectional interest–public relationships.

I have suggested that, to start with, we need to bring public co-operation out of an intellectual darkness and to propel it on to the centre stage of our economic understanding. In a sense, this is no more than a coming to terms with realities, a case of concepts and theories 'catching up'. Minimally, it would provide us with an essential clue as to why some modern economies have achieved a relatively balanced performance over long periods, in conditions of freedom, whilst others have not.

The required intellectual shift means much more than some vague admission of public co-operation's 'importance', its ritual inclusion in a list of final 'credits'. A distinctive set of concepts is necessary, a reinforced vocabulary, a fully fledged model or 'ideal type', backed up by empirical yardsticks and measures.

As we have seen, the relevant concepts start with the grass roots. A zone of freedom for the economic decision units is seen to begin at the many points where the prima donnas of competition and state direction have no more to say, or get into deadlocks, or even sabotage the entire performance. Within this discretionary zone, social expectations accumulate in both preceptual and organizational forms: the public factors which call for variations or sensitive improvisations. Then comes the 'ideal-type' format for public co-operation itself, and its core processes: a corporate reckoning with the public factors; a social dialogue; an operational response; some assumption of immediate cost. The overall co-operativeness of an organization emerges as a multiple of the diversity of public factors deferred to and the depth of immediate sacrifice, through these processes (chapter 4).

The concepts go on to depict the social benefits when public co-operation gathers force around individual organizations and sectors, and more particularly when, exceptionally, it reaches an economy-wide mass over fairly long peacetime periods. The primary historical example of the latter is public co-operation's major contribution to interest group participation, industrial peace and incomes restraint in certain West European countries from the late 1940s to the 1970s, in conditions of steady non-inflationary growth, high employment and rough-cut democracy. But although this is the principal exhibit so far, and an impressive one, it is far from being the last word. Public co-operation's roles are likely to go on being richly diverse.

To incorporate all this into our economic understanding requires a considerable intellectual shift. Let us imagine an economics textbook of the future, after the shift had taken place. In interpreting how things 'work', the textbook would abandon the virtual duopoly of competitive and *dirigiste* concepts. No longer, in accounts of micro-economic behaviour, would the tiniest minutiae of competition elbow out even the broadest outlines of public co-operation. Internal consistency, mathematical elegance, historical links with wider economic theorizing, even the pursuit of intellectual athleticism, would no longer entitle these models to saturation treatment. In the macro-field, the models of Keynesianism, monetarism, regulated competition or socialist central command (important as they are) would no longer totally dominate the story of how public interests are promoted.

Indeed, the shift would go still further. The idea that these long regnant, endlessly repeated formulas are purely descriptive or 'value free' would be discarded. There would be a recognition that to interpret economic co-ordination solely in terms of acquisitiveness, price systems and central manipulation (in various forms and mixtures) is likely to have some behavioural effects; that it tends to encourage people to follow these pathways and to neglect other routes.

Thus, economic communitarianism advocates a new set of basic understandings. But it also prescribes a distinctive array of reforms.

The increasing interconnections of an advanced mixed economy are grossly short-changed by its institutions. National politics, technology, advancing social aspirations and perennial social ideals, all engender a labyrinthine criss-crossing of interests. Between those interests sensitivity is persistently needed, and often demanded. Yet the arrangements for actual connecting up the parts, let alone fostering their civilized interaction, are still puny, primitive or even subverted. For democratic communitarians, one task is to refine and extend those institutions for public collaboration which have already shown their paces through modern history. In looking forward to the twenty-first century, a further priority is to innovate new institutional forms among those I have classified.

Yet an elaborate top dressing of would-be collaborative institutions makes little sense if the underlying socio-economic geography is marred by boulders and quicksands, fragmented into islands, and divided by uncrossable fissures and deep ravines. That is why economic communitarianism seeks to remove the structural obstacles to public co-operation as well as to nurture institutions aimed at promoting it more directly.

Economic communitarianism is not a panacea. It does not eliminate other approaches. As frequently explained, public co-operation works as a harmonizing complement to a competition and a state direction which it can never wholly replace. Substantial improvements in it would take time to implement. Even then, the advanced mixed economies' problems are so complex that the other methods of social co-ordination would still be needed on a major scale. There would still be a requirement for improved as well as existing categories of price mechanisms and competition policy, regulation and laws, fiscal policy, and macro-techniques for managing both demand and monetary flows.

The scope for markets is welcomed, in the economy. Not only does public co-operation, *qua* 'archway', presuppose a 'pillar' of market systems for the sake of efficiency. Democratic communitarianism supports multiple sources of economic initiative as a matter of principle. It offers 'two cheers for the price mechanism'.[3] This acceptance of markets forms more than a *mariage de convenance*, even though it is considerably less than a deep affair of the heart. A search for unity in diversity presupposes diversity. After all, the players have to be dispersed across the field before the collaborative game can begin.

Yet economic communitarianism is very different from a 'middle way' or mere compromise between the competitive and *dirigiste* cults. This tired, apologetic notion immediately surrenders to the polarized view – precisely what is to be escaped from – that if something is neither pure competition nor pure direction, it can only be a 'mixture'. A 'middle way' label denies the distinctiveness of economic communitarianism as a critique with its own value assumptions, empirical analysis and reform priorities. Rather, economic communitarianism stands 'at a tangent' to both the marketeering and the centralizing cults. In the architectural analogy already employed, public co-operation is to be the surmounting, unifying 'archway'; it is not the vacant space lying between the competition and state direction 'pillars'!

Economic communitarianism rejects a split between an essentially market-conceived economy and a notion of social correctives applied exclusively through taxation and 'welfare'. The hard-and-fast 'economy/society' distinction that lies behind this is misconceived. Still less acceptable is it to give top prominence, in thinking about policy, to a combination of more abrasive competition in 'the economy' and a greater egalitarian redistribution in 'society' (on the basis of individualistic assumptions about both).[4] This threatens to exacerbate the dichotomy, not just to maintain it.

Instead, the belief is that economics should be subordinate to democratic politics, and that both should pursue a communitarian social ethic. The social principle is to permeate right through to the inner workings of a decentralized, primarily market-based economic system, flowing through its bloodstream, penetrating to its roots. A communitarian integration aims to suffuse that living, sentient, yet profoundly morally ambiguous organism with a delicate public tissue. It does not accept either that the system can be totally levered from the centre, or that it can be made over in the eighteenth-century concept of a clockwork universe, or that it can be relegated to some amoral, purely technical backyard.

Economic communitarianism means more than just ending the pretence which has had such anti-communal, anti-democratic and even corrupt consequences, namely that the economic system is, or ever could be, 'autonomous'. It means developing a social fabric in and around the economic system which would, at the very least, make such interactions as are bound to exist between economic units and government and society more open, constitutional and accountable. At best, such a fabric would be designed to facilitate fraternity, inter-institutional associateship and democratic participation whilst also nurturing a balanced, sustained form of economic development.

## PRIORITIES FOR LONG-TERM REFORM

At various points in this book I have indicated priorities for reform, assuming that more public co-operation in the economy is desired.

There is no question of a detailed blueprint, let alone a political programme, but clear directions for long-term policy thinking do emerge. I will now draw these together, in roughly ascending order of importance, commenting briefly on some of their implications.

A more co-operative economy demands (1) *institutional continuity along its major intersections.* Despite much unavoidable flux in an economic system, the institutions which promote its civic responsibility must be able to rely on a decent degree of stability. A streak of deliberate conservation and tradition nurturing is evident here. An attitude which regards collaborative institutions as disposable or 'throwaway' is rejected; so is a restless radicalism towards the persons who form the relevant linkages. Where there is even greater discontinuity on the public side of the relevant frontiers, the concern becomes still more acute (chapter 6).

In some advanced western economies, the principal contemporary threat to this norm comes from the cult of privatism. This exalts the real or alleged ethos of the 'entrepreneurial' sectors and denigrates the values of public service. It subjects the people who are supposed to monitor or persuade sectional interests to quasi-manufacturing or marketing criteria even while it dramatically plays around with their agencies. A mixture of private apotheosis and public demotivation gets reinforced. Its symbol is a shabby, undermanned public office, dwarfed by an extravagant corporate skyscraper. The bad effects on threshold continuity are palpable. Able young people are less inclined to stay; the experienced are more likely to retire early; it becomes less unusual to soften one's stance towards private interests with a canny eye to later employment by them.

Like so much else in a commercialized, 'marketized' political economy, even the inner sanctums of public expertise, indeed the very bearers of that expertise, become tradeable or purchaseable, and so more vagrant and less constant. Where these tendencies were extreme, threshold continuity criteria would require some public reprovisioning; better staffing, pay and conditions, coupled with morale boosting.

(2) *Village-type formations of the principal sectional organizations*, the next desideratum, presents differing national priorities (chapter 6). In the USA, national public co-operation would imply a lot of aggregation not only of representative institutions of business, labour and pressure groups, but also of federal regulatory bodies and government itself. In the UK, many sectional interests would require national consolidation. In France and Italy, one major need would be to unify the fragmented institutions of organized labour.

Some other countries already approach a village-like compactness even among the directly responsible economic units (qualified by a greater emphasis on regional focuses and intermediate agencies in the 'big economy' case of West Germany). A widely recognized need is for economic interests to organize for representation and participation at the level of the EEC. For a democratic communitarian, it is even more important that the fast-developing EEC focus should also embody transparency, monitoring, forums and other public safeguards. But meantime, in terms of the numbers criterion alone, it is worth noting that, paradoxically, European integration may itself encourage sectional economic organizations to get together, nationally.

A further implication of village-type formations is less obvious. Almost everywhere, the socially deprived groups tend to be institutionally fragmented and under-represented, so that the very term 'group' becomes a mockery. Unless the deprived elements, too, achieve national corporate representation, the 'publicness' of such co-operativeness as occurs is impaired; the more fortunate sections are still further sheltered; the communitarian principle of public policy access is denied. To promote some corporative salience for the non-privileged is therefore vital. This becomes all the more important where, as often happens, a country's political system persistently fails the deprived by entrenching a majority electoral coalition of middle-income 'haves', to the detriment of the poorest, the immigrants and the unemployed.

Thus, more continuity along the key frontiers and a village-like population of the major organizations would remove some major impediments (while far from guaranteeing public co-operation's increase). Further structural–institutional priorities take us closer to the heart of the theory of public co-operation.

Outside the limited sectors of inherent transparency, as I have shown, there are no 'natural' tendencies towards the sort of illumination that aids public co-operation by working on the sense that one is observable by counterparts, public opinion or government. Such transparency as exists mostly arises from accident, past abuse, or unthinking convention. Where basic information about economic organizations is chronically uneven, free riders flourish; prisoners' dilemmas abound; public non-co-operativeness finds endless dark corners in which to hide. The more opaque units exploit others' susceptibility to searchlighting; many co-operative initiatives are stillborn out of a natural fear that disclosure will not be reciprocated. This brings us to (3), *a massive extension of statutory disclosure requirements*. Many sectors would have to reveal more; many others would have to open themselves up for the first time.

For example, in the case of large company mergers and take-overs, far from 'information loss' being taken for granted, more information would have to be regularly provided. Both financial institutions and major movements of capital would be drawn into the disclosure net; so would trade unions, professions and pressure groups (see chapter 7).

In pushing for more statutory transparency, the economic communitarian should find partial allies. Enthusiasts for efficient markets, 'fair competition' or consumers' rights will travel some of the way with him. An environmentalist will initiate parts of the task; so will pursuers of particular abuses. Yet in the end the case has to be made on the general interest grounds that comprehensive information is a universal benefit, not unlike clean air or decent sewage. The macro-rationale should be made clear. Some good actions would be uncovered; subject to other changes, many bad things would be discouraged. In the long run, the cause of a diffused or decentralized, and also economical, form of social control would be advanced.

A closely related priority is (4), *improved social monitoring of sectional organizations.* In some countries, more institutions would be enlisted to do the monitoring; always, more sectors would come within its purview. Two special needs have been pinpointed: widespread civic–economic education so that public opinion can play a more active part; and a 'monitor of the monitors'. In the last case, the aim would be to uncover abuses and gaps, to provide guidelines for the monitored, and, in some contexts, to reduce tendencies for monitoring itself to become too competitive and adversarial (chapter 7).

None of these changes could improve matters quickly. They would contribute towards critical mass over a long period. The same is true of strategies to enhance social proximity. Here, too, the economic communitarian's objectives should be clear. But if anything, a cumulative, intricate process of social bridge building is even more central to his grand design (chapter 8).

Thus we come to (5), *greatly extended networks for background social mixing.* There is a need to improve the existing channels for contact across classes, races, regions and economic groups, and to create new ones. For example, it should be possible to incorporate social microcosm, 'one-nation' elements in many forms of job training, whether for basic work skills, the professions or top administration. These would juxtapose workers in different sectors, the shop steward and the managing director, the merchant banker and the industrialist, the manager and the public regulator. Indeed, some existing institutions should be redesigned for this purpose, notably the business schools.

An interrelated objective is (6), *a nexus of strategically located, properly constituted forums*, including a national forum of the principal social partners. The case for forums, a vital part of the communitarian project, reflects many of my arguments about village-type proportions, transparency and contiguity, along with those relating to counterpart group control and long-term social learning.

Ideally, forums would be attached to every large company, trade union or pressure group organization, and to every region and major local community. Many pseudo-forums at less strategic points, and with trivial or outmoded briefs and tenuous public attributes, would be dismantled. A national forum would be the main consultative body for incomes restraint and public co-operation issues generally.

The national economic forum would be the principal arena for the leading sectional organizations to discipline and influence each other. It should further promote their public awareness and their social transparency, making them more vivid and interesting to the public. It should also improve the public and parliamentary accountability of their relationships with government. In helping to bridge the gulf between economic life and a national culture, it would draw heavily on history, ceremony and symbolism.

(7) *Supportive symbols and celebrations are desirable in the surrounding economic culture.* Durkheim was right: a sturdy pursuit of economic associativeness will be manifest only when ceremonial, festive and aesthetic elements help to give it expression and nourishment.

Thus, solemn ceremonies might attend the economy's major reunions. Sectional interest–public relationships might have major festive anniversaries. Public processions might symbolize the system's complementarities and its orders of precedence: parliament and constitutional authorities, then public officials, monitors, intermediaries, then representatives of all the main sectors. Here and elsewhere, notably in forums, 'invented traditions' which celebrated public responsibility and reciprocity could respond to widespread emotional needs: needs which the (often managerially manipulative) cult of purely 'corporate cultures' fulfils only partially or sidetracks socially.

The potential contribution of the arts should not be neglected. A bad sign has been the absence of a literature of social and civic choice in the economy. This has implied either that difficult moral dilemmas do not exist in economic life, or that they exist but are not confronted, even by those intimately concerned.

A final desideratum is (8), *educational norms and exemplars of a co-operative nature.* A shift in the emphasis of economic studies would be helpful here (see p. 188). But there are counterpart ideas in business studies and managerial cultures which equally require demotion.

At the heart of this problem is an essentially island concept of management. If recognized at all by the conventional models, public factors are viewed as diversions, constraints, obstacles to be transacted, barrier reefs to be steered around. The excitement, the urgency and the moral commitment are reserved for what goes on inside the organization, and for the techniques it needs in order to get its way in the environment. The heroics, the rhetoric and the assumptions are predominantly sectionalist. Sometimes there are Hobbesian, macho or wargame overtones, as in typical approaches to marketing or competitive strategy.[5] More often, the norms are merely organizationally introverted, corporate utopian and, above all, narrowly technical.

Economic communitarianism points to a major change of emphasis here as well. The concepts and measures of public co-operation would be inserted. There would be a recognition that economic organizations are also surrounded by an analysable, if usually primitive, nexus of public–ethical precepts, pushes and pulls. The concepts of forethought, colloquy and operational adjustment would provide an alternative normative guide: a format for the part that managers could play (and sometimes already play) in the co-operative nexus, but as citizens, social beings and moral agents.

That ideal, too, would require fillips to the imagination, models to emulate or avoid, eloquent moral tales. It should find its own personal and organizational exemplars, and resonant ways of celebrating them. In thinking about 'management' in the twenty-first century, a minimal step forward would be to grasp the nature of the co-operative fabric. A more expansive aim would be for sectional decision makers themselves to seek ways to improve it.

## THE CHANCES OF A TURNAROUND

What are the chances for a major structural, institutional and cultural shift of the sort I have just outlined?

Much of my historical argument has been astringent or at any rate bitter-sweet. I was driven by the evidence to reject a progressivist interpretation of public co-operation. Even a cyclical tendency would have been moderately pleasing, if only aesthetically. But for public co-operation, as distinct from the counterpart forces of competition and state direction, no such tendency could be detected.

Whilst major and sustainable ascents are possible and have happened, they depend on precarious conjunctions of luck, tragedy and moral effort. If a decisive advance towards more public co-operation is sought, it is important to have a good starting legacy (country size, background structures, civic ethos), *and* the potential advantage of a shock with tragic overtones (national emergency), *and* an upsurge of social ideas without which the former would lie fallow and the latter would turn sour (a communitarian political focus).

This theory's predictive content is limited. It offers a somewhat gloomy message for some of the advanced mixed economies. If a system is large, structurally malformed and culturally adverse, the required dose of both emergency and social idealism would be particularly heavy. But since the latter tends to have limits, a major onus would have to lie with the emergency factor, implying a propulsion, not a rapid promotion (see chapter 10). This has unpleasant implications even if the anticipated categories of 'crisis' are less shattering than those which applied to Austria, and more particularly Germany, and less cataclysmic than in some near-apocalyptic vision of a new Dark Ages.[6]

It is possible that a series of major environmental disasters may hammer the need home, or grave threats from a resurgent 'hard right', or even threats of civil war. Some country-wide state of regret, sorrow or even contrition would be helpful, but emphatically not a national mood of complacency or self- righteousness. In countries where 'New Right' policies had persisted over a long period, the eventual crises might well include underclass revolts, debt mountains, collapsing public services, commercial scandals, even deaths and disasters attributable to private acquisitiveness and/or governmental neglect.

However, the other side of my historical interpretation allows a wide, if demanding, place for voluntary effort. That is the thesis, equally based on a lot of past experience, that a communitarian movement of thought and action has to develop. Such a movement would be a necessity, whether or not a national emergency eventually called on it to perform a regenerative role in government. Those West European systems which are still relatively co-operative are not exempt from this need either. Despite many merits, they have patently underfulfilled the hopes invested in them; some would see them as already retreating or under threat. They, too, require a new communitarian impetus.

The relevant political changes are unlikely to occur quickly. The list of background preconditions is a long one: a massive priority for education, anti-poverty, investment and publicly responsible enterprise: a parallel emphasis on communal schooling and health, and on local community; a thrust towards the wider mixing of social classes and new networks for participation. A sustainable upward shift towards more public co-operation would require 'one nation', economically encompassing sorts of governments and, of course, a pre-conversion to the ideas and priorities summarized above.

This is a tall order. It would take time for party and political systems to move towards a full communitarian agenda. They could not do so unless the general climate of thought and opinion had changed first.

The auguries for a democratic communitarian movement of thought are not wholly bleak. Indeed, some faintly hopeful signs may be detected. In academic circles, there is a retreat from the trivializing 'end of ideology' mood; a decline of utilitarianism and of much economic hubris; a glimmer of new interest in Aristotelian and medieval ways of thinking about 'virtues' as opposed to 'interests'. In the sphere of religion, the decline of institutional Christianity is ambivalent. After all, democratic communitarianism owes a massive debt to Christian sources and inspirations. But a more clearly minority status for the churches has helped the Christian social message, with its fundamental communitarian overtones, to be reaffirmed more boldly.[7]

Democratic communitarianism could provide a focus for a large group of ideological malcontents and migrants: those who reject both the 'New Right' and the old 'Old Left' but who yearn for something more principled and dynamic than a tepid pragmatism 'in the middle'. This aspiration also applies to the advanced western countries' own collaborative efforts and their external duties. Democratic communitarianism could be seen as an apt ideology for both halves of a new Europe in the making: a western half already groping for unity in diversity and for a 'social dimension' over and above its economic mechanisms; an eastern half which deserves better than to jump from a bankrupted 'socialism' to a crudely reactive 'capitalism'.

The 'green tendency' is a further potentially favourable current which badly needs a democratic communitarian framework. This is true of both ideals and methods. In terms of ideals, the 'green' tendency is highly relevant and urgent; its communitarian implications are profound. Yet a concern for man's *habitat* and for future generations cannot stand apart from other expressions of community. A responsible use of resources is relevant not just to the ecology but to the mutual duties of human beings from day to day. Economic restraint is needed to reduce not only pollution but also stagflation, exploitation, neglect of the poor, cultural impoverishment, even abuse of the self.

In terms of methods, the 'green tendency' could fall short even on its own ground without economic community's wider pursuit. Like much else, 'green' priorities demand a wide array of tax penalties, fiscal inducements, and legal controls. But these devices are vulnerable to avoidance or manipulation. Alternatively, pushed to the draconian extremes which environmentalism might well require, they are inimical to personal liberty and basic human values (as with some proposed measures to reduce population and family size). Yet 'green' concerns cannot afford to rely too much either on spasms of popular altruism or on small enclaves of plain-living devotees. The moral is clear: 'greenness' also badly needs the whole panoply or public co-operation and its structural, institutional and cultural supports.

In the contemporary situation a primary question is, how can myriads of fairly well-off individuals and organizations find it in themselves to moderate their appetites for higher pay, profits and consumption, lower taxes, or a sheer outsmarting of neighbours? It is vain to exhort them to co-operate merely for the sake of private economic gains (which tend to be marginal, tenuous and distant), let alone collective abstractions like 'GNP', 'anti-inflation' or 'the balance of payments'. Even to invoke the vast social causes which are at stake is not enough. Most people would find it difficult to modify their economic ambitions and actions just for the sake of sustainable growth, environmental protection, help for the poor, or solidarity with the Third World.

In this situation, the more intimate as well as unfolding insight of democratic communitarianism could become increasingly attractive: that the specific processes of expressing economic responsibility, through forethought, colloquy and moderation, are enlarging in themselves; that as both organizations and persons ponder, discuss and adjust to public interests, in companionable or at least convergent ways, so they can discover moral vitality, spiritual progress and self-respect; that it is not only the distant social advantages but also the correlated immediate experiences which can be captivating, deepening and enlarging. But of course such a grass roots discovery needs the aid of cultural changes, structures to make the relevant experiences less elusive, and institutions to bring them home.

A fully fledged, if minority, democratic communitarian tendency has a sporting chance of coming into being. How politically focal it might become is more speculative. The auspices are no worse than they have been for a long time; in some ways, perhaps, better. But a lot of patient groundwork would be needed. Communitarians would have to be prepared to be prophets and preachers, and to play things long.[8]

## A WAY FORWARD

A more communitarian economic system would entail some costs. Its institutions, and still more its people, would be rather less mobile than theorists of economic efficiency would prefer. Such a system would often 'sub-maximize' immediate opportunities for rather greater profit, growth or wealth. Its decision processes would tend to be slower. Along single and specialized tracks, during short phases, its economic performance would tend to be less brilliant than in countries with fewer qualms, less balance and narrower aims.

As against this, there would be major gains in terms of the diversity of economic aims carried through to moderate success, the stability of the system, the social reintegration of economic institutions, and the chances for personal growth in community.

For the past 200 years or more, an abstract 'economic man' has been viewed as a competitive, would-be 'maximizing' creature, whether as 'entrepreneur', 'worker', 'consumer', or generic calculator. These cult figures have long held the centre stage of our economic imaginations. But a new model has to break free of them. It has to enfold such inescapable modern phenomena as increasing interdependence, large-scale corporate groups, and constant interactions with government. It has to put at the centre of our picture of wealth creation and resource allocation ideals of balance, responsibility and restraint.

An idea of 'economic citizenship' expresses this alternative quite well. For 'the entrepreneur', 'the worker' and 'the consumer' may well be loners. Individually or collectively, they may be free riders, jungle fighters, exploiters. But the overtones of 'economic citizen' tend to exclude such things. An idea of economic rights and entitlements is implied, including much free initiative, a fair share of resources, personal and corporate property, a say in the running of one's firm or office, a collectively mediated voice in national economic affairs. But equally present and no less clear is the implication as to economic responsibility, stewardship, trusteeship and mutuality.

Ideologically, co-operativism has been badly served by its practitioners among both institutional intermediaries and political 'centrists'. They have interpreted it with faint pastel, even weasel words like 'conciliation', 'compromise' and 'consensus'. They have portrayed it as incremental, operational and (like so much else) *technical*: a tackling of 'current' problems which takes existing institutions as given and which lets the agenda be fixed by tougher or more ideologically determined forces. The resulting impression is of something essentially conservative, timid or tactical, even of the co-operators themselves as natural fixers or fudgers. The contrast could hardly be more marked with the confidence shown by the ideologists of marketism and state direction.

I have outlined a different approach. In human understanding, crucial importance attaches to the shape of our initial interrogation of a social world that has to be interpreted, to the first questions we choose to ask about the world. In this book that first question has been, what happens to our social thinking if we assign supreme value to free relationships of community between persons?

The most basic answer is that fraternity, or personal development through companionship, mutual aid and shared ethical commitment, would be accepted as both a central phenomenon and the primary ethical norm. From the valleys we inhabit, it is this mountain which seems to tower above the other peaks. Glimpsing it, we begin to see that whilst fraternity between persons cannot be engineered, still less commandeered, at least the removal of obstacles to it must be the initial, minimal goal. Then, as we think through fraternity, two further core principles clearly follow: complementary association, or a balanced diversity of communally extending groupings, large as well as small; and democratic participation not just as a right but also as a duty for both persons and key groupings, with 'duty' redefined and rescued from certain historical taints.

From these three central axioms, various implications flow. If we take them seriously, liberty would be freed from its frequently separatist–individualist undertones. It would be seen as a vital correlate or essential precondition for democratic community, but not in itself the highest good. Likewise, equality would be embraced cordially but selectively. Possessive egalitarianism would be discarded. Instead, abilities to promote fraternity, complementary association and democratic participation would be the main yardstick, and an amply convincing one, for redistributive measures and anti-poverty.

Once these principles are adopted, it becomes a travesty to see the common good as an aggregate of private goods. Its main essence lies, rather, in mutual help, conviviality, and virtues practised together. In politics, this implies the nurturing of public traditions; the building up of shared services; the pursuit of civility and coalitionism as intrinsic goods; the promotion of both citizen and sectional group participation in public life as a cardinal aim. It means that the economic system can no longer be viewed purely as a wealth begetter, or a provisioner for liberty or equality. It, too, has to be recognized as a potential developer through community of persons and groups, a testing ground for fraternity and democratic participation.

A search for economic community would involve much imperfection and backsliding. It could never be a complete panacea for the complex problems of advanced mixed economies. It would doubtless attract much lip service and even hypocrisy. It would certainly involve many disappointments, and its achievements would always be both incomplete and vulnerable. But at least it would substitute a higher set of goals and would back these up in practical ways.

I have suggested that many institutional and structural changes would be needed along the way. But apart from the emergency factor, the main route to those changes has to be cultural. A belief system is needed that celebrates human relationships and free associativeness in the economy, as elsewhere, as morally paramount, a primary art form, and a source of personal virtue, enjoyment and play.

If balanced, sustained economic performance is sought, it seems that to desire it primarily for its own sake is unwise, even self-defeating, not to mention ethically unsound. If we seriously want it, it appears that we should want something else far more, namely a social change extending particularly, though not exclusively, to the economic system itself. We would accept that enterprise makes full practical and ethical sense only *in* and *with* as well as *for* community. We would acknowledge that economic health and a community renaissance are inseparable, and that of the two it is a community renaissance that would come first.

# Notes

## 1 THE RECOVERY OF COMMUNITY

1 In chapter 3 I explain why these terms are selected, including 'fraternity', despite an objection that it is 'sexist'.
2 A more community-related concept of equality emerges as an important element of democratic communitarianism in chapter 3.
3 For some of these concepts, see P.C. Schmitter and G. Lehmbruch (eds) (1979) *Trends towards Corporate Intermediation*, (1982) *Patterns of Corporatist Policy Making*, and (1985) *Private Interest Government, beyond market and state*, all Beverly Hills and London; Michael Beesley and Tom Evans (1978) *Corporate Social Responsibility*, London; John M. Clark (1957) *Economic Institutions and Human Welfare*, New York; and Kenneth E. Boulding (1948) *Beyond Economics*, New York, and (1985) *Human Betterment*, New York.

## 2 THE ROOTS OF DEMOCRATIC COMMUNITARIANISM

1 Even this element of 'community' finds little place in 'New Right' thinking.
2 The main alternatives are equally, if not more, clumsy, and shackled by their historical associations; for example, 'solidarism', 'communalism', 'associationalism'.
3 An excellent detailed study is Steven Lukes (1973) *Emile Durkheim, his life and work*, London. A useful introduction is Kenneth Thompson (1982) *Emile Durkheim*, London. The most relevant major works are Emile Durkheim (1911) *The Division of Labour in Society*, 4th edn., trans. (1933) by G. Simpson, New York and London; and *Leçons de Sociologie*, trans. as (1957) *Professional Ethics and Civic Morals*, by Cornelia Brookfield, London.
4 'Solidarity' had already enjoyed some popularity: see J.E.S. Hayward (1959) 'Solidarity: the social history of an idea in 19th century France', *International Review of Social History* IV: (2).
5 *The Division of Labour in Society*, op. cit., p. 360.
6 ibid., pp. 202–4, 365, 228.
7 ibid., p. 224.

8    This programme appears in Durkheim's classic preface to the second edition of *The Division of Labour in Society*, 1902, entitled 'Quelques remarques sur les groupements professionels'.

9    Matthew Elbow (1953) *French Corporative Theory, 1789–1948*, New York. Ralph Bowen (1947) *German Theories of the Corporatist State*. Peter J. Williamson (1985) *Varieties of Corporatism, theory and practice*, Cambridge. Philippe C. Schmitter (1979) 'Still the century of corporatism?', in Philippe S. Schmitter and Gerhard Lehmbruch (eds) *Trends towards Corporate Intermediation*, Beverly Hills and London.

10   G.D.H. Cole (1920) *Guild Socialism*, New York. Richard H. Tawney (1921) *The Acquisitive Society*, London, and see also Ross Terrill (1974) *R.H. Tawney and His Times, socialism as fellowship*, London. For Scandinavian social democracy and 1930s social Toryism, see chapter 9.

11   John M. Clark (1936) *Preface to Social Economics*, New York; (1939) *Social Control of Business*, 2nd edn., New York; (1948) *Alternative to Serfdom*, New York; (1957) *Economic Institutions and Human Welfare*, New York. Andrew Shonfield (1965) *Modern Capitalism*, London, and (1983) *In Defence of the Mixed Economy*, ed. Zuzanna Shonfield, London.

12   A useful introduction: Pierre Létamendia (1977) *La Démocratie Chrétienne*, Paris. Important: R.E.M. Irving (1979) *The Christian Democratic Parties of Western Europe*, London, and Jean Marie Mayeur (1980) *Mayerur, Des Partis Catholiques à la Démocratie Chrétienne*, Paris. Still very useful: Mario Einaudi and Francois Goguel (1952) *Christian Democracy in Italy and France*, Notre Dame, IN; Maurice Vaussard (1956) *Histoire de la Démocratie Chrétienne*, Paris; Michael P. Fogarty (1957) *Christian Democracy in Western Europe*, London.

13   Influential statements after *Rerum Novarum* were Pius XI's *Octogesimo Anno*, 1931, and Pius XII's radio message on democracy, 1944. For a useful discussion, see Richard L. Camp (1969) *The Papal Ideology of Social Reform*, Leiden.

14   Giuseppe Toniolo (1900) *La Democrazia Cristiana*, Rome; Luigi Sturzo (1938) *Politics and Morality*, trans. Barbara B. Carter, London, and M. Moos (1945) 'Luigi Sturzo, Christian Democrat', *American Political Science Review* 39: (2); Richard E. Mulcahy (1952) *The Economics of Heinrich Pesch*, New York; Albert de Mun (1895–1904) *Discours*, and (1909) *Ma Vocation Sociale*, Paris; Marc Sangnier (1907) *L'Esprit Démocratique*, Paris; Emanuel Mounier (1951) *Be Not Afraid, studies in personalist sociology*, trans. Cynthia Rowland, London. For Maritain, see notes below. For non-Roman Catholic parallels, see particularly William Temple (1942) *Christianity and the Social Order*, London, V.A. Demant (1948) *Religion and the Decline of Capitalism*, London, also Maurice B. Reckitt (ed.) (1945) *Prospect for Christendom*, London; and for a leading Protestant view, Rheinhold Niebuhr (1936) *Moral Man and Immoral Society*, New York.

15   Jacques Maritain (1944) *The Rights of Man and Natural Law*, London, p. 7. Etienne Gilson, cited in *Christian Democracy in Italy and France*, op. cit., p. 126.

16   Marc Sangnier (1907) *Le Plus Grand Sillon*, Paris, p. 228. *Histoire de la Démocratie Chrétienne*, op. cit., p. 246; Louis Biton (1954) *La Démocratie*

*Chrétienne dans la Politique Française*, Angers, pp. 92–3; Richard Webster (1961) *Christian Democracy in Italy, 1860–1960*, London.

17  Maritain's dispersed writings in this field are well represented in Joseph W. Evans and Leo R. Ward (1956) *The Social and Political Philosophy of Jacques Maritain, selected readings*, London. His 'post-capitalist' stance was outlined in *Humanisme Intégral*, trans. as (1938) *True Humanism*, by M.R. Adamson, London.

18  *True Humanism*, op. cit., pp. 130–1.

19  Maritain's work over 60 years embraced metaphysics, theology and aesthetics as well as political philosophy, and attracted adherents in the USA and Latin America as well as Europe. His influence on Catholic thinking anticipated many of the changes in the Second Vatican Council. His reformism also emerged through successive public controversies: over Action Française, anti-semitism and racism, religious liberty, Austria, Ethiopia, the Spanish Civil War, Vichy, and the post-1945 movement for an international declaration of human rights.

20  *True Humanism*, op. cit., pp. 2–3, 20–2.

21  Yves R. Simon (1951) *Philosophy of Democratic Government*, Chicago, pp. 49, 64–6.

22  Etienne Gilson, cited in *Christian Democracy in Italy and France*, op. cit., pp. 126–8.

23  *Christian Democracy in Italy and France*, ibid., p. 129.

24  See chapter 9.

25  *True Humanism*, op. cit.

26  For example, many of its British exponents from the late nineteenth century onwards were 'liberals', despite the strong historical links between this term and classical individualism and privatist ideas in earlier phases in the UK, and up to present times in Europe. For the British 'social liberals', see Michael Freeden (1978) *The New Liberalism, an ideology of social reform*, Oxford.

27  Andrew Vincent and Raymond Plant (1984) *Philosophy, Politics and Citizenship, the life and thought of the British idealists*, Oxford, p. 2. Thomas Hill Green, *Lectures on the Principles of Political Obligation*, cited in ibid., pp. 22, 23.

28  Green, cited in ibid., pp. 31, 80.

29  William M. Sullivan (1986) *Reconstructing Public Philosophy*, Berkeley, CA, pp. 10, 21, 157, 214.

30  Robert N. Bellah *et al.* (1986) *Habits of the Heart, individualism and commitment in American life*, Berkeley, CA, and *Reconstructing Public Philosophy*, op. cit. For further transatlantic variations on these themes, see Robert Paul Wolff (1968) *The Poverty of Liberalism*, Boston, MA; George C. Lodge (1978) *The New American Ideology*, Boston, MA; Michael Sandel (1983) *Liberalism and the Limits of Justice*, Cambridge; Michael Walzer (1983) *Spheres of Justice*, New York; Benjamin Barber (1984) *Strong Democracy, participatory politics for a new age*, Berkely, CA; Charles Taylor (1985) *Philosophy and the Human Sciences*, vol. 2, Cambridge.

31  Carole Pateman (1970) *Participation and Democratic Theory*, Cambridge. C.B. Macpherson (1973) *Democratic Theory, essays in retrieval*, Oxford, and (1977) *The Life and Times of Liberal Democracy*, Oxford. Some of

these themes are stimulatingly restated in David Marquand (1988) *The Unprincipled Society, new demands and old politics*, London.
32  *The Life and Times of Liberal Democracy*, op. cit., pp. 99–100.
33  Edwin T. Cone (1968) *Musical Form and Musical Performance*, New York, pp. 34–6.


## 3  FRATERNITY, ASSOCIATIVENESS AND PARTICIPATION

1  Max Scheler (1954) *The Nature of Sympathy*, trans. P. Heath, London. See further, Max Scheler, *Vom Ewigen im Menschen*, trans. as (1960) *On the Eternal in Man* by Bernard Noble, London. A useful study: John Raphael Staude (1967) *Max Scheler, 1874–1928, an intellectual portrait*, New York.
2  Aristotle (1953) *Nichomachean Ethics*, trans. J.A.K. Thompson, London, Book 8. See also St Thomas Aquinas (1951) *Philosophical Texts*, sel. and trans. by Thomas Gilby, London, pp. 732, 758, 942–55. Bernard Crick (1964) *In Defence of Politics*, 2nd edn, London, p. 227.
3  *In Defence of Politics*, op. cit., pp. 230–1.
4  William Morris (1968) *A Dream of John Ball*, ed. A.L. Morton, p. 51. W.J.H. Sprott (1958) *Human Groups*, London, p. 191. Ivan Illich (1973) *Deschooling Society*, London, p. 68.
5  Michael Young and Peter Willmott (1960) *Family and Class in a London Suburb*, London, pp. 132–3. Huw Beynon (1984) *Working for Ford*, 2nd edn, London, p. 128.
6  Robert N. Bellah *et al.* (1986) *Habits of the Heart, individualism and commitment in American life*, Berkeley, CA, pp. 72, 197.
7  Ross Terrill (1974) *R.H. Tawney and His Times, socialism as fellowship*, London, pp. 216–19.
8  Michael Taylor (1982) *Community, Anarchy and Liberty*, Cambridge, p. 32. Ferdinand Tönnies (1963) *Community and Society*, ed. and trans. C.P. Loomis, New York. Alasdair Macintyre (1981) *After Virtue, a study in moral theory*, London. Glynceiriog appears in Ronald Frankenberg (1966) *Communities in Britain*, Harmondsworth, Middlesex, pp. 86–112.
9  H.D.F. Kitto (1951) *The Greeks*, Harmondsworth, Middlesex, in David W. Minar and Scott Greer (1969) *The Concept of Community, readings with interpretations*, Chicago, p. 76.
10  Emmanuel Le Roy Ladurie (1978) *Montaillou, Cathars and Catholics in a French Village*, trans. B. Bray, London. Michael Zuckerman (1970) *Peaceable Kingdoms, New England towns in the 18th century*, New York. Thorstein Veblen (1948) 'The country town', from *Absentee Ownership and Business Enterprise in Modern Times*, in *The Portable Veblen*, New York. See also Rosabeth M. Kanter (1972) *Commitment Community, communes and utopias in sociological perspective*, Cambridge, MA.
11  J.E.S. Hayward and R.W. Berki (1979) *State and Society in Contemporary Europe*, London, p. 266. Jacques Maritain (1948) *The Person and the Common Good*, trans. J.F. Fitzgerald, London, p. 39. Emile Durkheim (1957) *Professional Ethics and Civic Morals*, trans. Cornelia Brookfield, London, p. 73.

12 Johannes Messner (1949) *Social Ethics*, trans. J.J. Doherty, St Louis MO, and London, p. 232.
13 These examples come from *Habits of the Heart*, op. cit., pp. 157–61, 192–3, 216, 239–40.
14 Edward Shils and Michael Young (1953) 'The Meaning of the Coronation', *Sociological Review*, 1: 64–7. The Durkheim quotation occurs there. For the sombre aspects of the 'crowd', see Elias Canetti (1962) *Crowds and Power*, trans. Carol Stewart, London.
15 Albert O. Hirschman (1982) *Shifting Involvements, private interest and public action*, Oxford, p. 84.
16 Alan Ryan (1977) 'Two concepts of democracy: James and John Stuart Mill', and James E. Krier and Edmund Ursin (1977) *Pollution and Policy*, both cited in *Shifting Involvements*, op. cit., p. 86.
17 *Shifting Involvements*, op. cit., pp. 85–8.
18 Michael Walzer (1970) *Obligations, essays on disobedience, war and citizenship*, Cambridge, MA, pp. 237–8. For a discussion of 'over-commitment' and, more particularly, the 'rebound effect' in this context, see *Shifting Involvements*, op. cit.
19 Leading statements of this viewpoint are, Friedrich von Hayek (1944) *The Road to Serfdom*, London, (1960) *The Constitution of Liberty*, London, and (1967) *Studies in Philosophy, Politics and Economics*, London. See also Milton Friedman (1962) *Capitalism and Freedom*, Chicago, and Milton and Rose Friedman (1980) *Free to Choose*, London.
20 'Expressive libertarianism' is interestingly discussed in an American context in *Habits of the Heart*, op. cit. The Emerson citation occurs there, p. 63; the other is of Gail Sheehy, p. 79.
21 Richard Tawney's link between redistribution and 'fellowship' is relevant here: see *R.H. Tawney and His Times*, op. cit. For a similar emphasis, see Gunnar Myrdal (1960) *Beyond the Welfare State*, London, and (1972) *Against the Stream, critical essays in economics*, New York.
22 *In Defence of Politics*, op. cit. pp. 221–2, 233.
23 The classic case for a consensus on distributive justice as the basis for community is made by John Rawls (1971) in *A Theory of Justice*, Cambridge, MA. Rawls remains firmly within the individualistic tradition in his starting assumptions about human nature, his reliance on a 'contract theory' of society, and his non-pursuit of the definition and priority of community between persons in itself.
24 De Tocqueville, cited in *Habits of the Heart*, op. cit., p. 194.
25 *After Virtue*, op. cit. Robert Paul Wolff (1968) *The Poverty of Liberalism*, Boston, MA, pp. 162–95.
26 Wolff, ibid., p. 192.
27 See also chapter 9.

## 4 PUBLIC CO-OPERATION IN THE ECONOMY

1 Andrew Shonfield (1965) *Modern Capitalism*, London.
2 ibid., particularly chapters 7–12, and part 4.
3 P.C. Schmitter and G. Lehmbruch, (eds) (1979) *Trends towards Corporate*

*Intermediation*, and (1982) *Patterns of Corporatist Policy Making*, both Beverly Hills and London.

4　(1981) *Industrial Relations in Europe*, European Industrial Relations Group, Oxford.

5　J.L. Fallick and R.F. Elliott (1980) *Incomes Policies, Inflation and Relative Pay*, London. A. Boltho (ed.) (1981) *The European Economy, Growth and Crisis*, Oxford. Specific intercountry comparisons on this and the other criteria are pursued in chapter 10.

6　Karl Stadler (1971) *Austria*, London; E. Barker (1973) *Austria, 1918–72*, London; Alfred Klose (1976) *Ein Weg zur Sozialpartnerschaft*, Wien; G. Lehmbruch in *Trends towards Corporate Intermediation*, op. cit.

7　H. Suppanz and D. Robinson (1972) *Prices and Incomes Policy, the Austrian Experience*, Paris, pp. 46–7, 49, 52–3, 55–6, 63–4, 66.

8　For the problems of measuring 'competition', see for example J.S. Bain (1956) *Barriers to New Competition*, Cambridge, MA, and W.J. Shepherd (1979) *The Economics of Industrial Organization*, Princeton, NJ.

9　J.S. Boswell (1983) *Business Policies in the Making, three steel companies compared*, London, chapter 9.

10　ibid., chapter 8.

11　J.S. Boswell and B.R. Johns (1982) 'Patriots or profiteers? British businessmen and the 1st World War', *Journal of European Economic History* 11: (2).

12　W.J. Reader (1970) *I.C.I., a History*, vol. 1, London. See also S.E. Koss (1970) *Sir John Brunner, Radical Plutocrat, 1842–1919*, Cambridge. For a general survey of this field, see J.S. Boswell (1983) 'The informal social control of business in Britain, 1880–1939', *Business History Review* LVII: (2).

13　Allen Nevins (1940) *Study in Power, John D. Rockefeller*, New York, Allen Nevins and F.E. Hill (1962) *Ford, Decline and Rebirth*, New York. Ward McAfee (1973) *The Californian Railroad Era*, San Marino, CA. K. McQuaid (1974) 'Businessman as reformer', *American Journal of Economics and Sociology* 33: (4). James E. Post (1978) *Corporate Behaviour and Social Change*, Boston, MA. B. Harvey, S. Smith and B. Wilkinson (1984) *UK Managers and Corporate Social Policy*, London.

14　Wolfgang Streeck (1984) *Industrial Relations in West Germany, a case study of the car industry*, London. Volker Schneider (1985) 'Corporatist and pluralist patterns of policy-making for chemicals control: a comparison between West Germany and the USA', in Alan Cawson (ed.) *Organized Interests and the State*, Beverly Hills and London. J.L. Badarocco Jr (1985) *Loading the Dice, a five-country study of vinyl chloride regulation*, Cambridge, MA.

15　J.S. Boswell (1978) 'Hope, inefficiency or public duty? The United Steel Companies and West Cumberland, 1918–39', *Business History* 22: (1).

16　*I.C.I., a History*, op. cit. See also Alfred Mond (1928) *Industry and Politics*, London, and H.H. Bolitho (1933) *Alfred Mond*, London. Discussions the author had in Vienna in 1982.

17　It should be noted that the definition of 'public co-operation' (see later) makes no restrictive assumptions about motivations; in psychological terms, it assumes no more than deliberateness.

18 *I.C.I., a History*, op. cit.
19 The pertinent public interests, although diffuse, can be conveniently grouped into a small number of policy areas, as typically in discussions of public policy.
20 This point is neglected by a purely 'political' or institutional approach, such as 'stakeholder analysis', as in, for example, G. Johnson and K. Scholes (1984) *Exploring Corporate Strategy*, London.
21 This is a familiar issue in the discussion of strategy formation: see J.B. Quinn (1980) *Strategies for Change, Logical Incrementalism*, Chicago, and Henry Mintzberg *et al.* (1978) 'Patterns in strategy formation', *Management Science* no. 4.
22 For example, in comparing organizations within a particular sector, immediate costs would be estimated as a ratio of net income or profit, or of senior personnel resources of time.
23 For the definitions of these various terms, see chapter 3.
24 Again, see chapter 3.
25 For a detailed example, see Carol E. Hoffecker (1974) *Wilmington, Delaware, portrait of an industrial community, 1830–1910*, University of Virginia.
26 Jacques Maritain (1938) *True Humanism*, London.

## 5 STRUCTURES, EMERGENCIES AND BELIEFS

1 W.H. Beveridge (1928) *British Food Control*, London; E.M.H. Lloyd (1924) *Experiments in State Control*, Oxford; J.S. Boswell and B.R. Johns (1982) 'Patriots or profiteers? British businessmen and the 1st World War', *Journal of European Economic History* 11: (2); Richard F. Kuisel (1981) *Capitalism and the State in Modern France*, Cambridge; Robert D. Cuff (1973) *The War Industries Board, Business–Government Relations during World War 1*, Baltimore, MD.
2 Earlier sketches of this framework are in J.S. Boswell (1980) 'Social co-operation in economic systems, a business history approach', *Review of Social Economy* 38: (2); (1983) 'The informal social control of business in Britain, 1880–1939', *Business History Review* LVII: (2); and (1986) 'Business behaviour and public co-operation, a structural perspective', *Journal of General Management* 12: (2).
3 It is worth pointing out that this theory differs a lot from another theory of the mixed economy, Mancur Olson's (1982) in *The Rise and Decline of Nations*, New Haven, CT. In essence, Olson's thesis is that special interest groups are harmful to economic growth unless vast upheavals enable a country to make a clean sweep of them. Olson makes brilliant observations about the frequently baneful effects of economic group organization, but his historical theory is inadequate. He concentrates just on economic growth as the dependent variable; over-exalts the economic virtues of competition; discounts much of the evidence that economic group organization can be beneficial both for growth, *and* for other, wider aims in which he is much less interested; and oversimplifies the benefits of the emergency factor. With the exception of the size variable (to be discussed in chapter 6), Olson

neglects those structural and institutional conditions which can be shown to have limited the bad effects of economic interest organization, and enhanced its positive aspects, over long periods, in certain modern economies. He also largely ignores the factor of communitarian beliefs, culture, and politics, including its influence on whether upheavals turn out 'well'.

4  Emile Durkheim (1911) *The Division of Labour in Society*, 4th edn, trans. (1933) by George Simpson, New York and London, pp. 368–9.

5  For the 'prisoner's dilemma', see T.C. Schelling (1962) *The Strategy of Conflict*, Cambridge, MA, and Robert Axelrod (1984) *The Evolution of Co-operation*, New York.

6  On the inescapability of social ideas, their degrees of coherence in 'belief systems', and their historical influence, see Martin Seliger (1976) *Ideology and Politics*, London.

7  See, for example, J.U. Nef (1963) *Western Civilisation since the Renaissance*, New York and Evanston, IL; Thomas C. Cochran (1972) *Business in American Life, a history*, New York; Kenneth E. Boulding (1953) *The Organizational Revolution*, New York; John M. Clark (1957) *Economic Institutions and Human Welfare*, New York.

8  See citations of Boswell, Reader, Mond and Koss in notes 12, 15 and 16 in chapter 4.

9  See chapter 10.

10  The 'demand' side has been much discussed by scholars of 'corporatism' in connection with public economic policies, and problems of governmental 'overload' and 'control deficits'.

11  I return to the last phenomenon in particular in chapter 9.

12  M.A. Utton (1982) *The Political Economy of Big Business*, Oxford, pp. 105, 216–17.

13  Susan Strange (1986) *Casino Capitalism*, Oxford, p. 144; see also pp. 111, 137–42.

14  Allen Nevins and F.E. Hill (1962) *Ford, Decline and Rebirth*, New York. James Weinstein (1968) *The Corporate Ideal in the Liberal State*, Boston, MA. A.G. Gardiner (1923) *Life of George Cadbury*, London. David Jeremy (1990) *Religion and Business in Britain*, Oxford.

15  David Brody (1960) *Steelworkers in America, the Non-Union Era*, Cambridge, MA. H.A. Mess (1926) *Factory Legislation and its Administration, 1891–1924*, London. T.R. Nevett (1979) 'The development of commercial advertising in Britain, 1880–1914'; PhD Thesis, London University. Otis Pease (1958) *The Responsibilities of American Advertising, private control and public influence, 1920–1940*, New Haven, CT. Morton R. Keller (1963) *The Life Insurance Enterprise, 1885–1910*, Cambridge, MA.

16  James E. Post (1978) *Corporate Behaviour and Social Change*, Boston, MA. Brent Fisse and John Braithwaite (1983) *The Impact of Publicity on Corporate Offenders*, Albany, NY. Volker Schneider (1985) 'Corporatist and pluralist patterns of policy-making for chemicals control', in Alan Cawson (ed.) *Organized Interests and the State*, Beverly Hills and London.

17  Wolfgang Streeck (1984) *Industrial Relations in West Germany, a case study of the car industry*, London.

18  This thesis is developed in chapter 10.

## 6 THRESHOLD CONTINUITY AND CONFORMABLE SIZE

1   Daniel Boorstin (1973) *The Americans, the democratic experience*, New York. T.C. Cochran (1972) *Business in American Life, a history*, New York. Oscar Håndlin (1954) *The American People in the 20th century*, Cambridge MA.
2   See chapter 4.
3   J.Z. Rubin and B.R. Brown (1975) *The Social Psychology of Bargaining and Negotiation*, New York and London, pp. 234–5. Emile Durkheim *Leçons de Sociologie*, trans. as (1957) *Professional Ethics and Civic Morals*, by Cornelia Brookfield, London, p. 13. Robert Axelrod (1984) *The Evolution of Co-operation*, New York.
4   For example, see Kevin Hawkins (1976) *British Industrial Relations, 1945–1975*, London, for indications of a marked instability of public sector institutions in post-war Britain.
5   Mancur Olson (1982) *The Rise and Decline of Nations*, New Haven, CT, pp. 47–53, 90–2. For a comment on Olson's general theory, see chapter 5, note 3.
6   Samuel Beer (1982) *Britain Against Itself, the contradictions of collectivism*, London, pp. 26–7, 31.
7   Peter Wiles (1977) *Economic Institutions Compared*, Oxford, p. 231.
8   For this argument, see particularly Wolfgang Streeck (1984) *Industrial Relations in West Germany, a case study of the car industry*, London, final chapter.

## 7 ORGANIZATIONAL TRANSPARENCY AND SOCIAL MONITORING

1   John Rawls (1971) *A Theory of Justice*, Cambridge, MA, p. 133. Kurt Baier (1958) *The Moral Point of View*, Ithaca, NY, p. 196. Sissela Bok (1979) *Lying, moral choices in public and private life*, New York, pp. 95–9 and footnote p. 322.
2   Charles J. Erasmus (1977) *In Search of the Common Good, utopian experiments, past and future*, New York, pp. 341, 344.
3   Susan Strange (1986) *Casino Capitalism*, Oxford, p. 144.
4   Arthur S. Dewing (1914) *Corporate Promotions and Reorganizations*, Cambridge, MA. B.M. Anderson Jr (1918) 'Value and Price Theory in relation to price fixing and war finance', *American Economic Review*, March. J.S. Boswell, unpublished paper on UK companies' annual reports and chairmen's speeches, 1914–18.
5   T.R. Nevett (1979) 'The development of commercial advertising in Britain, 1880–1914', PhD Thesis, London University. Joseph C. Palamountain Jr (1955) *The Politics of Distribution*, Cambridge, MA, p. 142. Richard Tedlow (1979) *Keeping the Company Image, public relations and business, 1900–1950*, Greenwich, CT. H. Larson and G. Porter (1959) *History of Humble Oil and Refining Company*, p. 343.
6   J.S. Boswell (1983) 'The informal social control of business in Britain,

1880–1939', *Business History Review*, Summer, and unpublished paper on UK company reports, 1914–18, op. cit. T.R. Nevett, op. cit. *The Politics of Distribution*, op. cit., pp. 95–6.

7 This emerges in the behaviour of the International Harvester Company in the early 1900s; Robert Ozanne (1967) *A Century of Labour Relations at International Harvester*, Chicago. Researches by the author in the company's archives in Chicago.

8 J.M. Keynes (1926) *Essays in Persuasion*, London. Annual Reports of Commissioner of Corporations, Washington, 1904–1905, p. 7. Ministry of Reconstruction (1919) *Report of Committee on Trusts* HMSO, Cmd. 9236, particularly study by John Hilton, pp. 26, 30.

9 Charles Perrow (1970) *Organizational Analysis*, London, p. 330.

10 Brent Fisse and John Braithwaite (1983) *The Impact of Publicity on Corporate Offenders*, Albany, NY.

11 Henry F. May (1949) *Protestant Churches and Industrial America*, New York. David Brody (1960) *Steelworkers in America, the non-union era*, Cambridge, MA. Otis Pease (1958) *The Responsibilities of American Advertising, private control and public interests*, New Haven, CT. *The Politics of Distribution*, op. cit. Federal Trade Commission, annual reports, 1920s. H.A. Mess (1926) *Factory legislation and its Administration, 1891–1924*, London.

12 I return to this tendency in chapter 10 in relation to the USA.

13 J.K. Galbraith (1952) *American Capitalism*, London.

# 8 SOCIAL PROXIMITY AND FORUMS

1 Benedict Nightingale (1973) *Charities*, London. Hermann Mannheim (1940) *Social Aspects of Crime in England between the wars*, London, pp. 115, 117, 197–8. John U. Nef (1963) *Western Civilisation since the Renaissance*, New York and Evanston, IL, pp. 250–5.

2 See chapter 5.

3 (1959) *Memoirs of the Earl of Woolton*, London, p. 1.

4 Albro Martin (1976) *James J. Hill and the Opening of the North West*, New York, p. 41. S.E. Koss (1970) *Sir John Brunner, Radical Plutocrat, 1842–1919*, Cambridge, p. 13. David Louth (1958) *Swope of G.E.*, New York, pp. 31–4, 51. Herbert Croly (1912) *Marcus Alonzo Hanna*, New York, pp. 78–9. F.H. and Mrs. Crittall (1934) *Fifty Years of Work and Play*, London, p. 29. J.S. Boswell (1985) 'Sir Walter Benton Jones, 1880–1967', *Dictionary of Business Biography*, vol. 2, London. Keith Middlemas (1969) *Baldwin, a biography*, London, p. 9.

5 W.J. Reader (1970) *I.C.I., a history*, vol. 1, London. Robert D. Cuff (1973) *The War Industries Board, Business–Government Relations during World War I*, Baltimore, MD. Stephen Blank (1973) *Industry and Government in Britain, the F.B.I. in politics, 1945–1965*, Farnborough, Hants, p. 48.

6 T.C. Cochran (1972) *Business in American Life*, New York, p. 72. Robert M. Wiebe (1967) *The Search for Order*, New York, pp. 37–8. F. Machin (1958) *The Yorkshire Miners, a history*, vol. 1, Barnsley, Yorkshire, pp.

12–13, 148. J.E. Williams (1962) *The Derbyshire Miners*, London, pp. 444, 797. H.A. Mess (1926) *Factory Legislation and its Administration*, London, p. 68. Francis Hyde (1975) *Cunard and the North Atlantic*, London, p. 75. R. Ozanne (1967) *A Century of Labor Relations at International Harvester*, Chicago. Graham Adams Jr (1966) *Age of Industrial Violence*, New York and London, pp. 148, 172. Allen Nevins (1940) *Study in Power, John D. Rockefeller*, New York.

7    Donald Read (1964) *The English Provinces, c.1760–1960*, London, pp. 233, 239, 256–7. J.M. Lee (1963) *Social Leaders and Public Persons*, Oxford, pp. 35–6, 42–3, 91–3. Asa Briggs (1963) *Victorian Cities*, London, pp. 64, 72, 115. Morrell Heald (1970) *Social Responsibilities of Business, company and community, 1900–60*, Cleveland, OH, pp. 186–8. John A. Williams (1976) *West Virginia, a bicentennial history*, New York.

8    Richard Kuisel (1981) *Capitalism and the State in Modern France*, Cambridge. Keith Middlemas (1983) *Industry, Unions and Government, 21 years of N.E.D.O.*, London. For Austria, see chapters 5 and 10.

9    Harry Eckstein (1966) *Division and Coherence in Democracy, a study of Norway*, Princeton, NJ, describes high degrees of interconnection between social classes and otherwise divided groups, through schooling and a dense network of participative organizations. Eckstein sees economic co-operativeness as one manifestation of this factor, as also of history, cultural symbols and beliefs (while probably underestimating the small population factor). M. Donald Hancock (1972) *Sweden, The Politics of Postindustrial Change*, London, whilst giving more attention to conflicts and mutations in this more complex case, also ascribes major importance to socialization through schooling and mass political party and occupational association memberships, through joint management–labour bodies, and through an exposure of economic interest groups to each other, government and 'a wider range of socio-political factors', within Royal Commissions and *remiss* (national consultative) procedures.

10   Jean Monnet (1978) *Memoirs*, trans. Richard Mayne, London.

11   W.J. Reader (1968) *Architect of Air Power, Life of 1st Viscount Weir of Eastwood*, London. Louis Galambos (1964) 'The Cotton Textile Institute and the Government', *Business History Review*, autumn. H.L. Hutchinson (1965) *Tariff-making and Industrial Reconstruction*, London *Industry and Government in Britain, the F.B.I. in politics, 1945–1965*, op. cit.

12   For forums, see Andrew Shonfield (1965) *Modern Capitalism*, London; J.E.S. Hayward (1966) *Private Interests and Public Policy, the French Economic and Social Council*, London; S. Howson and D. Winch (1977) *The Economic Advisory Council, 1930–1939*, Cambridge; John P. Windmuller (1969) *Labour Relations in the Netherlands*, Ithaca, NY, and W. Singh (1972) *Policy Development, a study of the Social and Economic Council of the Netherlands*, Rotterdam; *Industry, Unions and Government, 21 years of N.E.D.O.*, op. cit.; (1981) *Industrial Democracy in Europe*, European Industrial Relations Group, Oxford, 1981.

13   See chapter 4.

# 9 IDEOLOGICAL BARRIERS AND SUPPORTS

1  J.M. Keynes (1926) 'The end of laissez-faire', in *Essays in Persuasion*, London.
2  For a fine analysis of this, see David Marquand (1988) *The Unprincipled Society*, London.
3  In what follows I focus on the most influential tendencies (democratic communitarianism's pure ideological antecedents were discussed in chapter 2). I do not claim 'comprehensiveness'. US political parties are excluded for reasons which should emerge in chapter 10. Modern 'liberalism' is not explicitly dealt with: it is too heterogeneous. I hope that readers will be able to relate aspects of these and other important tendencies to the categories I do discuss.
4  Richard Kuisel (1981) *Capitalism and the State in Modern France*, Cambridge, pp. 40–5.
5  *Capitalism and the State in Modern France*, op. cit.
6  Robert Wiebe (1969) *The Search for Order, 1877–1920*, New York. Ellis Hawley (1966) *The New Deal and the Problem of Monopoly*, Princeton, NJ. Andrew Shonfield (1965) *Modern Capitalism*, London. Samuel Beer (1965) *British Politics in the Collectivist Age*, New York, and (1982) *Britain Against Itself*, London. Keith Middlemas (1979) *Politics in Industrial Society, the experience of the British system since 1911*, London.
7  *Britain Against Itself*, op. cit., p. 126.
8  A few leading economists have criticized some of these limitations. See Edmund S. Phelps (ed.) (1965) *Altruism, Morality and Economic Theory*, New York; Edward Mishan (1967) *The Costs of Economic Growth*, London; Fred Hirsch (1976) *Social Limits to Growth*, Cambridge MA; Tibor Scitovsky (1976) *The Joyless Economy*, New York; Albert O. Hirschman (1982) *Shifting Involvements, private interest and public action*, Oxford; and Amartya Sen (1987) *On Ethics and Economics*, Oxford. However, positive alternatives are another matter. The very few economists who become major theorists of co-operation and community tended to draw their assumptions from outside economics, indeed to travel 'beyond the camp'; notably, J.M. Clark, Kenneth E. Boulding and Gunnar Myrdal (see notes to chapter 2).
9  'The end of laissez-faire', op. cit. John Diebold (1959) *The Schuman Plan, a study in economic co-operation, 1950–1959*, New York, pp. 268–9. *Modern Capitalism*. op. cit., particularly part 4. *Capitalism and the State in Modern France*, op. cit., pp. 39–40.
10 J.E.S. Hayward (1959) 'Solidarity: the social history of an idea in 19th century France', *International Review of Social History*, IV: (2). Theodore Zeldin (1974) *France 1848–1945, Politics and Anger*, Oxford, chapter 8. Petr Kropotkin (1902) *Mutual Aid, a factor of evolution*, London. Charles Cooley (1912) *Human Nature and Social Order*, New York, and (1924) *Social Process*, New York.
11 For Durkheim's views, see chapter 2.
12 Henry Bentinck (1918) *Tory Democracy*, London; various authors (1927) *Industry and the State, a Conservative View*, London; Harold Macmillan

(1938) *The Middle Way*, London, also (1932) *The State and Industry*, London. Nigel Fisher (1982) *Harold Macmillan, a biography*, London, p. 53. For recent restatements, see Ian Gilmour (1977) *Inside Right*, London, and (1983) *Britain Can Work*, London.

13  S.G. Hobson (1919) *National Guilds*, London; G.D.H. Cole (1920) *Self-Government in Industry*, London; G.D.H. Cole (1948) *History of the Labour Party from 1914*, London. Peter J. Williamson (1985) *Varieties of Corporatism*, Cambridge. Robert M. Wiebe (1962) *Businessmen and Reform*, Cambridge MA; Morrell Heald (1970) *Social Responsibilities of Business, company and community, 1900–1960*, Cleveland, OH. Samuel Courtauld (1949) *Ideals and Industry*, Cambridge.

14  The mystique and its rich symbols emerge in detail in E.P. Thompson (1963) *The Making of the English Working Class*, London.

15  R.H. Tawney was a partial exception to this: see (1921) *The Acquisitive Society*, London.

16  See chapter 3.

17  Albert S. Lindemann (1983) *A History of European Socialism*, New Haven, CT, and London.

18  Hendrik de Man (1935) *Corporatisme et Socialisme*, Brussels, and Peter Dodge (1966) *Beyond Marxism, The faith and works of Hendrik de Man*, The Hague; Evan Durbin (1940) *The Politics of Democratic Socialism*, London; Gunnar Myrdal (1960) *Beyond the Welfare State*, London. The ideology of individualism, as a fillip to sectionalism in the British Labour movement, is illuminated by Robert M. Currie (1979) *Industry and Politics*, Oxford.

19  Spencer M. Di Scala (1988) *Renewing Italian Socialism, Nenni to Craxi*, New York, and Richard Bellamy (1987) *Modern Italian Social Theory*, Oxford. Hugh Gaitskell (1956) *Recent Developments in British Socialist Thinking*, London, and Philip Williams (1979) *Hugh Gaitskell, a political biography*, London. Willy Brandt (1978) *People and Politics*, London, p. 446. Douglas Jay (1962) *Socialism and the New Society*, London, pp. 2, 4–5, 7. See also Roy Hattersley (1987) *Choose Freedom, the future for democratic socialism*, London. In this sense modern French socialism does not appear to have experienced an ideological rebirth either: see D.S. Bell and B. Criddle (1984) *The French Socialist Party, resurgence and victory*, Oxford.

20  Anthony Crosland (1956) *The Future of Socialism*, London, pp. 89–91, 110–11.

21  *The Future of Socialism*, op. cit. pp. 90, 106–8, 111–12.

22  ibid., pp. 90, 106, 113.

23  ibid., p. 111.

24  ibid., pp. 105, 113, 528.

25  Herbert Tingsten (1973) *The Swedish Social Democrats, their ideological development*, Princeton, NJ, pp. 265, 312–13, 707.

26  Marquis Childs (1936) *Sweden, the Middle Way*, New Haven, CT; F.G. Castles (1978) *The Social Democratic Image of Society, a study of the achievements and origins of Scandinavian Social Democracy*, London; M. Donald Hancock (1972) *Sweden, The Politics of Postindustrial Change*,

London. Also, D.A. Rustow (1955) *The Politics of Compromise, politics and government in Sweden*, Princeton, NJ.

27  For sources on Christian democracy up to and during this period, see notes 12 and 16 in chapter 2.

28  Parti Social Chrétien (1945) *Les Chantiers Sont Ouverts ... quel sera l'architecte?*, Noel. The French MRP's emphasis at this time was similar: see Mario Einaudi and Francois Goguel (1952) *Christian Democracy in Italy and France*, Notre Dame, IN; Louis Biton (1954) *La Démocratie Chrétienne dans la politique Française*, Angers; R.E.M. Irving (1973) *Christian Democracy in France*, London.

29  For this last concept see chapter 6.

30  In addition to sources already cited, particularly Irving, Mayeur, Vaussard and Létamendia (see chapter 2, note 12), the following are very useful for general trends in post-1950s Christian democracy: Jean Marie Mayeur (1986) *Catholicisme Social et Démocratie Chrétienne*, Paris, and Roberto Papini (1988) *L'Internationale Démocrate-Chrétienne 1925–86*, Paris. See also, John H. Whyte (1981) *Catholics in Western Democracies*, Dublin; Geoffrey Pridham (1977) *Christian Democracy in West Germany*, London; R. Morgan and S. Silvestri (eds) (1982) *Moderates and Conservatives in Western Europe*, London; Donald Sassoon (1986) *Contemporary Italy*, London; H. Portelli and T. Jensen (eds) (1986) *La Démocratie Chrétienne, force internationale*, Nanterre. For changing views on economic reform, see (1981) *La Démocratie Chrétienne en Europe, la doctrine fondamentale et la politique economique*, C.I.D.C.I.D., Rome; and Albert Kalaydjian and Hugues Portelli (eds) (1988) *Les Démocrates-Chrétiens et l'économie sociale de marché*, Paris.

31  Brian Davies and M. Walsh (eds) (1984) *Proclaiming Justice and Peace, documents from John XXIII to John Paul II*, London, includes the main Catholic statements since 1961 by Popes and the 2nd Vatican Council. John Paul II's *Sollicitudo Rei Socialis*, 1987, continued the themes of 'social justice', 'participation' and, more particularly, 'solidarity'. Other important sources include: *Economic Justice for All, Catholic Social Teaching and the U.S. Economy, National Conference of U.S. Catholic Bishops, 1986*. Leading Anglican circles have emphasized similar themes: a notable example is *Faith in the City*, (1985) General Synod of the Church of England, London, particularly pp. 51–6. The principles involved have also featured in the World Council of Churches' deliberations at various times.

# 10  WESTERN EUROPE, THE USA AND THE UK

1  See chapter 5.

2  This discounts single-trend theories pointing towards an eventual triumph of one or the other principle.

3  See chapter 4.

4  Frank Blackaby (ed.) (1980) *The Future of Pay Bargaining*, London. Charles Carter and John Pinder (1982) *Policies for a Constrained Economy*, London. James E. Meade (1982) *Stagflation*, vol. 1, *Wage-Fixing*, London.

Andrea Boltho (ed.) (1981) *The European Economy, growth and crisis*, Oxford.

5  This factor was foreshadowed in chapters 1 and 5.

6  This classification of the French and Italian economic systems as 'less co-operativist', overall, through the whole period, reflects the criteria of (1) interest group representation and participation (or 'corporatism'), (2) industrial relations peace, and (3) voluntary incomes restraint: see chapter 4.

7  Of course, this is not to deny the various imperfections of the more co-operativist countries, let alone the achievements in other fields of the less co-operativist ones.

8  E.H. Kossman (1978) *The Low Countries, 1780–1940*, Oxford. Arend Lijphart (1968) *The Politics of Accommodation*, Los Angeles and London. Johan de Vries (1978) *The Netherlands Economy in the 20th Century*. John P. Windmuller (1978) *Labour Relations in the Netherlands*, Ithaca, NY. R.T. Griffiths (1980) *The Political Economy of the Netherlands since 1945*, The Hague.

9  *The Low Countries, 1780–1940*, op. cit. *Labour Relations in the Netherlands*, op. cit. Willem Verkade (1965) *Democratic Parties in the Low Countries and Germany*, Leiden. Jean Beaufays (1973) *Les Partis Catholiques en Belgique et aux Pays Bas, 1918–1958*, Brussels. H. Bakvis (1987) *Catholic Power in the Netherlands since 1945*, New York.

10  Johan Goudsblom (1967) *Dutch Society*, New York. *The Low Countries, 1780–1940*, op. cit.

11  *The Low Countries, 1780–1940*, op. cit. *Democratic Parties in the Low Countries and Germany*, op. cit. Vernon Mallinson (1969) *Belgium*, London. J. Fitzmaurice (1983) *The Politics of Belgium*, London. Raymond Riley (1976) *Belgium*, London.

12  *Les Partis Catholiques en Belgique et aux Pays Bas, 1918–1958*, op. cit. R.E.M. Irving (1979) *The Christian Democratic Parties of Western Europe*, London. John H. Whyte (1981) *Catholics in Western Democracies*, Dublin. Peter Dodge (1966) *Beyond Marxism, the faith and works of Hendrik de Man*, The Hague.

13  M. Donald Hancock (1972) *Sweden, The Politics of Postindustrial Change*, London, pp. ix, 45.

14  Ernest Barker (1973) *Austria, 1918–1972*, London. Karl R. Stadler (1971) *Austria*, London. P.C. Schmitter and G. Lehmbruch (eds) (1979) *Trends towards Corporate Intermediation*, Beverly Hills and London. Kurt L. Shell (1967) *The Transformation of Austrian Socialism*, Buffalo, NY. William T. Bluhm (1973) *Building an Austrian Nation*, New Haven, CT, and London. Charles Maier (1984) in John Goldthorpe (ed.) *Order and Conflict in Contemporary Capitalism*, Oxford, p. 52.

15  J. Hayward and R.W. Berki (1979) *State and Society in Europe*, Oxford, p. 257. Volker Berghahn and Detlev Karsten (1987) *Industrial Relations in West Germany*, Oxford, New York and Hamburg, p. 222. *Order and Conflict in Contemporary Capitalism*, op. cit., p. 47.

16  M. Edelman and R.W. Fleming (1965) *The Politics of Wage-Price Decisions*, Urbana, IL, pp. 96–7. Andrew Shonfield (1965) *Modern Capitalism*, London, pp. 246, 263. *Industrial Relations in West Germany*, op. cit., pp. 211–12, 222. K. Dyson (1982) in J. Richardson (ed.) *Policy*

*Styles in Western Europe*, London, p. 34. Vaclav Holesovsky (1977) *Economic Systems, analysis and comparison*, New York, p. 281. G. Lehmbruch, in *Order and Conflict in Contemporary Capitalism*, op. cit., p. 66.

17  *Trends towards Corporate Intermediation*, op. cit. Lewis J. Edinger (1986) *West German Politics*, New York. David P. Conradt (1978) *The German Polity*, New York and London. E. Hartmann (1959) *Authority and Organization in German Management*, Princeton, NJ. Volker Berghaan (1982) *Modern Germany*, Cambridge, and (1986) *The Americanisation of West German Industry, 1945–1973*, Leamington Spa and New York.

18  *Modern Capitalism*, op. cit., pp. 244, 246.

19  *The Christian Democratic Parties of Western Europe*, op. cit. Arnold J. Heidenheimer (1960) *Adenauer and the C.D.U.*, The Hague. Geoffrey Pridham (1977) *Christian Democracy in West Germany*, London. Herbert S. Spiro (1958) *The Politics of German Co-determination*, Cambridge, MA. Susanna Miller and Heinrich Potthoff (1986) *A History of German Social Democracy from 1848 to the Present*, trans. J.A. Underwood, Leamington Spa.

20  Daniel Boorstin (1973) *The Americans, the democratic experience*, New York, pp. 26, 78, 85, 135, 273. Robert M. Wiebe (1975) *The Segmented Society*, New York, pp. 17, 29. Other influences on the interpretation which follows include Wiebe (1967) *The Search for Order*, New York; T.C. Cochran (1972) *Business in American Life, a history*, New York; Grant McConnell (1970) *Private Power and American Democracy*, New York; William Letwin (1965) *Law and Economic Policy in America*, New York; Edwin Epstein (1969) *The Corporation in American Politics*, Princeton, NJ.

21  Wilson Carey McWilliams (1973) *The Idea of Fraternity in America*, Berkeley, CA. James E. Post (1978) *Corporate Behavior and Social Change*, Boston, MA. Robert N. Bellah *et al.* (1986) *Habits of the Heart, individualism and commitment in American life*, Berkeley, CA.

22  Robert Paul Wolff (1968) *The Poverty of Liberalism*, Boston, MA; Theodore J. Lowi (1969) *The End of Liberalism*, New York; George C. Lodge (1976) *The New American Ideology*, Cambridge, MA; Robert B. Reich (1983) *The Next American Frontier*, New York; Charles K. Wilber and Kenneth P. Jameson (1983) *An Inquiry into the Poverty of Economics*, Notre Dame, IN; *Habits of the Heart, individualism and commitment in American life*, op. cit.

23  Sidney Checkland (1983) *British Public Policy, 1776–1939*, Cambridge; Keith Middlemas (1979) *Politics in Industrial Society, the experience of the British system since 1911*, London, and (1983) *Industry, Unions and Government, 21 years of NEDO*, London; Andrew Shonfield (1965) *Modern Capitalism*, London, and (1983) *In Defence of the Mixed Economy*, ed. Z. Shonfield, London; Samuel H. Beer (1982) *Britain Against Itself, the political contradictions of collectivism*, London; Wilfred Beckerman (1972) *The Labour Government's Economic Record 1964–1970*, London; Peter Hall (1986) *Governing the Economy, the politics of state intervention in Britain and France*, Cambridge; David Marquand (1988) *The Unprincipled Society, new demands and old politics*, London.

24  See chapter 9.

## 11  IMPLICATIONS AND PROSPECTS

1   Market competitive approaches imply higher degrees of organizational fragmentation and conflict, less inclusiveness, and less socio-political incorporation. The economic discipline of unemployment reduces abuses of trade union power but at an unacceptably severe human and social as well as economic cost.

2   The cyclical relationship between competition and state direction was discussed in chapter 10.

3   So far as I know, this phrase originated in James E. Meade (1975) *The Intelligent Radical's Guide to Economic Policy, the mixed economy,* London, p. 123.

4   This combination emerges in some discussions of the amorphous concept of the 'social market economy'.

5   See, for example, Michael E. Porter (1980) *Competitive Strategy,* New York.

6   For the last, see Alasdair Mcintyre (1981) *After Virtue, a study in moral theory,* London, chapter 18.

7   See chapter 9, note 31.

8   A lot more work is needed on the areas discussed in this book. I am aware that I have done no more than sketch a framework. More work is needed on the principles of fraternity, complementary association and democratic participation, and their relationships with other social ideas. The processes of public co-operation – internal forethought, external colloquy, operational adjustment and immediate cost bearing – require further investigation. More research is needed on the nature, influence and interactions of the structural–institutional factors I have identified: threshold continuity and conformable size; organizational transparency and social monitoring; social proximity and forums. The historical development of communitarian ideas invites further enquiry. The theory of the long-term dynamics of public co-operation in advanced mixed economies, including the role of national emergency, and the relationships with competition and state direction, requires further development and application to additional cases.

# Index